2020 CASELAW AND STATUTORY SUPPLEMENT TO
COMPUTER CRIME LAW

Fourth Edition

■ ■ ■

Orin S. Kerr

Professor
University of California, Berkeley
School of Law

AMERICAN CASEBOOK SERIES®

WEST
ACADEMIC
PUBLISHING

American Casebook Series is a trademark registered in the U.S. Patent and Trademark Office.

© 2020 LEG, Inc. d/b/a West Academic
    444 Cedar Street, Suite 700
    St. Paul, MN 55101
    1-877-888-1330

West, West Academic Publishing, and West Academic are trademarks of West Publishing Corporation, used under license.

Printed in the United States of America

ISBN: 978-1-68467-926-3

PREFACE

This supplement serves two purposes. First, it provides caselaw updates for materials that appeared after the early 2018 publication of the Fourth Edition of *Computer Crime Law*. Second, it provides the current text of the relevant federal computer crime statutes.

ORIN S. KERR

October 2019

TABLE OF CONTENTS

PREFACE III

TABLE OF CASES IX

PART A. CASELAW SUPPLEMENT

Chapter 2. Computer Misuse Crimes 3
C.   Unauthorized Access Statutes 3
     4.   What Is Authorization? The Case of Contract-Based Restrictions ... 3
F.   18 U.S.C. § 1030(a)(5) and Computer Damage Statutes 7
     1.   18 U.S.C. § 1030(a)(5) Misdemeanor Liability 7
        United States v. Thomas 7
     2.   18 U.S.C. § 1030(a)(5) Felony Liability 12

Chapter 3. Traditional Crimes 13
A.   Economic Crimes 13
     1.   Property Crimes 13
B.   Crimes Against Persons 14
     1.   Threats and Harassment 14
       c)   Revenge Porn Laws 14
         State v. Van Buren 14
         Notes and Questions 26
C.   Vice Crimes 29
     3.   Prostitution 29
         Notes and Questions 30

Chapter 4. Sentencing 33
C.   Sentencing in Computer Misuse Cases 33

Chapter 5. The Fourth Amendment 35
A.   The Requirement of Government Action 35
B.   Defining Searches and Seizures 37
     1.   Searches 37
       c)   Searches in the Network Context 37
         Carpenter v. United States 37
         Notes and Questions 48
C.   Exceptions to the Warrant Requirement 51
     2.   Exigent Circumstances 51
     4.   Border Searches 52
D.   Searching and Seizing Computers with a Warrant 60
     1.   Probable Cause 60
     5.   Ex Ante Restrictions on Computer Warrants 64
     6.   Encryption 65

      b)   Fifth Amendment Issues 65

Chapter 6. Statutory Privacy Protections 69
D.   The Stored Communications Act 69
    1.   The Basic Structure 69
    3.   Voluntary Disclosure Under § 2702 70

Chapter 7. Jurisdiction 73
B.   State Power 73
    2.   Procedural Limits 73
C.   International Computer Crimes 74
    2.   Statutory Privacy Laws 74
    4.   Mutual Legal Assistance and International Treaties 76

PART B. STATUTORY SUPPLEMENT

18 U.S.C. § 641. Public Money, Property or Records 79
18 U.S.C. § 875. Interstate Communications 79
18 U.S.C. § 1028. Fraud and Related Activity in Connection with Identification Documents, Authentication Features, and Information 80
18 U.S.C. § 1028A. Aggravated Identity Theft 84
18 U.S.C. § 1029. Fraud and Related Activity in Connection with Access Devices 85
18 U.S.C. § 1030. Fraud and Related Activity in Connection with Computers 88
18 U.S.C. § 1084. Transmission of Wagering Information; Penalties 96
18 U.S.C. § 1343. Fraud by Wire, Radio, or Television 97
18 U.S.C. § 1462. Importation or Transportation of Obscene Matters 97
18 U.S.C. § 1465. Production and Transportation of Obscene Matters for Sale or Distribution 98
18 U.S.C. § 1831. Economic Espionage 98
18 U.S.C. § 1832. Theft of Trade Secrets 99
18 U.S.C. § 1839. Definitions 99
18 U.S.C. § 2251. Sexual Exploitation of Children 100
18 U.S.C. § 2252. Certain Activities Relating to Material Involving the Sexual Exploitation of Minors 102
18 U.S.C. § 2252A. Certain Activities Relating to Material Constituting or Containing Child Pornography 104
18 U.S.C. § 2256. Definitions for Chapter 109
18 U.S.C. § 2258A. Reporting Requirements of Electronic Communication Service Providers and Remote Computing Service Providers 111
18 U.S.C. § 2261A. Stalking 117
18 U.S.C. § 2314. Transportation of Stolen Goods, Securities, Moneys, Fraudulent State Tax Stamps, or Articles Used in Counterfeiting 117
18 U.S.C. § 2319. Criminal Infringement of a Copyright 118
17 U.S.C. § 506. Criminal Offenses 120

18 U.S.C. § 2422. Coercion and Enticement.. 121

18 U.S.C. § 2423. Transportation of Minors.. 122

18 U.S.C. § 2510. Definitions.. 123

18 U.S.C. § 2511. Interception and Disclosure of Wire, Oral, or Electronic
Communications Prohibited 126

18 U.S.C. § 2512. Manufacture, Distribution, Possession, and
Advertising of Wire, Oral, or Electronic Communication Intercepting
Devices Prohibited.. 133

18 U.S.C. § 2513. Confiscation of Wire, Oral, or Electronic
Communication Intercepting Devices 134

18 U.S.C. § 2515. Prohibition of Use as Evidence of Intercepted Wire or
Oral Communications 135

18 U.S.C. § 2516. Authorization for Interception of Wire, Oral, or
Electronic Communications.. 135

18 U.S.C. § 2517. Authorization for Disclosure and Use of Intercepted
Wire, Oral, or Electronic Communications... 139

18 U.S.C. § 2518. Procedure for Interception of Wire, Oral, or Electronic
Communications.. 141

18 U.S.C. § 2519. Reports Concerning Intercepted Wire, Oral, or
Electronic Communications.. 148

18 U.S.C. § 2520. Recovery of Civil Damages Authorized............................ 150

18 U.S.C. § 2521. Injunction Against Illegal Interception 151

18 U.S.C. § 2522. Enforcement of the Communications Assistance for
Law Enforcement Act... 152

18 U.S.C. § 2523. Executive Agreements on Access to Data by Foreign
Governments.. 153

18 U.S.C. § 2701. Unlawful Access to Stored Communications.................... 162

18 U.S.C. § 2702. Voluntary Disclosure of Customer Communications or
Records 163

18 U.S.C. § 2703. Required Disclosure of Customer Communications or
Records 165

18 U.S.C. § 2704. Backup Preservation 170

18 U.S.C. § 2705. Delayed Notice... 172

18 U.S.C. § 2706. Cost Reimbursement.. 174

18 U.S.C. § 2707. Civil Action 175

18 U.S.C. § 2708. Exclusivity of Remedies 176

18 U.S.C. § 2711. Definitions for Chapter 176

18 U.S.C. § 2713. Required Preservation and Disclosure of
Communications and Records 177

18 U.S.C. § 3121. General Prohibition on Pen Register and Trap and
Trace Device Use; Exception 177

18 U.S.C. § 3122. Application for an Order for a Pen Register or a Trap
and Trace Device 178

18 U.S.C. § 3123. Issuance of an Order for a Pen Register or a Trap and
Trace Device 179

18 U.S.C. § 3124. Assistance in Installation and Use of a Pen Register or
a Trap and Trace Device 181

18 U.S.C. § 3125. Emergency Pen Register and Trap and Trace Device Installation 182

18 U.S.C. § 3126. Reports Concerning Pen Registers and Trap and Trace Devices 183

18 U.S.C. § 3127. Definitions for Chapter 184

47 U.S.C. § 223. Obscene or Harassing Telephone Calls in the District of Columbia or in Interstate or Foreign Communications........................ 185

6 U.S.C. § 1501. Definitions.. 190

6 U.S.C. § 1503. Authorizations for Preventing, Detecting, Analyzing, and Mitigating Cybersecurity Threats 194

6 U.S.C. § 1505. Protection from Liability.................................... 198

6 U.S.C. § 1507. Construction and Preemption............................... 199

6 U.S.C. § 1510. Effective Period 202

Federal Rule of Criminal Procedure 41 202

TABLE OF CASES

The principal cases are in bold type.

———————

Aleynikov, People v., 13, 14
Andrews v. Sirius XM Radio Inc., 12
Bosyk, United States v., 60
Brown, United States v., 33
California v. Riley, 39
Cano, United States v., 57
Carpenter v. United States, 37
Casillas v. Berkshire Hathaway
    Homestate Cos., 69
Casillas v. Cypress Ins. Co., 69
Facebook v. Superior Court, 70
Fair Housing Council of San Fernando
    Valley v. Roommates.Com, LLC, 31
hiQ Labs, Inc. v. LinkedIn Corp., 3
Hood, United States v., 48
Hupp v. Cook, 51
Jobe, United States v., 51
Jones, Commonwealth v., 65
Jones, Ex parte, 27
Jones, United States v., 40, 50
Kinslow v. State, 51
Knotts, United States v., 39
Kolsuz, United States v., 52, 56, 58
Kyllo v. United States, 39
LVRC Holdings LLC v. Brekka, 10
McIntyre v. Ohio Elections Comm'n,
    73
Miller v. California, 17
Miller, United States v., 40, 46
Mixton, State v., 73
Morel, United States v., 49
Nexans Wires S.A. v. Sark-USA, Inc.,
    12
Olmstead v. United States, 45
Phillips, United States v., 11
Pittman, State v., 66
Riley v. California, 53
Sandvig v. Sessions, 5, 6
Search of a Residence in Oakland,
    Cal., In the Matter of the, 68
Search Warrant, In re Application for
    a, 68
Shaffer, Commonwealth v., 36
Sims v. State, 51
Smith v. Maryland, 39, 40, 46
Stetkiw, United States v., 64
Stevens, United States v., 18
Terrell, State v., 35
Thomas, United States v., 7
Touset, United States v., 53
Van Buren, State v., 14

Wellbeloved-Stone, United States v.,
    49
Yoder & Frey Auctioneers, Inc. v.
    EquipmentFacts, LLC, 12

2020 CASELAW AND STATUTORY SUPPLEMENT TO

COMPUTER CRIME LAW

Fourth Edition

PART A

CASELAW SUPPLEMENT

■ ■ ■

CHAPTER 2

COMPUTER MISUSE CRIMES

■ ■ ■

C. UNAUTHORIZED ACCESS STATUTES

4. WHAT IS AUTHORIZATION? THE CASE OF CONTRACT-BASED RESTRICTIONS

On page 72, before Section 5, add the following new Notes 8–11:

8. *Can the CFAA apply at all to accessing a public website, even when a cease-and-desist letter prohibits access?* The Ninth Circuit handed down an important precedent on visiting public websites in hiQ Labs, Inc. v. LinkedIn Corp., 938 F.3d 985 (9th Cir. 2019). hiQ Labs ("HiQ") is a data analytics company that scrapes the LinkedIn profiles of users who have set their profiles to be available to the public without the need to log in to a LinkedIn account. HiQ then analyzes the data and sells it. In an effort to stop HiQ's accessing LinkedIn's site, LinkedIn sent a cease-and-desist letter to HiQ warning that HiQ was not permitted to access the public profiles on LinkedIn's site and that accessing LinkedIn's website violated the CFAA and other laws.

HiQ then sued LinkedIn, seeking a declaratory judgment that LinkedIn could not stop HiQ from visiting LinkedIn's public profiles. HiQ also sought a preliminary injunction requiring LinkedIn to continue to provide access to LinkedIn's website. The district court granted the preliminary injunction, effectively barring LinkedIn from blocking HiQ's access to its website while the litigation was pending. LinkedIn appealed the district court's preliminary injunction, and the Ninth Circuit affirmed. Ninth Circuit precedent limited the court's review to a narrow question about the CFAA: Whether HiQ's conduct "clearly" violated the CFAA or there was at least a "serious question" about it. The Ninth Circuit held that there was a serious question as to whether HiQ violated the CFAA.

The Ninth Circuit's ruling is important because it reflects a specific theory of the CFAA: Access to "websites that are accessible to the general public" is inherently authorized and cannot violate the CFAA. An unauthorized access can occur only when access occurs to "private computer networks and websites" that are "protected by a password authentication system and not visible to the public." *Id.* at 1003. This is the correct interpretation of the CFAA, the Ninth Circuit reasoned, because the CFAA is focused on virtual "breaking and entering." *Id.* at 1001. The concept of "breaking and entering" only makes sense when there is an authentication system such as a password gate that requires bypassing. Accessing information available to the public, like a public LinkedIn page, is therefore authorized:

> The legislative history of section 1030 makes clear that the prohibition on unauthorized access is properly understood to apply only to private information—information delineated as private through use of a permission requirement of some sort. As one prominent commentator has put it, "an authentication requirement, such as a password gate, is needed to create the necessary barrier that divides open spaces from closed spaces on the Web." Orin S. Kerr, *Norms of Computer Trespass*, 116 Colum. L. Rev. 1143, 1161 (2016). Moreover, elsewhere in the statute, password fraud is cited as a means by which a computer may be accessed without authorization, *see* 18 U.S.C. § 1030(a)(6), bolstering the idea that authorization is only required for password-protected sites or sites that otherwise prevent the general public from viewing the information.
>
> Put differently, the CFAA contemplates the existence of three kinds of computer information: (1) information for which access is open to the general public and permission is not required, (2) information for which authorization is required and has been given, and (3) information for which authorization is required but has not been given (or, in the case of the prohibition on exceeding authorized access, has not been given for the part of the system accessed). Public LinkedIn profiles, available to anyone with an Internet connection, fall into the first category. With regard to such information, the "breaking and entering" analogue invoked so frequently during congressional consideration has no application, and the concept of "without authorization" is inapt.
>
> For all these reasons, it appears that the CFAA's prohibition on accessing a computer "without authorization" is violated when a person circumvents a computer's generally applicable rules regarding access permissions, such as username and password requirements, to gain access to a computer. It is likely that when a computer network generally permits public access to its data, a user's accessing that publicly available data will not constitute access without authorization under the CFAA.

Id. at 1001–03.

The Ninth Circuit then distinguished *Nosal II* (see Note 6 on pages 51–52 in the main text) and *Power Ventures* (see Note 5 on pages 67–69 in the main text) on the ground that both of those precedents involved access limited by a username and password. The court's basis for distinguishing *Power Ventures* is particularly interesting. In *Power Ventures*, Facebook had sent Power Ventures a cease-and-desist letter prohibiting Power Ventures from accessing the Facebook accounts that Facebook users had permitted Power Ventures to access. The Ninth Circuit held that Power Ventures had violated the CFAA by ignoring the cease-and-desist letter. According to the Ninth Circuit in *hiQ Labs v. LinkedIn*, however, a different result was appropriate when the cease-and-desist letter tried to limit access to areas of a public website that were not protected by a username and password:

> Facebook requires its users to register with a unique username and password, and Power Ventures required that Facebook users provide their Facebook username and password to access their Facebook data on Power Ventures' platform. While Power Ventures was gathering user data that was protected by Facebook's username and password authentication system, the data hiQ was scraping was available to anyone with a web browser.

> In sum, *Nosal II* and *Power Ventures* control situations in which authorization generally is required and has either never been given or has been revoked. As *Power Ventures* indicated, the two cases do not control the situation present here, in which information is presumptively open to all comers.

Id. at 1002.

9. *Summarizing Ninth Circuit caselaw on the CFAA.* After the decision in *hiQ Labs*, an effort to summarize Ninth Circuit CFAA caselaw might go something like this. When information is available to the public, accessing it is authorized even if the computer owner has made clear that it does not want the access to occur (*hiQ Labs*). When information is available only to an employee or a specific person, that person is authorized to access the information until the relationship entitling the person to access the information has ended (*Brekka*). After that permission has ended, the person cannot access the information even with the permission of a current account holder (*Nosal II*). And when information is not available to the public, authorization to access it can be withdrawn expressly by a cease-and-desist letter (*Power Ventures*) but cannot be withdrawn implicitly by terms of service (*Nosal I*).

Assuming this is an accurate statement of current Ninth Circuit law, do these cases provide a sensible interpretation of the CFAA?

10. *Does the First Amendment limit how courts must construe unauthorized access?* In Sandvig v. Sessions, 315 F.Supp.3d 1 (D.D.C. 2018), Judge Bates concluded that the First Amendment does not apply to computer access that circumvents a code-based restriction, but that it may require a narrow construction of unauthorized access when no code-based restriction is involved:

> Rifling through a business's confidential files is no less a trespass merely because those files are located in the cloud. A hacker cannot legally break into a Gmail account and copy the account-holder's emails, just as a busybody cannot legally reach into someone else's mailbox and open her mail. The First Amendment does not give someone the right to breach a paywall on a news website any more than it gives someone the right to steal a newspaper.

But simply placing contractual conditions on accounts that anyone can create, as social media and many other sites do, does not remove a website from the First Amendment protections of the public Internet. Rather, only code-based restrictions, which carve out a virtual private space within the website or service that requires proper authentication to gain access, remove those protected portions of a site from the public forum. Stealing another's credentials, or breaching a site's security to evade a code-based restriction, therefore remains unprotected by the First Amendment.

Note the similarity between how Judge Bates reads the CFAA as limited by the First Amendment in *Sandvig* and how the Ninth Circuit construed the CFAA as a matter of statutory interpretation in *hiQ Labs*. Both opinions limit unauthorized access to acts that bypass code-based restrictions.

11. *Creating fictitious user accounts under the CFAA.* Imagine a website allows anyone to register for an account on the condition, expressed in the terms of service, that they must provide their real names and identities on registration. Anyone with an account can enter a username and password to see nonpublic information available to those with accounts. A person creates an account using a fictitious identity, and he uses that account to access nonpublic information on the website. Does the act of accessing the information using the account count as bypassing a code-based restriction (because it was used to access hidden information), or is it merely violating a contractual restriction (because it violated the terms of service)? And does that classification determine whether they violate the CFAA?

In Sandvig v. Sessions, 315 F.Supp.3d 1 (D.D.C. 2018), a group of researchers regularly visited public websites for academic purposes in ways that violated the websites' terms of service. In some cases, they created fictitious accounts before using the accounts to gather information. Judge Bates concluded that merely visiting public websites in violation of terms of service, as well as using "bots" to access the sites in violation of terms of service, was authorized. "Employing a bot to crawl a website or apply for jobs," Judge Bates explained, "may run afoul of a website's ToS, but it does not constitute an access violation when the human who creates the bot is otherwise allowed to read and interact with that site." On the other hand, creating a fictitious user account could exceed authorized access:

> Unlike plaintiffs' other conduct, which occurs on portions of websites that any visitor can view, creating false accounts allows [a computer user] to access information on those sites that is both limited to those who meet the owners' chosen authentication requirements and targeted to the particular preferences of the user. Creating false accounts and obtaining information through those accounts would therefore [be a prohibited act of exceeding authorized access.]

Id. at 27.

F. 18 U.S.C. § 1030(a)(5) AND COMPUTER DAMAGE STATUTES

1.   18 U.S.C. § 1030(a)(5) MISDEMEANOR LIABILITY

At the bottom of page 109, replace *United States v. Carlson* with the following new decision:

18 U.S.C. § 1030(a)(5)(A) is different from other provisions of § 1030 because it prohibits unauthorized damage instead of unauthorized access. This raises obvious questions: When is a person authorized to damage a computer? How clear must authorization be, and how can it be provided? The following recent case sheds light on the answers.

UNITED STATES V. THOMAS
United States Court of Appeals for the Fifth Circuit, 2017.
877 F.3d 591.

GREGG COSTA, CIRCUIT JUDGE.

Michael Thomas worked as the Information Technology Operations Manager for ClickMotive, LP, a software and webpage hosting company. Upset that a coworker had been fired, Thomas embarked on a weekend campaign of electronic sabotage. He deleted over 600 files, disabled backup operations, eliminated employees from a group email a client used to contact the company, diverted executives' emails to his personal account, and set a "time bomb" that would result in employees being unable to remotely access the company's network after Thomas submitted his resignation. Once ClickMotive discovered what Thomas did, it incurred over $130,000 in costs to fix these problems.

A jury found Thomas guilty of knowingly causing the transmission of a program, information, code, or command, and as a result of such conduct, intentionally causing damage without authorization, to a protected computer. 18 U.S.C. § 1030(a)(5)(A). Thomas challenges the "without authorization" requirement of this provision of the Computer Fraud and Abuse Act. He contends that because his IT job gave him full access to the system and required him to "damage" the system—for example, at times his duties included deleting certain files—his conduct did not lack authorization. But we conclude that Thomas's conduct falls squarely within the ordinary meaning of the statute and affirm his conviction.

I.

Thomas's duties at ClickMotive included network administration; maintaining production websites; installing, maintaining, upgrading, and troubleshooting network servers; ensuring system security and data integrity; and performing backups. He was granted full access to the network operating system and had the authority to access any data and change any setting on the system. Thomas was expected to perform his duties using his "best efforts and judgment to produce maximum benefit" to ClickMotive.

Thomas was not happy when his friend in the IT department was fired. It was not just a matter of loyalty to his former colleague; a smaller IT staff meant more work for Thomas. So Thomas, to use his word, "tinkered" with the company's system. The tinkering, which started on a Friday evening and continued through Monday morning, included the following:

- He deleted 625 files of backup history and deleted automated commands set to perform future backups.

- He issued a command to destroy the virtual machine that performed ClickMotive's backups for one of its servers and then Thomas failed to activate its redundant pair, ensuring that the backups would not occur.

- He tampered with ClickMotive's pager notification system by entering false contact information for various company employees, ensuring that they would not receive any automatically-generated alerts indicating system problems.

- He triggered automatic forwarding of executives' emails to an external personal email account he created during the weekend.

- He deleted pages from ClickMotive's internal "wiki," an online system of internal policies and procedures that employees routinely used for troubleshooting computer problems.

- He manually changed the setting for an authentication service that would eventually lead to the inability of employees to work remotely through VPN. Changing the setting of the VPN authentication service set a time bomb that would cause the VPN to become inoperative when someone rebooted the system, a common and foreseeable maintenance function.

- And he removed employees from e-mail distribution groups created for the benefit of customers, leading to customers' requests for support going unnoticed.

Thomas was able to engage in most of this conduct from home, but he did set the VPN time bomb on Sunday evening from ClickMotive's office, which he entered using another employee's credentials. It was during this visit to the office that Thomas left his resignation letter that the company would see the next day. When the dust settled, the company incurred over

$130,000 in out-of-pocket expenses and employees' time to undo the harm Thomas caused. In a subsequent interview with the FBI, Thomas stated that he engaged in this conduct because he was frustrated with the company and wanted to make the job harder for the person who would replace him.

A grand jury eventually charged Thomas with the section 1030(a)(5)(A) offense. But two days before the grand jury met, Thomas fled to Brazil. Nearly three years later, Thomas was arrested when he surrendered to FBI agents at Dallas/Fort Worth International Airport.

At trial, company employees and outside IT experts testified that none of the problems ClickMotive experienced as a result of Thomas's actions would be attributable to a normal system malfunction. They further stated that Thomas's actions were not consistent with normal troubleshooting and maintenance or consistent with mistakes made by a novice. ClickMotive employees asserted that it was strange for the wiki pages to be missing and that someone in Thomas's position would know that changing the setting of the VPN authentication service would cause it to become inoperative when someone rebooted the system.

ClickMotive's employee handbook was not offered at trial and there was no specific company policy that governed the deletions of backups, virtual machines, or wiki modifications. Employees explained, however, that there were policies prohibiting interfering with ClickMotive's normal course of business and the destruction of its assets, such as a virtual machine or company data. Thomas's own Employment Agreement specified he was bound by policies that were reasonably necessary to protect ClickMotive's legitimate interests in its clients, customers, accounts, and work product.

The jury instructions included the statutory definition of "damage," which is "any impairment to the integrity or availability of data, a program, a system, or information." 18 U.S.C. § 1030(e)(8). The district court denied Thomas's proposed instruction for "without authorization," which was "without permission or authority." It did not define the phrase.

After the jury returned a guilty verdict, the district court sentenced Thomas to time served (which was the four months since he had been detained after returning to the country), plus three years of supervised release, and ordered restitution of $131,391.21.

II.

A.

Because Thomas's argument that he was authorized to damage a computer seems nonsensical at first glance, it is helpful at the outset to explain the steps he takes to get there. He first points out that his job duties included "routinely deleting data, removing programs, and taking systems offline for diagnosis and maintenance." Thomas says this conduct damaged the computer within the meaning of the Computer Fraud and Abuse Act because damage is defined to just mean "any impairment to the integrity or availability of data, a program, a system, or information," 18 U.S.C. § 1030(e)(8); there is no requirement of harm. And the damage he caused by engaging in these routine tasks was not "without authorization" because it was part of his job. So far, so good.

Next comes the critical leap: Thomas argues that because he was authorized to damage the computer when engaging in these routine tasks, *any* damage he caused while an employee was not "without authorization." Thus he cannot be prosecuted under section 1030(a)(5)(A). This argument is far reaching. If Thomas is correct, then the damage statute would not reach any employee who intentionally damaged a computer system as long as any part of that employee's job included deleting files or taking systems offline.

Thomas's support for reading the statute to cover only individuals who had no rights, limited or otherwise to impair a system comes from cases addressing the separate "access" provisions of section 1030. *See, e.g., LVRC Holdings LLC v. Brekka*, 581 F.3d 1127, 1133 (9th Cir. 2009) ("A person who uses a computer 'without authorization' has no rights, limited or otherwise, to access the computer in question."). But there are important differences between the "access" and "damage" crimes that make it inappropriate to import access caselaw into the damage statute.

Section 1030(a)(5)(A) is the only independent "damage" provision, meaning it does not also require a lack of authorization to access the computer. *Contrast* 18 U.S.C. § 1030(a)(5)(B), (C) (both applying to damage that results from unauthorized access of a computer). It prohibits intentionally causing damage without authorization. As discussed, the statute defines damage. And as numerous courts have recognized in discussing both the damage and access provisions, the ordinary meaning of "without authorization" is "without permission." Indeed, Thomas asked that the jury be told that "without authorization" means "without permission or authority"; he did not seek an instruction that "without authorization" is limited to those who have no rights to ever impair a system.

As the caselaw and Thomas's proposed instruction recognize, the plain meaning of the damage provision is that it makes it a crime to intentionally impair a computer system without permission. And notably, it applies to particular acts causing damage that lacked authorization. *See* 18 U.S.C. § 1030(e)(8) (defining damage to include a single impairment of the system). Nothing in the statutory text says it does not apply to intentional acts of damage that lacked permission if the employee was allowed to engage at other times in other acts that impaired the system.

"Without authorization" modifies damage rather than access. Section 1030(a)(5)(A) makes no distinction between all-or-nothing authorization and degrees of authorization. Its text therefore covers situations when the individual never had permission to damage the system (an outsider) or when someone who might have permission for some damaging acts causes other damage that is not authorized (an insider). Tellingly, other subsections of the same damage statute are limited to those who inflict damage while "intentionally access[ing] a protected computer without authorization." 18 U.S.C. § 1030(a)(5)(B), (C). Because section 1030(a)(5)(A) is the one subsection of the damage statute that also applies to insiders, it would make no sense to import a limitation from the access statutes that is aimed at excluding insider liability.

Nor is there a significant threat that liability under the damage statute would extend to largely innocuous conduct because the requirement of "intentionally causing damage" narrows the statute's reach.

We conclude that Section 1030(a)(5)(A) prohibits intentionally damaging a computer system when there was no permission to engage in that particular act of damage. To the extent more is needed to flesh out the scope of "permission" when a defendant has some general authority to impair a network, there is helpful guidance in one of our cases addressing an access statute, which if anything should define authorization more narrowly for the reasons we have discussed. *United States v. Phillips*, 477 F.3d 215, 219 (5th Cir. 2007), says to look at the expected norms of intended use.

B.

There is overwhelming evidence to support the jury's view that Thomas did not have permission to engage in the weekend damage campaign.

The nature of Thomas's conduct is highly incriminating. No reasonable employee could think he had permission to stop the system from providing backups, or to delete files outside the normal protocols, or to falsify contact information in a notification system, or to set a process in motion that would prevent users from remotely accessing the network. Thomas emphasizes the unlimited access he had to the system that gave him the ability to inflict this damage. But it is not conceivable that any employee, regardless of their level of computer access, would be authorized to cause these problems. The incidents for which Thomas was held liable were nothing like the periodic acts he performed as part of his duties. Those tasks may have impaired the system on a limited basis in order to benefit the computer network in the long run. Routine deletions of old files provide that benefit by increasing storage space. Taking systems offline allows for necessary maintenance.

In contrast, the various types of damage Thomas caused during the last few days before he resigned resulted in over $130,000 in remediation costs. Regardless of whether the definition of "damage" under the statute requires a showing of harm, impairments that harm the system are much less likely to be authorized than those that benefit the system. It would rarely if ever make sense for an employer to authorize an employee to harm its computer system.

The harmful acts themselves would be enough to support the verdict, but Thomas's words and conduct in response to the criminal investigation provide additional support. When questioned by federal agents, he acknowledged the distinction we have just made. He did not say that he caused the damage in order to maintain or improve the system; instead, his motive was to make things more difficult for the person hired to replace him. And his flight to Brazil is not what is expected of someone who had permission to engage in the conduct being investigated.

The circumstances surrounding the damaging acts provide even more support for the finding of guilt. Thomas committed the various acts one after the other in a concentrated time span beginning Friday evening and continuing through the weekend. Thomas did most of this from home, but the one time he had to go the office he did so using another employee's credentials. One of his acts—falsification of contact information in the alert system—prevented Thomas's conduct from being detected during the weekend as employees would not receive notifications about the damage to the system. He submitted his resignation immediately after completing the damage spree and timed the most damaging act—the one that would prevent remote access—so that it would not occur until he was gone. Why this sequence of events if Thomas had permission to cause the damage? All of this provided ample support to conclude that Thomas lacked permission to inflict the damage he caused.

The judgment of the district court is affirmed.

2.   18 U.S.C. § 1030(a)(5) FELONY LIABILITY

On page 131, at the end of Note 6, add the following new material:

Several courts of appeals have held that "revenue lost" must be limited to those losses that occurred because of interruption of service. *See* Andrews v. Sirius XM Radio Inc., 932 F.3d 1253, 1263 (9th Cir. 2019); Yoder & Frey Auctioneers, Inc. v. EquipmentFacts, LLC, 774 F.3d 1065, 1073–74 (6th Cir. 2014); Nexans Wires S.A. v. Sark-USA, Inc., 166 Fed. App'x 559, 562 (2d Cir. 2006). Note that this does not answer the broader question in Note 6 of whether *all* losses must be the result of interruption of service.

CHAPTER 3

TRADITIONAL CRIMES

■ ■ ■

A. ECONOMIC CRIMES

1. PROPERTY CRIMES

On page 159, at the end of Note 5, add the following material as an addendum to Note 5:

On appeal to the New York Court of Appeals, New York's highest state court, the court affirmed the conviction. *See* People v. Aleynikov, 104 N.E.3d 687 (N.Y. 2018). The Court of Appeals agreed with the Appellate Division that Aleynikov made a "tangible reproduction" by copying the source code:

> Ideas begin in the mind. By its very nature, an idea, be it a symphony or computer source code, begins as intangible property. However, the medium upon which an idea is stored is generally physical, whether it is represented on a computer hard drive, vinyl record, or compact disc. The changes made to a hard drive or disc when information is copied onto it are physical in nature. The representation occupies space. Consequently, a statute that criminalizes the making of a tangible reproduction or representation of secret scientific material by electronically copying or recording applies to the acts of a defendant who uploads proprietary source code to a computer server.

> A rational jury could have found that the "reproduction or representation" that defendant made of Goldman's source code, when he uploaded it to the German server, was tangible in the sense of "material" or "having physical form." The jury heard testimony that the representation of source code has physical form. Kumar, the computer engineer, testified that while source code, as abstract intellectual property, does not have physical form, the representation of it is material. He explained that when computer files are stored on a hard drive or CD, they are physically present on that hard drive or disc, and further stated that data is visible in aggregate when stored on such a medium. The jury also heard testimony that source code that is stored on a computer takes up physical space in a computer hard drive. Given that a reproduction of computer code takes up space on a drive, it is clear that it is physical in nature. In short, the changes that are made to the hard drive or disc, when code or other information is stored, are physical.

Id. at 688, 697.

Are the results of the federal and state cases against Aleynikov inconsistent? *See* People v. Aleynikov, ___ N.Y.S.3d ___, 2019 WL 4935986 (N.Y. App. Div. 2019) (concluding that the state charges against Aleynikov after his federal conviction was overturned did not violate Double Jeopardy principles because "there is no inconsistency between the Second Circuit's determination that the codes were intangible when transported and this Court's determination that defendant made a tangible reproduction when he uploaded them to the German server, where they resided within a physical medium.").

B. CRIMES AGAINST PERSONS

1. THREATS AND HARASSMENT

c) Revenge Porn Laws

From the bottom of page 245 through the top of page 248, replace the Superior Court's ruling in *State v. Van Buren* and the associated notes with the following new opinion and notes:

STATE V. VAN BUREN
Vermont Supreme Court, 2019.
214 A.3d 791.

ROBINSON, J.

This case raises a facial challenge to Vermont's statute banning disclosure of nonconsensual pornography, 13 V.S.A. § 2606. We conclude that the statute is constitutional on its face and grant the State's petition for extraordinary relief.

I. "REVENGE-PORN," OR NONCONSENSUAL PORNOGRAPHY GENERALLY

"Revenge porn" is a popular label describing a subset of nonconsensual pornography published for vengeful purposes. "Nonconsensual pornography" may be defined generally as "distribution of sexually graphic images of individuals without their consent." D. Citron & M. Franks, *Criminalizing Revenge Porn*, 49 Wake Forest L. Rev. 345, 346 (2014). The term "nonconsensual pornography" encompasses images originally obtained without consent (e.g., hidden recordings or recordings of sexual assaults) as well as images originally obtained with consent, usually within the context of a private or confidential relationship. The nonconsensual dissemination of such intimate images—to a victim's employer, coworkers, family members, friends, or even strangers—can cause "public degradation, social isolation, and professional humiliation for the victims."

C. Alter, *It's Like Having an Incurable Disease': Inside the Fight Against Revenge Porn*, Time.com. The images may haunt victims throughout their lives.

This problem is widespread, with one recent study finding that "4% of U.S. internet users-roughly 10.4 million Americans-have been threatened with or experienced the posting of explicit images without their consent." Data & Society, *New Report Shows That 4% of U.S. Internet Users Have Been a Victim of 'Revenge Porn*, Dec. 13, 2016. *See also* C. Alter, *supra* (stating that "Facebook received more than 51, 000 reports of revenge porn in January 2017 alone"). Revenge porn is overwhelmingly targeted at women. D. Citron & M. Franks, *supra*, at 353–54 (citing data that victims of revenge porn are overwhelmingly female).

Forty states, including Vermont, have enacted legislation to address this issue. Federal legislation has also been proposed. *See* Intimate Privacy Protection Act of 2016, H.R. 5896, 114th Cong. (2016) (proposing to "amend the federal criminal code to make it unlawful to knowingly distribute a photograph, film, or video of a person engaging in sexually explicit conduct or of a person's naked genitals or post-pubescent female nipple with reckless disregard for the person's lack of consent if the person is identifiable from the image itself or from information displayed in connection with the image," with certain exceptions).

II.　VERMONT'S STATUTE

Vermont's law, enacted in 2015, makes it a crime punishable by not more than two years' imprisonment and a fine of $2,000 or both to "knowingly disclose a visual image of an identifiable person who is nude or who is engaged in sexual conduct, without his or her consent, with the intent to harm, harass, intimidate, threaten, or coerce the person depicted, and the disclosure would cause a reasonable person to suffer harm." 13 V.S.A. § 2606(b)(1). "Nude" and "sexual conduct" are both expressly defined. The law makes clear that "consent to recording of the visual image does not, by itself, constitute consent for disclosure of the image." *Id.* Violation of § 2606(b)(1) is a misdemeanor, unless a person acts "with the intent of disclosing the image for financial profit," in which case it is a felony.

Section 2606 does not apply to:

(1)　Images involving voluntary nudity or sexual conduct in public or commercial settings or in a place where a person does not have a reasonable expectation of privacy.

(2)　Disclosures made in the public interest, including the reporting of unlawful conduct, or lawful and common practices of law enforcement, criminal reporting, corrections, legal proceedings, or medical treatment.

(3) Disclosures of materials that constitute a matter of public concern.

(4) Interactive computer services, as defined in 47 U.S.C. § 230(f)(2), or information services or telecommunications services, as defined in 47 U.S.C. § 153, for content solely provided by another person. This subdivision shall not preclude other remedies available at law.

Id. § 2606(d)(1)–(4).

III. FACTS AND PROCEEDINGS BEFORE THE TRIAL COURT

In late 2015, defendant was charged by information with violating 13 V.S.A. § 2606(b)(1). The police officer averred as follows. Complainant contacted police after she discovered that someone had posted naked pictures of her on a Facebook account belonging to Anthony Coon and "tagged" her in the picture. Complainant called Mr. Coon and left a message asking that the pictures be deleted. Shortly thereafter, defendant called complainant back on Mr. Coon's phone; she called complainant a "moraless pig" and told her that she was going to contact complainant's employer, a child-care facility. When complainant asked defendant to remove the pictures, defendant responded that she was going to ruin complainant and get revenge.

Complainant told police that she had taken naked pictures of herself and sent them to Mr. Coon through Facebook Messenger. She advised that the pictures had been sent privately so that no one else could view them. Defendant admitted to the officer that she saw complainant's pictures on Mr. Coon's Facebook account and that she posted them on Facebook using Mr. Coon's account. Defendant asked the officer if he thought complainant had "learned her lesson."

In her sworn statement, complainant provided additional details concerning the allegations above. She described her efforts to delete the pictures from Facebook and to delete her own Facebook account. Complainant stated that the night before the pictures were publicly posted, she learned through a friend that defendant was asking about her. Defendant described herself as Mr. Coon's girlfriend. Complainant asked Mr. Coon about defendant, and Mr. Coon said that defendant was obsessed with him and that he had never slept with her. Complainant "took it as him being honest so we moved on." The next day, complainant discovered that defendant posted her nude images on Mr. Coon's Facebook page.

IV. FACIAL VALIDITY OF SECTION 2606

The State argues that nonconsensual pornography, as defined in the Vermont statute, falls outside of the realm of constitutionally protected speech for two reasons: such speech amounts to obscenity, and it constitutes an extreme invasion of privacy unprotected by the First

Amendment. Second, the State argues that even if nonconsensual pornography falls outside of the categorical exclusions to the First Amendment's protection of free speech, the statute is narrowly tailored to further a compelling State interest. Defendant counters each of these points.

For the reasons set forth below, we conclude that "revenge porn" does not fall within an established categorical exception to full First Amendment protection, and we decline to predict that the U.S. Supreme Court would recognize a new category. However, we conclude that the Vermont statute survives strict scrutiny as the U.S. Supreme Court has applied that standard.

A.   Categorical Exclusions

1.   Obscenity

Although some nonconsensual pornography may meet the constitutional definition of obscenity, we reject the State's contention that the Vermont statute categorically regulates obscenity and is thus permissible under the First Amendment. The purposes underlying government regulation of obscenity and of nonconsensual pornography are distinct, the defining characteristics of the regulated speech are accordingly quite different, and we are mindful of the U.S. Supreme Court's recent rejection of efforts to expand the definition of obscenity to include new types of speech that may engender some of the harms of obscenity.

The Supreme Court has recognized the government's "legitimate interest in prohibiting dissemination or exhibition of obscene material when the mode of dissemination carries with it a significant danger of offending the sensibilities of unwilling recipients or of exposure to juveniles." *Miller v. California*, 413 U.S. 15, 18–19 (1973). The Court has consistently recognized that a state's interest in regulating obscenity relates to protecting the sensibilities of those exposed to obscene works, as opposed to, for example, protecting the privacy or integrity of the models or actors depicted in obscene images. By contrast, a state's interest in regulating nonconsensual pornography has little to do with the sensibilities of the people exposed to the offending images; the State interest in this case focuses on protecting the privacy, safety, and integrity of the victim subject to nonconsensual public dissemination of highly private images.

In that sense, Vermont's statute is more analogous to the restrictions on child pornography that the Supreme Court has likewise categorically excluded from full First Amendment protection. Given these disparate interests, the test for obscenity that may be regulated consistent with the First Amendment is different from that for nonconsensual pornography under the Vermont statute. In considering whether expression is obscene for the purposes of the categorical exclusion from the full protections of the First Amendment, a trier of fact must consider:

> (a) whether "the average person, applying contemporary community standards" would find that the work, taken as a whole, appeals to the prurient interest; (b) whether the work depicts or describes, in a patently offensive way, sexual conduct specifically defined by the applicable state law; and (c) whether the work, taken as a whole, lacks serious literary, artistic, political or scientific value.

Miller, 413 U.S. at 24 (quotation and citations omitted).

The offending disclosures pursuant to Vermont's statute, by contrast, need not appeal to the prurient interest or be patently offensive. Typically, their purpose is to shame the subject, not arouse the viewer. *See* 13 V.S.A. § 2606(b)(1) (disclosure is prohibited if undertaken with intent to "harm, harass, intimidate, threaten, or coerce the person depicted"). Although, by definition, the nonconsensual pornography must include images of genitals, the pubic area, anus, or female nipple, or depictions of sexual conduct as defined in 13 V.S.A. §§ 2606(a)(3)–(4), those depictions need not appeal to the prurient interest applying contemporary community standards or be patently offensive in and of themselves.

We agree with the State's assertion that the privacy invasion and violation of the consent of the person depicted in revenge porn are offensive, but the viewer of the images need not know that they were disseminated without the consent of the person depicted in order to satisfy the revenge porn statute. Although the context in which images are disseminated may inform the obscenity analysis, the circumstances of their procurement and distribution fall outside of the typical obscenity assessment. For these reasons, the category of obscenity is ill-suited to include the nonconsensual pornography regulated here.

Given the ill fit between nonconsensual pornography and obscenity, and the Supreme Court's reluctance to expand the contours of the category of obscenity, we conclude that the speech restricted by Vermont's statute cannot be fairly categorized as constitutionally unprotected obscenity.

2.   Extreme Invasion of Privacy

Although many of the State's arguments support the proposition that the speech at issue in this case does not enjoy full First Amendment protection, we decline to identify a new categorical exclusion from the full protections of the First Amendment when the Supreme Court has not yet addressed the question.

The Supreme Court recognized in *United States v. Stevens*, 559 U.S. 460 (2010), that there may be "some categories of speech that have been historically unprotected, but have not yet been specifically identified or discussed as such in our case law." In deciding whether to recognize a new category outside the First Amendment's full protections for depictions of animal cruelty, the Court focused particularly on the absence of any history of regulating such depictions, rather than the policy arguments for and against embracing the proposed new category.

Notwithstanding these considerations, we decline to predict that the Supreme Court will add nonconsensual pornography to the list of speech categorically excluded. We base our declination on two primary considerations: The Court's recent emphatic rejection of attempts to name previously unrecognized categories, and the oft-repeated reluctance of the Supreme Court to adopt broad rules dealing with state regulations protecting individual privacy as they relate to free speech.

More than once in recent years, the Supreme Court has rebuffed efforts to name new categories of unprotected speech. In *Stevens*, the Court emphatically refused to add depictions of animal cruelty to the list, rejecting the notion that the court has "freewheeling authority to declare new categories of speech outside the scope of the First Amendment." The Court explained, "Maybe there are some categories of speech that have been historically unprotected, but have not yet been specifically identified or discussed as such in our case law. But if so, there is no evidence that 'depictions of animal cruelty' is among them." A year later, citing *Stevens*, the Court declined to except violent video games sold to minors from the full protections of the First Amendment. And a year after that, the Court declined to add false statements to the list.

More significantly, in case after case involving a potential clash between the government's interest in protecting individual privacy and the First Amendment's free speech protections, the Supreme Court has consistently avoided broad pronouncements, and has defined the issue at hand narrowly, generally reconciling the tension in favor of free speech in the context of speech about matters of public interest while expressly reserving judgment on the proper balance in cases where the speech involves purely private matters. The considerations that would support the Court's articulation of a categorical exclusion in this case may carry great weight in the strict scrutiny analysis, see below. But we leave it to the Supreme Court in the first instance to designate nonconsensual pornography as a new category of speech that falls outside the First Amendment's full protections.

B.　Strict Scrutiny

Our conclusion that nonconsensual pornography does not fall into an existing or new category of unprotected speech does not end the inquiry. The critical question is whether the First Amendment permits the regulation at issue. The remaining question is whether § 2606 is narrowly tailored to serve a compelling State interest.

1. Compelling Interest

We conclude that the State interest underlying § 2606 is compelling. We base this conclusion on the U.S. Supreme Court's recognition of the relatively low constitutional significance of speech relating to purely private matters, evidence of potentially severe harm to individuals arising from nonconsensual publication of intimate depictions of them, and a litany of analogous restrictions on speech that are generally viewed as uncontroversial and fully consistent with the First Amendment.

Although we decline to identify a new category of unprotected speech on the basis of the above cases, the decisions are relevant to the compelling interest analysis in that they reinforce that the First Amendment limitations on the regulation of speech concerning matters of public interest do not necessarily apply to regulation of speech concerning purely private matters. Time and again, the Supreme Court has recognized that speech concerning purely private matters does not carry as much weight in the strict scrutiny analysis as speech concerning matters of public concern, and may accordingly be subject to more expansive regulation.

The proscribed speech in this case has no connection to matters of public concern. By definition, the proscribed images must depict nudity or sexual conduct, § 2606(b)(1); must be disseminated without the consent of the victim, *id.*; cannot include images in settings in which a person does not have a reasonable expectation of privacy, *id.* § 2606(d)(1); cannot include disclosures made in the public interest, including reporting concerning various specified matters, *id.* § 2606(d)(2); and may not constitute a matter of public concern, *id.* § 2606(d)(3). By definition, the speech subject to regulation under § 2606 involves the most private of matters, with the least possible relationship to matters of public concern.

The harm to the victims of nonconsensual pornography can be substantial. Images and videos can be directly disseminated to the victim's friends, family, and employers; posted and "tagged" (as in this case) so they are particularly visible to members of a victim's own community; and posted with identifying information such that they catapult to the top of the results of an online search of an individual's name. In the constellation of privacy interests, it is difficult to imagine something more private than images depicting an individual engaging in sexual conduct, or of a person's genitals, anus, or pubic area, that the person has not consented to sharing publicly. The personal consequences of such profound personal violation and humiliation generally include, at a minimum, extreme emotional distress. Amici cited numerous instances in which the violation led the victim to suicide.

Finally, the government's interest in preventing the nonconsensual disclosure of nude or sexual images of a person obtained in the context of a confidential relationship is at least as strong as its interest in preventing the disclosure of information concerning that person's health or finances obtained in the context of a confidential relationship; content-based restrictions on speech to prevent these other disclosures are uncontroversial and widely accepted as consistent with the First Amendment. From a constitutional perspective, it is hard to see a distinction between laws prohibiting nonconsensual disclosure of personal information comprising images of nudity and sexual conduct and those prohibiting disclosure of other categories of nonpublic personal information. The government's interest in protecting all from disclosure is strong.

For the above reasons, we conclude that the State interest underlying § 2606 is compelling.

2.   Narrowly Tailored

Section 2606 defines unlawful nonconsensual pornography narrowly, including limiting it to a confined class of content, a rigorous intent element that encompasses the nonconsent requirement, an objective requirement that the disclosure would cause a reasonable person harm, an express exclusion of images warranting greater constitutional protection, and a limitation to only those images that support the State's compelling interest because their disclosure would violate a reasonable expectation of privacy. Our conclusion on this point is bolstered by a narrowing interpretation of one provision that we offer to ensure that the statute is duly narrowly tailored.

The images subject to § 2606 are precisely defined, with little gray area or risk of sweeping in constitutionally protected speech. Moreover, disclosure is only criminal if the discloser knowingly discloses the images without the victim's consent. We construe this intent requirement to require knowledge of both the fact of disclosing, and the fact of nonconsent. Individuals are highly unlikely to accidentally violate this statute while engaging in otherwise permitted speech. In fact, § 2606 goes further, requiring not only knowledge of the above elements, but a specific intent to harm, harass, intimidate, threaten, or coerce the person depicted or to profit financially.

In addition, the disclosure must be one that would cause a reasonable person "physical injury, financial injury, or serious emotional distress." *Id.* § 2606(a)(2), (b)(1). The statute is not designed to protect overly fragile sensibilities, and does not reach even knowing, nonconsensual disclosures of images falling within the narrow statutory parameters unless disclosure would cause a reasonable person to suffer harm.

Two additional limitations assuage any concern that some content meeting all of these requirements may nonetheless implicate a matter of public concern. First, the statute does not purport to reach "disclosures made in the public interest, including the reporting of unlawful conduct, or lawful and common practices of law enforcement, criminal reporting, corrections, legal proceedings, or medical treatment." *Id.* § 2606(d)(2). This broad and nonexclusive list of permitted disclosures is designed to exclude from the statute's reach disclosures that do implicate First Amendment concerns—those made in the public interest.

Second, even if a disclosure is not made "in the public interest," if the materials disclosed "constitute a matter of public concern," they are excluded from the statute's reach. *Id.* § 2606(d)(3). The Legislature has made every effort to ensure that its prohibition is limited to communication of purely private matters with respect to which the State's interest is the strongest and the First Amendment concerns the weakest.

Finally, to ensure that the statute reaches only those disclosures implicating the right to privacy the statute seeks to protect, it expressly excludes "images involving voluntary nudity or sexual conduct in public or commercial settings or in a place where a person does not have a reasonable expectation of privacy." *Id.* § 2606(d)(1). Where an individual does not have a reasonable expectation of privacy in an image, the State's interest in protecting the individual's privacy interest in that image is minimal. The statute recognizes this fact.

In connection with this factor, we offer a narrowing construction, or clarification of the statute to ensure its constitutional application while promoting the Legislature's goals. The statute's exclusion of otherwise qualifying images involving voluntary nudity or sexual conduct in settings in which a person does not have a reasonable expectation of privacy, 13 V.S.A. § 2606(d)(1), does not clearly reach images recorded in a private setting but distributed by the person depicted to public or commercial settings or in a manner that undermines any reasonable expectation of privacy. From the perspective of the statute's goals, there is no practical difference between a nude photo someone voluntarily poses for in the public park and one taken in private that the person then voluntarily posts in that same public park.

Given the Legislature's clear intent to protect peoples' reasonable expectations of privacy in intimate images of them, and to exclude from the statute's reach those images in which a person has no such reasonable expectation, it seems clear that the Legislature intends its exclusion to apply to images the person has distributed to the public, as well as those recorded in public. This construction also ensures that the scope of the statute is no broader than necessary to advance the State's interest in protecting reasonable expectations of privacy with respect to intimate images.

Given this narrowing construction, as well as all the express limitations on the statute's reach built into § 2606, we conclude that it is narrowly tailored to advance the State's compelling interest.

For the above reasons, the statute is narrowly tailored to advance the State's interests, does not penalize more speech than necessary to accomplish its aim, and does not risk chilling protected speech on matters of public concern. We accordingly conclude that 13 V.S.A. § 2606 is constitutional on its face.

* * *

We now resolve the question of whether the trial court's dismissal of the State's charge against defendant for nonconsensual disclosure of images of an identifiable nude person under 13 V.S.A. § 2606 was proper on the basis that the State failed to present sufficient evidence to show that complainant, the person depicted in the images, had a reasonable expectation of privacy in those images.

We conclude that because the State's evidence, taken in the light most favorable to the State, does not establish that complainant had a reasonable expectation of privacy in the images, the State has failed to make out a prima facie case. Accordingly, we affirm the dismissal of the charge pursuant to Vermont Rule of Criminal Procedure 12(d) and deny the State's petition for relief.

The evidence before the trial court in connection with the motion to dismiss reflects the following. Complainant sent nude pictures of herself to Anthony Coon via Facebook Messenger, Facebook's private messaging service. Her sworn statement reflects that on October 8, 2015, multiple people contacted her to report that the nude photos of her had been publicly posted on Mr. Coon's Facebook page and she had been tagged in them. Complainant initially tried to untag herself but was unable to. She eventually deleted her account. She left Mr. Coon a telephone message asking that he delete the pictures from Facebook.

Complainant then received a call from Mr. Coon's phone number. The caller was defendant. Defendant called complainant a pig and said she was going to tell complainant's employer, a child-care facility, about "what kind of person worked there." Defendant said that she had left her "ex" for Mr. Coon. Complainant asked defendant to remove the pictures from Facebook, and defendant replied that she was going to "ruin" complainant and "get revenge." After that call ended, complainant contacted the police.

Complainant reported that the night before the pictures were publicly posted, a friend told her defendant was asking about her and claiming Mr. Coon was her boyfriend. Upon learning this, complainant asked Mr. Coon about defendant, and Mr. Coon said that defendant was obsessed with him and he never slept with her. Complainant "took it as him being honest so we moved on."

The investigating officer spoke with defendant over the phone. Defendant admitted that she saw the nude pictures of complainant through

Mr. Coon's Facebook account and that she posted the pictures on Facebook through Mr. Coon's account. Defendant stated to the officer, "you think she learned her lesson."

In reviewing the State's motion, the trial court later asked the parties to stipulate to additional facts, if possible, concerning when the photographs were sent, whether complainant sent them while in or after ending a relationship with Mr. Coon, and how defendant had access to Mr. Coon's Facebook account. The parties stipulated that complainant sent Mr. Coon the photos on October 7, and they were posted on a public Facebook page on October 8. They further stipulated that "complainant was not in a relationship with Mr. Coon at the time the photographs were sent to Mr. Coon." Finally, they stipulated that defendant did not have permission to access Mr. Coon's Facebook account, and Mr. Coon believes defendant gained access to his account through her phone, which had his Facebook password saved on it.

We conclude that dismissal is appropriate because the State has not established that it has evidence showing that complainant had a reasonable expectation of privacy in the images she sent to Mr. Coon. The statutory exception for images taken in a setting where there was no reasonable expectation of privacy, or previously distributed in a manner that undermined that expectation of privacy, is fundamental to the constitutionality and purpose of this statute, and must be understood as an element of the crime. The State bears the burden of establishing that it has evidence as to each element of the offense, including this one. Because the State has stipulated that complainant and Mr. Coon were not in a relationship at the time complainant sent Mr. Coon the photo, and there is no evidence in the record showing they had any kind of relationship engendering a reasonable expectation of privacy, we conclude the State has not met its burden.

The requirement that the images at issue be subject to a reasonable expectation of privacy is central to the statute's constitutional validity under a strict-scrutiny standard. A content-based restriction on First Amendment-protected speech like § 2606 can withstand strict scrutiny only if it is narrowly tailored to serve a compelling state interest. Because the protection of reasonable expectations of privacy in intimate images is central to the statute's constitutionality and purpose, the reasonable-expectation-of-privacy provision must be understood as an element of the crime.

We acknowledge that the structure of § 2606, as set forth below, weighs in favor of finding the reasonable-expectation-of-privacy requirement to be a defense because its positioning makes it appear to be an excuse or exception to the definition of the crime. But the very essence of this crime is that it is a violation of the depicted person's reasonable expectation of privacy. As the State aptly put it in its opening brief, "the conduct regulated by 13 V.S.A. § 2606" is "publicly disseminating someone's private nude pictures without their consent" and "Section 2606 thus generally prohibits disclosing a person's nude or sexually explicit pictures if the person had a reasonable expectation of privacy in the picture and did not consent to its disclosure." Although phrased as an exception, it is an essential ingredient which constitutes the offense." It is an element of the crime.

The State has not shown it has evidence that complainant had a reasonable expectation of privacy in the images she sent to Mr. Coon. We understand this to be an objective standard, and find no evidence in the record showing that complainant had such a relationship with Mr. Coon that distributing the photos to him did not undermine any reasonable expectation of privacy that she had in them.

We interpret the reasonable-expectation-of-privacy standard as a purely objective one because the Legislature specified that the statute shall not apply to "images involving voluntary nudity or sexual conduct where a person does not have a reasonable expectation of privacy." § 2606(d)(1) This reflects a decision by the Legislature that the expectation-of-privacy determination should be based on what a reasonable person would think, not what the person depicted thought.[15] We do not attempt to precisely define here where and when a person may have a reasonable expectation of privacy for the purposes of § 2606(d)(1), except to note that it generally connotes a reasonable expectation of privacy within a person's most intimate spheres. Privacy here clearly does not mean the exclusion of all others, but it does mean the exclusion of everyone but a trusted other or few.

We conclude that the State has not shown, as we held it must, that the images were not distributed by the person depicted in a manner that undermined any reasonable expectation of privacy. As the State acknowledged in its briefing, "it is difficult to see how a complainant would have a reasonable expectation of privacy in pictures sent to a stranger." But the State has not presented evidence to demonstrate that, in contrast to a stranger, Mr. Coon had a relationship with complainant of a sufficiently intimate or confidential nature that she could reasonably assume that he would not share the photos she sent with others. Nor has it offered evidence of any promise by Mr. Coon, or even express request by complainant, to keep the photos confidential.

---

[15] We note that case law construing a criminal defendant's reasonable expectation of privacy for the purposes of the Fourth Amendment is of little help in determining whether the subject of an image has a reasonable expectation of privacy under § 2606(d)(1). Because a reasonable expectation of privacy under § 2606(d)(1) requires no analogous balancing of legitimate law-enforcement interests, the tests are fundamentally different. Although we are using the same phrase—"reasonable expectation of privacy"—it does not necessarily have the same meaning in this context that it would in the Fourth Amendment setting.

The State stipulated that complainant and Mr. Coon were not in a relationship at the time complainant sent the pictures. In the face of this stipulation, the facts that complainant and Mr. Coon apparently knew each other, had each other's contact information, and had a conversation about whether Mr. Coon was sleeping with defendant, are not sufficient to support an inference that she had a reasonable expectation of privacy. In sum, the State has not offered sufficient evidence to permit a jury to conclude beyond a reasonable doubt that complainant had a reasonable expectation of privacy in the photos she sent to Mr. Coon.

The petition for extraordinary relief is denied, and the decision below is affirmed.

NOTES AND QUESTIONS

1. *The case for a categorical exclusion.* Should the U.S. Supreme Court carve out a new categorical exclusion from First Amendment scrutiny for nonconsensual pornography? If so, how far should it extend?

2. *The Vermont law's narrow tailoring.* The Vermont Supreme Court concludes that the state's revenge pornography law survives strict scrutiny under the First Amendment because it advances a compelling interest and is narrowly tailored to advance the State's interests, it does not penalize more speech than necessary to accomplish its aim, and it does not risk chilling protected speech on matters of public concern. Are you convinced? If so, could the law be drafted more broadly than it is and still survive strict scrutiny? If not, is there a way to narrow the law to have it pass strict scrutiny?

3. *The debate over including an intent-to-harm element.* The Vermont law applies to one who "knowingly disclose[s] a visual image of an identifiable person who is nude or who is engaged in sexual conduct, without his or her consent, with the intent to harm, harass, intimidate, threaten, or coerce the person depicted." 13 V.S.A. § 2606(b)(1). Unlike the Vermont law, several state revenge pornography laws do not include an intent-to-harm element. As a matter of policy, which is better: The narrower laws that include an intent-to-harm element, or the broader laws that do not include this as an element?

Consider one argument for not including an intent-to-harm element:

Consider what it would look like if laws protecting other forms of private information were treated similarly. Imagine allowing doctors to post patients' pre-op photos to Facebook—photos in which the patients are clearly identifiable by face or name or other identifying information—to amuse friends, make money, or provide sexual gratification, or any other motive other than to harm the patient. If that seems absurd, it is no less absurd here.

Danielle Citron & Mary Anne Franks, *Evaluating New York's "Revenge Porn" Law: A Missed Opportunity to Protect Sexual Privacy*, Harvard Law Review Blog, March 19, 2019. On the other hand, is it currently a crime for a doctor to post patients' pre-op photos to Facebook? If so, what crime is it? And is the case for criminalizing a physician's disclosure of patient photographs based on doctors having special responsibilities over the medical records of their patients, or is it because people should have an inherent right to control their photos?

Next consider the First Amendment implications of including an intent-to-harm element. *Van Buren* upholds the Vermont law that includes an intent-to-harm element. If the Vermont legislature removed that element, would the Vermont Supreme Court still rule that the statute was narrowly tailored and therefore constitutional? Or, based on the *Van Buren* decision, does the First Amendment require the intent-to-harm element?

4   *The Texas "revenge porn" law has been struck down on First Amendment grounds.* Compare the Vermont Supreme Court's decision upholding the Vermont revenge pornography law in *Van Buren* with the Texas Court of Appeals ruling invalidating the Texas revenge pornography law in Ex parte Jones, ___ S.W.3d___, 2018 WL 2228888 (Tx. Ct. App. 2018). The law, Tex. Penal Code § 21.16(b), reads as follows:

A person commits an offense if:

(1) without the effective consent of the depicted person, the person intentionally discloses visual material depicting another person with the person's intimate parts exposed or engaged in sexual conduct;

(2) the visual material was obtained by the person or created under circumstances in which the depicted person had a reasonable expectation that the visual material would remain private;

(3) the disclosure of the visual material causes harm to the depicted person; and

(4) the disclosure of the visual material reveals the identity of the depicted person in any manner.

In defending the statute against a First Amendment facial challenge, the state conceded that the law was a regulation of speech that was not content-neutral. The court accepted the concession and agreed with it: "Section 21.16(b)(1) penalizes only a subset of disclosed images, those which depict another person with the person's intimate parts exposed or engaged in sexual conduct. Therefore, we conclude that Section 21.16(b)(1) discriminates on the basis of content."

The court struck down the Texas law on the ground that it failed strict scrutiny. "Because Section 21.16(b) does not use the least restrictive means of achieving what we have assumed to be the compelling government interest of preventing the intolerable invasion of a substantial privacy interest," the court held, "it is an invalid content-based restriction in violation of the First Amendment."

According to the court, the biggest problem with the statute was the disjunctive test in Section 21.16(b)(2). That language required that "the visual material was obtained by the person *or* created under circumstances in which the depicted person had a reasonable expectation that the visual material would remain private" (emphasis added). The difficulty with this language, the court explained, is that a person could be liable under the statute even if they did not know that the depicted person had a reasonable expectation that the visual material would remain private. The court explained the flaw in the statute with the following hypothetical:

> Adam and Barbara are in a committed relationship. One evening, in their home, during a moment of passion, Adam asks Barbara if he can take a nude photograph of her. Barbara consents, but before Adam takes the picture, she tells him that he must not show the photograph to anyone else. Adam promises that he will never show the picture to another living soul, and takes a photograph of Barbara in front of a plain, white background with her breasts exposed.
>
> A few months pass, and Adam and Barbara break up after Adam discovers that Barbara has had an affair. A few weeks later, Adam rediscovers the topless photo he took of Barbara. Feeling angry and betrayed, Adam emails the photo without comment to several of his friends, including Charlie. Charlie never had met Barbara and, therefore, does not recognize her. But he likes the photograph and forwards the email without comment to some of his friends, one of whom, unbeknownst to Charlie, is Barbara's coworker, Donna. Donna recognizes Barbara and shows the picture to Barbara's supervisor, who terminates Barbara's employment.
>
> Meanwhile, Adam also emails the picture to Ed. This time, however, Adam writes in the body of the email, "She thought I never would show anyone." Ed reads the email and forwards it with the attachment to several friends.
>
> In this scenario, Adam and Ed can be charged under Section 21.16(b), but so can Charlie and Donna. Charlie has a First Amendment right to share a photograph. Charlie had no reason to know that the photograph was created under circumstances under which Barbara had a reasonable expectation that the photograph would remain private. Charlie was not aware of Barbara's conditions posed to Adam immediately prior to the photograph's creation, nor did he receive the photograph with any commentary from Adam that would make him aware of this privacy expectation on Barbara's part.
>
> In fact, there is nothing to suggest that Charlie could not reasonably have believed that Adam found this picture on a public website or had been given permission by the depicted person to share the image with others. Further still, Charlie did not intend to harm the depicted person. Lastly, Charlie did not and could not identify the depicted person because he did not know Barbara. Yet, under the disjunctive language used in Section 21.16(b)(2), Charlie nonetheless is culpable despite his having no knowledge of the circumstances surrounding

the photograph's creation or the depicted person's privacy expectation arising thereunder.

Although the court struck down the statute on the ground that it did not use the least restrictive means of protecting privacy, the court also found that the statute was fatally overbroad:

> Section 21.16 is extremely broad, applying to any person who discloses visual material depicting another person's intimate parts or a person engaged in sexual conduct, but where the disclosing person has no knowledge or reason to know the circumstances surrounding the material's creation, under which the depicted person's reasonable expectation of privacy arose. Furthermore, its application is not attenuated by the fact that the disclosing person had no intent to harm the depicted person or may have been unaware of the depicted person's identity.

If the court's First Amendment analysis is correct, do you think the constitutional defect would be cured if the statute added a statutory requirement of intent to harm?

C. VICE CRIMES

On page 283, before the beginning of Part D., add the following new section:

3. PROSTITUTION

In 2018, Congress enacted a new federal law designed to limit the use of websites that further prostitution. Here is the new law, now codified at 18 U.S.C. § 2421A:

§ 2421A. Promotion or facilitation of prostitution and reckless disregard of sex trafficking

(a) In general.—Whoever, using a facility or means of interstate or foreign commerce or in or affecting interstate or foreign commerce, owns, manages, or operates an interactive computer service (as such term is defined in defined in section 230(f) the Communications Act of 1934 (47 U.S.C. 230(f))), or conspires or attempts to do so, with the intent to promote or facilitate the prostitution of another person shall be fined under this title, imprisoned for not more than 10 years, or both.

(b) Aggravated violation.—Whoever, using a facility or means of interstate or foreign commerce or in or affecting interstate or foreign commerce, owns, manages, or operates an interactive computer service (as such term is defined in defined in section 230(f) the Communications Act of 1934 (47 U.S.C. 230(f))), or conspires or attempts to do so, with the intent to promote or facilitate the prostitution of another person and—

(1) promotes or facilitates the prostitution of 5 or more persons; or

(2) acts in reckless disregard of the fact that such conduct contributed to sex trafficking, in violation of 1591(a),

shall be fined under this title, imprisoned for not more than 25 years, or both.

(c) Civil recovery.—Any person injured by reason of a violation of section 2421A(b) may recover damages and reasonable attorneys' fees in an action before any appropriate United States district court.

(d) Mandatory restitution.—Notwithstanding sections 3663 or 3663A and in addition to any other civil or criminal penalties authorized by law, the court shall order restitution for any violation of subsection (b)(2). The scope and nature of such restitution shall be consistent with section 2327(b).

(e) Affirmative defense.—It shall be an affirmative defense to a charge of violating subsection (a), or subsection (b)(1) where the defendant proves, by a preponderance of the evidence, that the promotion or facilitation of prostitution is legal in the jurisdiction where the promotion or facilitation was targeted.

Pub.L. 115–164, § 3(a), Apr. 11, 2018, 132 Stat. 1253.

NOTES AND QUESTIONS

1. 18 U.S.C. § 2421A(a) was passed as part of the Allow States And Victims To Fight Online Sex Trafficking Act, Pub. L. 115–164, known colloquially as "FOSTA." The passage of FOSTA reflects a concern that authorities lacked the tools to combat prostitution and sex trafficking online. In particular, websites such as Backpage.com hosted thousands of prostitution advertisements. Much of the new statute is addressed to limiting the immunity of such websites against civil and state liability under Section 230 of the Communications Decency Act. But part of the law also includes this new federal criminal provision. Do you think the new federal law was necessary? Should running a website that promotes prostitution be left to state law, or is it appropriate for Congress to punish such conduct at the federal level?

2. *Interactive computer service.* 47 U.S.C. § 230(f)(2) defines "interactive computer service" as

any information service, system, or access software provider that provides or enables computer access by multiple users to a computer server, including specifically a service or system that provides access to the Internet and such systems operated or services offered by libraries or educational institutions.

Under this definition, a website is the most common type of interactive computer service. *See* Fair Housing Council of San Fernando Valley v. Roommates.Com, LLC, 521 F.3d 1157, 1163 n.6 (9th Cir. 2003). As a result, the prohibition in 18 U.S.C. § 2421A(a) has the effect of making it a federal crime to own, manage, or operate a website with the intent of furthering illegal prostitution.

3.   *The affirmative defense.* Like most vice crimes, prostitution is typically a matter of state law rather than federal law. To that end, the new statute provides an affirmative defense to a charge of violating subsection (a), or subsection (b)(1), "where the defendant proves, by a preponderance of the evidence, that the promotion or facilitation of prostitution is legal in the jurisdiction where the promotion or facilitation was targeted."

Compare the affirmative defense in § 2421A(e) to the somewhat analogous treatment of state law in the context of the federal prohibition on running an interstate sports betting operation in violation of the Wire Act, 18 U.S.C. § 1084. Recall from the materials on Internet gambling that the Wire Act provides the following exception:

> Nothing in this section shall be construed to prevent the transmission in interstate or foreign commerce of information for use in news reporting of sporting events or contests, or for the transmission of information assisting in the placing of bets or wagers on a sporting event or contest from a State or foreign country where betting on that sporting event or contest is legal into a State or foreign country in which such betting is legal.

18 U.S.C. § 1084(b). The text of this provision, as construed in the *Cohen* case on page 255 of your casebook, suggests that the government has the burden of showing that gambling is illegal according to at least one of the laws of the state or country where the bet was placed or received. In contrast, § 2421A(e) places the burden on the defendant to show by a preponderance of the evidence that the promotion or facilitation of prostitution is legal. Which is the better approach? Does it matter in practice, given that the issue is the state of the law rather than a fact?

CHAPTER 4

SENTENCING

■ ■ ■

C. SENTENCING IN COMPUTER MISUSE CASES

On page 383 at the bottom, add the following new Note 11:

11. *Enhancements for "substantial disruption of a critical infrastructure."* Section 2B1.1(b)(18)(A)(iii) provides a six-level enhancement for a violation of § 1030 that causes a "substantial disruption of a critical infrastructure." (Note that page 372 of your casebook lists this language as being in Section 2B1.1(b)(17). Recent changes to 2B1.1 not relevant to our discussion have since moved this text to 2B1.1(b)(18). The language remains the same.) The harsh extra penalty when a § 1030 violation substantially disrupts a critical infrastructure prompts two questions: When does a computer count as a critical infrastructure, and what is the standard for when a CFAA violation substantially disrupts it?

The Fifth Circuit answered these questions in United States v. Brown, 884 F.3d 281 (5th Cir. 2018). The defendant, a system specialist at Citibank's Global Control Center, reacted to a negative review of his job performance by sending commands that intentionally disrupted network traffic on Citibank's network. The defendant's act of sabotage, which started at about 6pm, resulted in a loss of connectivity to some but not all of Citibank's North American data centers, campuses, call centers, and sixty-nine ATMs. By about 10 p.m., Citibank was able to restore ninety percent of the lost connectivity. By 4:30 a.m. the next morning, the network was back up and running normally. At sentencing, the trial court applied the enhancement for substantial disruption of a critical infrastructure.

On appeal, the Fifth Circuit ruled that this enhancement was improperly applied to the facts of Brown's case. On one hand, it was clear from the Guidelines definition that Citibank's computers involved critical infrastructure:

> The commentary to the 2015 Sentencing Guidelines defines "critical infrastructure" as "systems and assets vital to national defense, national security, economic security, public health or safety, or any combination of these matters." U.S. Sentencing Guidelines Manual § 2B1.1(b)(18) cmt. n.14 (U.S. Sentencing Comm'n 2015). The enumerated examples include public and private "financing and banking systems."

Id. at 285. Despite this, the enhancement was improperly applied because Brown's conduct did not cause a "substantial disruption" of that critical infrastructure:

> Brown's conduct did not constitute a substantial disruption of a critical infrastructure. There is no indication that Brown's conduct affecting a portion of Citibank's operations for a short period of time could have had a serious impact on national economic security. As a result of Brown's actions, Citibank suffered relatively minor financial losses and was temporarily unable to optimally serve its customers. Neither of these harms threatened to disrupt the nation's economy, and, in light of Citibank's demonstrated ability to quickly resolve the disruption and mitigate in the interim, there is no other evidence that Brown's conduct had the potential to do so. Accordingly, we hold that the district court erred by applying an enhancement that we conclude is reserved for conduct that disrupts a critical infrastructure in a way that could have a serious impact on national economic security.

Id. at 287.

CHAPTER 5

THE FOURTH AMENDMENT

■ ■ ■

A. THE REQUIREMENT OF GOVERNMENT ACTION

On page 399, after Note 4, add the following new note 4.1:

4.1. *When reenacting a private search, does it matter whether the officer conducts the search or asks the private party to do so?* Note 4 on page 398 discusses how the Fourth Amendment applies when a private party finds evidence of crime on a computer and brings the evidence to the police. As Note 4 explains, lower courts are divided on whether and how much the police can search the computer without a warrant on the ground that they are merely reconstructing a private search. Now consider another wrinkle: Should the answer to that question depend on whether the police search the computer themselves or merely ask the private party to show the police the digital evidence previously found?

Contrast two recent cases. In the first case, State v. Terrell, 831 S.E.2d 17 (N.C. 2019), the government did the searching. A woman named Ms. Jones found a suspicious image on her boyfriend's thumb drive and brought the thumb drive to the police to investigate. Detective Bailey searched the thumb drive in order to locate the image Ms. Jones had found. On the way to locating the suspicious image, the detective observed additional suspicious images. The Supreme Court of North Carolina ruled that the detective's search violated the boyfriend's Fourth Amendment rights because Ms. Jones's search of the thumb drive had been limited in scope:

> Following the mere opening of a thumb drive by a private individual, an officer cannot proceed with "virtual certainty that nothing else of significance" is in the device "and that a manual inspection of the [thumb drive] and its contents would not tell him anything more than he already had been told." *Jacobsen*, 466 U.S. at 119. Rather, there remains the potential for officers to learn any number and all manner of things that had not previously been learned during the private search. Accordingly, the extent to which an individual's expectation of privacy in the contents of an electronic storage device is frustrated depends upon the extent of the private search and the nature of the device and its contents.

> It is clear that Ms. Jones's limited search did not frustrate defendant's legitimate expectation of privacy in the entire contents of

his thumb drive and that Detective Bailey's follow-up search to locate the image of was not permissible under Jacobsen because he did not possess "a virtual certainty that nothing else of significance was in the [thumb drive] and that a manual inspection of the [thumb drive] and its contents would not tell him anything more than he already had been told" by Jones. *Jacobsen*, 466 U.S. at 119. The requirement that an officer possess "virtual certainty that nothing else of significance" is in a container is central to *Jacobsen* because the private-search doctrine, unlike other exceptions to the Fourth Amendment's warrant requirement, is premised fundamentally on the notion that the follow-up search is not a "search" at all. *Jacobsen*, 466 U.S. at 120 ("It infringed no legitimate expectation of privacy and hence was not a 'search' within the meaning of the Fourth Amendment."). If a container continues to support a reasonable expectation of privacy, it is a necessary corollary that an officer cannot proceed with a "search" of that container absent virtual certainty that he will not infringe upon that expectation of privacy.

Id. at 26–27.

Compare *Terrell* with Commonwealth v. Shaffer, 209 A.3d 957 (Pa. 2019), a case in which the officer asked the private party to do the search. After a computer repairman found suspected child pornography on a computer and brought the computer to the police, the officer asked the repairman to show the officer exactly what images the repairman had previously seen. The repairman complied, searching the computer "using the exact route taken to find the images" previously. *Id.* at 960. The repairmen then showed the officer the images he had previously discovered. According to the Pennsylvania Supreme Court, the officer did not violate the Fourth Amendment. The officer "merely viewed the images that [the repairman] presented to him," and therefore he did not exceed the repairman's private search. *Id.* at 974–76.

Does it make sense that these two cases should reach different results?

B. DEFINING SEARCHES AND SEIZURES

1. SEARCHES

c) Searches in the Network Context

On page 431, replace Note 5 with the following new decision:

CARPENTER V. UNITED STATES

Supreme Court of the United States, 2018.
138 S.Ct. 2206.

CHIEF JUSTICE ROBERTS delivered the opinion of the Court.

This case presents the question whether the Government conducts a search under the Fourth Amendment when it accesses historical cell phone records that provide a comprehensive chronicle of the user's past movements.

I

A

There are 396 million cell phone service accounts in the United States—for a Nation of 326 million people. Cell phones perform their wide and growing variety of functions by connecting to a set of radio antennas called "cell sites." Although cell sites are usually mounted on a tower, they can also be found on light posts, flagpoles, church steeples, or the sides of buildings. Cell sites typically have several directional antennas that divide the covered area into sectors.

Cell phones continuously scan their environment looking for the best signal, which generally comes from the closest cell site. Most modern devices, such as smartphones, tap into the wireless network several times a minute whenever their signal is on, even if the owner is not using one of the phone's features. Each time the phone connects to a cell site, it generates a time-stamped record known as cell-site location information (CSLI). The precision of this information depends on the size of the geographic area covered by the cell site. The greater the concentration of cell sites, the smaller the coverage area. As data usage from cell phones has increased, wireless carriers have installed more cell sites to handle the traffic. That has led to increasingly compact coverage areas, especially in urban areas.

Wireless carriers collect and store CSLI for their own business purposes, including finding weak spots in their network and applying "roaming" charges when another carrier routes data through their cell sites. In addition, wireless carriers often sell aggregated location records to data brokers, without individual identifying information of the sort at issue here. While carriers have long retained CSLI for the start and end of incoming calls, in recent years phone companies have also collected location information from the transmission of text messages and routine data connections. Accordingly, modern cell phones generate increasingly vast amounts of increasingly precise CSLI.

B

In 2011, police officers arrested four men suspected of robbing a series of Radio Shack and (ironically enough) T-Mobile stores in Detroit. One of the men confessed that, over the previous four months, the group (along with a rotating cast of getaway drivers and lookouts) had robbed nine different stores in Michigan and Ohio. The suspect identified 15 accomplices who had participated in the heists and gave the FBI some of their cell phone numbers; the FBI then reviewed his call records to identify additional numbers that he had called around the time of the robberies.

Based on that information, the prosecutors applied for court orders under the Stored Communications Act to obtain cell phone records for petitioner Timothy Carpenter and several other suspects. That statute, as amended in 1994, permits the Government to compel the disclosure of certain telecommunications records when it "offers specific and articulable facts showing that there are reasonable grounds to believe" that the records sought "are relevant and material to an ongoing criminal investigation." 18 U.S.C. § 2703(d). Federal Magistrate Judges issued two orders directing Carpenter's wireless carriers—MetroPCS and Sprint—to disclose cell/site sector information for Carpenter's telephone at call origination and at call termination for incoming and outgoing calls during the four-month period when the string of robberies occurred. The first order sought 152 days of cell-site records from MetroPCS, which produced records spanning 127 days. The second order requested seven days of CSLI from Sprint, which produced two days of records covering the period when Carpenter's phone was "roaming" in northeastern Ohio. Altogether the Government obtained 12,898 location points cataloging Carpenter's movements—an average of 101 data points per day.

Carpenter was charged with six counts of robbery and an additional six counts of carrying a firearm during a federal crime of violence. At trial, seven of Carpenter's confederates pegged him as the leader of the operation. In addition, FBI agent Christopher Hess offered expert testimony about the cell-site data. Hess explained that each time a cell phone taps into the wireless network, the carrier logs a time-stamped record of the cell site and particular sector that were used. With this information, Hess produced maps that placed Carpenter's phone near four of the charged robberies. In the Government's view, the location records clinched the case: They confirmed that Carpenter was "right where the robbery was at the exact time of the robbery." App. 131 (closing argument).

Carpenter was convicted on all but one of the firearm counts and sentenced to more than 100 years in prison.

The Court of Appeals for the Sixth Circuit affirmed. The court held that Carpenter lacked a reasonable expectation of privacy in the location information collected by the FBI because he had shared that information with his wireless carriers. Given that cell phone users voluntarily convey cell-site data to their carriers as "a means of establishing communication," the court concluded that the resulting business records are not entitled to Fourth Amendment protection. (quoting *Smith v. Maryland,* 442 U.S. 735, 741 (1979)).

II

A

As technology has enhanced the Government's capacity to encroach upon areas normally guarded from inquisitive eyes, this Court has sought to "assure preservation of that degree of privacy against government that existed when the Fourth Amendment was adopted." *Kyllo v. United States,* 533 U.S. 27, 34 (2001). For that reason, we rejected in *Kyllo* a mechanical interpretation of the Fourth Amendment and held that use of a thermal imager to detect heat radiating from the side of the defendant's home was a search. Because any other conclusion would leave homeowners at the mercy of advancing technology, we determined that the Government—absent a warrant—could not capitalize on such new sense-enhancing technology to explore what was happening within the home.

Likewise in *California v. Riley,* 134 S.Ct. 2473 (2014), the Court recognized the immense storage capacity of modern cell phones in holding that police officers must generally obtain a warrant before searching the contents of a phone. We explained that while the general rule allowing warrantless searches incident to arrest strikes the appropriate balance in the context of physical objects, neither of its rationales has much force with respect to the vast store of sensitive information on a cell phone.

B

The case before us involves the Government's acquisition of wireless carrier cell-site records revealing the location of Carpenter's cell phone whenever it made or received calls. This sort of digital data—personal location information maintained by a third party—does not fit neatly under existing precedents. Instead, requests for cell-site records lie at the intersection of two lines of cases, both of which inform our understanding of the privacy interests at stake.

The first set of cases addresses a person's expectation of privacy in his physical location and movements. In *United States v. Knotts,* 460 U.S. 276 (1983), we considered the Government's use of a "beeper" to aid in tracking a vehicle through traffic. Police officers in that case planted a beeper in a container of chloroform before it was purchased by one of Knotts's co-conspirators. The officers (with intermittent aerial assistance) then followed the automobile carrying the container from Minneapolis to Knotts's cabin in Wisconsin, relying on the beeper's signal to help keep the vehicle in view. The Court concluded that the augmented visual surveillance did not constitute a search because a person traveling in an automobile on public thoroughfares has no reasonable expectation of privacy in his movements from one place to another. Since the movements of the vehicle and its final destination had been voluntarily conveyed to anyone who wanted to look, Knotts could not assert a privacy interest in the information obtained.

This Court in *Knotts,* however, was careful to distinguish between the rudimentary tracking facilitated by the beeper and more sweeping modes of surveillance. The Court emphasized the limited use which the government made of the signals from this particular beeper during a discrete automotive journey. Significantly, the Court reserved the question whether different constitutional principles may be applicable if twenty-four hour surveillance of any citizen of this country were possible.

Three decades later, the Court considered more sophisticated surveillance of the sort envisioned in *Knotts* and found that different principles did indeed apply. In *United States v. Jones,* 565 U.S. 400 (2012), FBI agents installed a GPS tracking device on Jones's vehicle and remotely monitored the vehicle's movements for 28 days. The Court decided the case based on the Government's physical trespass of the vehicle. At the same time, five Justices agreed that related privacy concerns would be raised by, for example, surreptitiously activating a stolen vehicle detection system in Jones's car to track Jones himself, or conducting GPS tracking of his cell phone. *Id.,* at 426, 428 (Alito, J., concurring in judgment); *id.,* at 415 (Sotomayor, J., concurring). Since GPS monitoring of a vehicle tracks every movement a person makes in that vehicle, the concurring Justices concluded that longer term GPS monitoring in investigations of most offenses impinges on expectations of privacy—regardless whether those movements were disclosed to the public at large. *Id.,* at 430, (opinion of Alito, J.); *id.,* at 415 (opinion of Sotomayor, J.).

In a second set of decisions, the Court has drawn a line between what a person keeps to himself and what he shares with others. We have previously held that a person has no legitimate expectation of privacy in information he voluntarily turns over to third parties. *Smith v. Maryland,* 442 U.S. 735, 743–744 (1979). That remains true even if the information is revealed on the assumption that it will be used only for a limited purpose. *United States v. Miller,* 425 U.S. 435, 443 (1976). As a result, the Government is typically free to obtain such information from the recipient without triggering Fourth Amendment protections.

This third-party doctrine largely traces its roots to *Miller*. While investigating Miller for tax evasion, the Government subpoenaed his banks, seeking several months of canceled checks, deposit slips, and monthly statements. The Court rejected a Fourth Amendment challenge to the records collection. For one, Miller could assert neither ownership nor possession of the documents; they were business records of the banks. For another, the nature of those records confirmed Miller's limited expectation of privacy, because the checks were not confidential communications but negotiable instruments to be used in commercial transactions, and the bank statements contained information exposed to bank employees in the ordinary course of business. The Court thus concluded that Miller had taken the risk, in revealing his affairs to another, that the information would be conveyed by that person to the Government.

Three years later, *Smith* applied the same principles in the context of information conveyed to a telephone company. The Court ruled that the Government's use of a pen register—a device that recorded the outgoing phone numbers dialed on a landline telephone—was not a search. Noting the pen register's limited capabilities, the Court doubted that people in general entertain any actual expectation of privacy in the numbers they dial. Telephone subscribers know, after all, that the numbers are used by the telephone company for a variety of legitimate business purposes, including routing calls. And at any rate, the Court explained, such an expectation is not one that society is prepared to recognize as reasonable. When Smith placed a call, he voluntarily conveyed the dialed numbers to the phone company by exposing that information to its equipment in the ordinary course of business. Once again, we held that the defendant assumed the risk that the company's records would be divulged to police.

III

The question we confront today is how to apply the Fourth Amendment to a new phenomenon: the ability to chronicle a person's past movements through the record of his cell phone signals. Such tracking partakes of many of the qualities of the GPS monitoring we considered in *Jones*. Much like GPS tracking of a vehicle, cell phone location information is detailed, encyclopedic, and effortlessly compiled.

At the same time, the fact that the individual continuously reveals his location to his wireless carrier implicates the third-party principle of *Smith* and *Miller*. But while the third-party doctrine applies to telephone numbers and bank records, it is not clear whether its logic extends to the qualitatively different category of cell-site records. After all, when *Smith* was decided in 1979, few could have imagined a society in which a phone goes wherever its owner goes, conveying to the wireless carrier not just dialed digits, but a detailed and comprehensive record of the person's movements.

We decline to extend *Smith* and *Miller* to cover these novel circumstances. Given the unique nature of cell phone location records, the fact that the information is held by a third party does not by itself overcome the user's claim to Fourth Amendment protection. Whether the Government employs its own surveillance technology as in *Jones* or leverages the technology of a wireless carrier, we hold that an individual maintains a legitimate expectation of privacy in the record of his physical movements as captured through CSLI. The location information obtained from Carpenter's wireless carriers was the product of a search.[3]

A

A person does not surrender all Fourth Amendment protection by venturing into the public sphere. To the contrary, what one seeks to preserve as private, even in an area accessible to the public, may be constitutionally protected. A majority of this Court has already recognized that individuals have a reasonable expectation of privacy in the whole of their physical movements. *Jones,* 565 U.S., at 430 (Alito, J., concurring in judgment); *id.,* at 415 (Sotomayor, J., concurring). Prior to the digital age, law enforcement might have pursued a suspect for a brief stretch, but doing so for any extended period of time was difficult and costly and therefore rarely undertaken. For that reason, society's expectation has been that law enforcement agents and others would not—and indeed, in the main, simply could not—secretly monitor and catalogue every single movement of an individual's car for a very long period.

Allowing government access to cell-site records contravenes that expectation. Although such records are generated for commercial purposes, that distinction does not negate Carpenter's anticipation of privacy in his physical location. Mapping a cell phone's location over the course of 127 days provides an all-encompassing record of the holder's whereabouts. As with GPS information, the time-stamped data provides an intimate window into a person's life, revealing not only his particular movements, but through them his familial, political, professional, religious, and sexual associations. These location records hold for many Americans the privacies of life. And like GPS monitoring, cell phone tracking is remarkably easy, cheap, and efficient compared to traditional investigative tools. With just the click of a button, the Government can access each carrier's deep repository of historical location information at practically no expense.

In fact, historical cell-site records present even greater privacy concerns than the GPS monitoring of a vehicle we considered in *Jones.*

---

[3] The parties suggest as an alternative to their primary submissions that the acquisition of CSLI becomes a search only if it extends beyond a limited period. As part of its argument, the Government treats the seven days of CSLI requested from Sprint as the pertinent period, even though Sprint produced only two days of records. We need not decide whether there is a limited period for which the Government may obtain an individual's historical CSLI free from Fourth Amendment scrutiny, and if so, how long that period might be. It is sufficient for our purposes today to hold that accessing seven days of CSLI constitutes a Fourth Amendment search.

Unlike the bugged container in *Knotts* or the car in *Jones,* a cell phone—almost a feature of human anatomy—tracks nearly exactly the movements of its owner. While individuals regularly leave their vehicles, they compulsively carry cell phones with them all the time. A cell phone faithfully follows its owner beyond public thoroughfares and into private residences, doctor's offices, political headquarters, and other potentially revealing locales. Accordingly, when the Government tracks the location of a cell phone it achieves near perfect surveillance, as if it had attached an ankle monitor to the phone's user.

Moreover, the retrospective quality of the data here gives police access to a category of information otherwise unknowable. In the past, attempts to reconstruct a person's movements were limited by a dearth of records and the frailties of recollection. With access to CSLI, the Government can now travel back in time to retrace a person's whereabouts, subject only to the retention polices of the wireless carriers, which currently maintain records for up to five years. Critically, because location information is continually logged for all of the 400 million devices in the United States—not just those belonging to persons who might happen to come under investigation—this newfound tracking capacity runs against everyone. Unlike with the GPS device in *Jones,* police need not even know in advance whether they want to follow a particular individual, or when.

Whoever the suspect turns out to be, he has effectively been tailed every moment of every day for five years, and the police may—in the Government's view—call upon the results of that surveillance without regard to the constraints of the Fourth Amendment. Only the few without cell phones could escape this tireless and absolute surveillance.

The Government and Justice Kennedy contend [in dissent] that the collection of CSLI should be permitted because the data is less precise than GPS information. Not to worry, they maintain, because the location records did not on their own suffice to place Carpenter at the crime scene; they placed him within a wedge-shaped sector ranging from one-eighth to four square miles. . . . [But] the rule the Court adopts must take account of more sophisticated systems that are already in use or in development. While the records in this case reflect the state of technology at the start of the decade, the accuracy of CSLI is rapidly approaching GPS-level precision. As the number of cell sites has proliferated, the geographic area covered by each cell sector has shrunk, particularly in urban areas. In addition, with new technology measuring the time and angle of signals hitting their towers, wireless carriers already have the capability to pinpoint a phone's location within 50 meters. Brief for Electronic Frontier Foundation et al. as *Amici Curiae* 12 (describing triangulation methods that estimate a device's location inside a given cell sector).

Accordingly, when the Government accessed CSLI from the wireless carriers, it invaded Carpenter's reasonable expectation of privacy in the whole of his physical movements.

B

The Government's primary contention to the contrary is that the third-party doctrine governs this case. In its view, cell-site records are fair game because they are "business records" created and maintained by the wireless carriers. The Government (along with Justice Kennedy) recognizes that this case features new technology, but asserts that the legal question nonetheless turns on a garden-variety request for information from a third-party witness.

The Government's position fails to contend with the seismic shifts in digital technology that made possible the tracking of not only Carpenter's location but also everyone else's, not for a short period but for years and years. Sprint Corporation and its competitors are not your typical witnesses. Unlike the nosy neighbor who keeps an eye on comings and goings, they are ever alert, and their memory is nearly infallible. There is a world of difference between the limited types of personal information addressed in *Smith* and *Miller* and the exhaustive chronicle of location information casually collected by wireless carriers today. The Government thus is not asking for a straightforward application of the third-party doctrine, but instead a significant extension of it to a distinct category of information.

The third-party doctrine partly stems from the notion that an individual has a reduced expectation of privacy in information knowingly shared with another. But the fact of diminished privacy interests does not mean that the Fourth Amendment falls out of the picture entirely. *Smith* and *Miller,* after all, did not rely solely on the act of sharing. Instead, they considered the nature of the particular documents sought to determine whether there is a legitimate 'expectation of privacy' concerning their contents. *Smith* pointed out the limited capabilities of a pen register; as explained in *Riley,* telephone call logs reveal little in the way of identifying information. *Miller* likewise noted that checks were not confidential communications but negotiable instruments to be used in commercial transactions. In mechanically applying the third-party doctrine to this case, the Government fails to appreciate that there are no comparable limitations on the revealing nature of CSLI.

The Court has in fact already shown special solicitude for location information in the third-party context. In *Knotts,* the Court relied on *Smith* to hold that an individual has no reasonable expectation of privacy in public movements that he "voluntarily conveyed to anyone who wanted to look. But when confronted with more pervasive tracking, five Justices [in *Jones*] agreed that longer term GPS monitoring of even a vehicle traveling on public streets constitutes a search. [T]his case is not about "using a phone" or a person's movement at a particular time. It is about a detailed chronicle of a person's physical presence compiled every day, every moment, over several years. Such a chronicle implicates privacy concerns far beyond those considered in *Smith* and *Miller.*

Neither does the second rationale underlying the third-party doctrine—voluntary exposure—hold up when it comes to CSLI. Cell phone location information is not truly "shared" as one normally understands the term. In the first place, cell phones and the services they provide are such a pervasive and insistent part of daily life that carrying one is indispensable to participation in modern society. Second, a cell phone logs a cell-site record by dint of its operation, without any affirmative act on the part of the user beyond powering up. Virtually any activity on the phone generates CSLI, including incoming calls, texts, or e-mails and countless other data connections that a phone automatically makes when checking for news, weather, or social media updates. Apart from disconnecting the phone from the network, there is no way to avoid leaving behind a trail of location data. As a result, in no meaningful sense does the user voluntarily assume the risk of turning over a comprehensive dossier of his physical movements.

We therefore decline to extend *Smith* and *Miller* to the collection of CSLI. Given the unique nature of cell phone location information, the fact that the Government obtained the information from a third party does not overcome Carpenter's claim to Fourth Amendment protection. The Government's acquisition of the cell-site records was a search within the meaning of the Fourth Amendment.

* * *

Our decision today is a narrow one. We do not express a view on matters not before us: real-time CSLI or "tower dumps" (a download of information on all the devices that connected to a particular cell site during a particular interval). We do not disturb the application of *Smith* and *Miller* or call into question conventional surveillance techniques and tools, such as security cameras. Nor do we address other business records that might incidentally reveal location information. Further, our opinion does not consider other collection techniques involving foreign affairs or national security.

As Justice Brandeis explained in his famous dissent, the Court is obligated—as "subtler and more far-reaching means of invading privacy have become available to the Government"—to ensure that the "progress of science" does not erode Fourth Amendment protections. *Olmstead v. United States,* 277 U.S. 438, 473–474 (1928). Here the progress of science has afforded law enforcement a powerful new tool to carry out its important responsibilities. At the same time, this tool risks Government encroachment of the sort the Framers, after consulting the lessons of history, drafted the Fourth Amendment to prevent.

We decline to grant the state unrestricted access to a wireless carrier's database of physical location information. In light of the deeply revealing nature of CSLI, its depth, breadth, and comprehensive reach, and the inescapable and automatic nature of its collection, the fact that such information is gathered by a third party does not make it any less deserving of Fourth Amendment protection. The Government's acquisition of the cell-site records here was a search under that Amendment.

JUSTICE KENNEDY, with whom JUSTICE THOMAS and JUSTICE ALITO join, dissenting.

This case involves new technology, but the Court's stark departure from relevant Fourth Amendment precedents and principles is, in my submission, unnecessary and incorrect, requiring this respectful dissent.

The new rule the Court seems to formulate puts needed, reasonable, accepted, lawful, and congressionally authorized criminal investigations at serious risk in serious cases, often when law enforcement seeks to prevent the threat of violent crimes. And it places undue restrictions on the lawful and necessary enforcement powers exercised not only by the Federal Government, but also by law enforcement in every State and locality throughout the Nation. Adherence to this Court's longstanding precedents and analytic framework would have been the proper and prudent way to resolve this case.

The Court has twice held that individuals have no Fourth Amendment interests in business records which are possessed, owned, and controlled by a third party. *United States v. Miller,* 425 U.S. 435 (1976); *Smith v. Maryland,* 442 U.S. 735 (1979). This is true even when the records contain personal and sensitive information. So when the Government uses a subpoena to obtain, for example, bank records, telephone records, and credit card statements from the businesses that create and keep these records, the Government does not engage in a search of the business's customers within the meaning of the Fourth Amendment.

Petitioner acknowledges that the Government may obtain a wide variety of business records using compulsory process, and he does not ask the Court to revisit its precedents. Yet he argues that, under those same precedents, the Government searched his records when it used court-approved compulsory process to obtain the cell-site information at issue here. Cell-site records, however, are no different from the many other kinds of business records the Government has a lawful right to obtain by compulsory process. Customers like petitioner do not own, possess, control, or use the records, and for that reason have no reasonable expectation that they cannot be disclosed pursuant to lawful compulsory process.

The Court today disagrees. It holds for the first time that by using compulsory process to obtain records of a business entity, the Government has not just engaged in an impermissible action, but has conducted a search of the business's customer. The Court further concludes that the search in this case was unreasonable and the Government needed to get a warrant to obtain more than six days of cell-site records.

In concluding that the Government engaged in a search, the Court unhinges Fourth Amendment doctrine from the property-based concepts that have long grounded the analytic framework that pertains in these cases. In doing so it draws an unprincipled and unworkable line between cell-site records on the one hand and financial and telephonic records on the other. According to today's majority opinion, the Government can acquire a record of every credit card purchase and phone call a person makes over months or years without upsetting a legitimate expectation of privacy. But, in the Court's view, the Government crosses a constitutional line when it obtains a court's approval to issue a subpoena for more than six days of cell-site records in order to determine whether a person was within several hundred city blocks of a crime scene. That distinction is illogical and will frustrate principled application of the Fourth Amendment in many routine yet vital law enforcement operations.

It is true that the Cyber Age has vast potential both to expand and restrict individual freedoms in dimensions not contemplated in earlier times. However, there is simply no basis here for concluding that the Government interfered with information that the cell phone customer, either from a legal or commonsense standpoint, should have thought the law would deem owned or controlled by him.

JUSTICE GORSUCH, dissenting.

Today the Court suggests that *Smith* and *Miller* distinguish between *kinds* of information disclosed to third parties and require courts to decide whether to "extend" those decisions to particular classes of information, depending on their sensitivity. But as the Sixth Circuit recognized and Justice Kennedy explains, no balancing test of this kind can be found in *Smith* and *Miller*. Those cases announced a categorical rule: Once you disclose information to third parties, you forfeit any reasonable expectation of privacy you might have had in it. And even if *Smith* and *Miller* did permit courts to conduct a balancing contest of the kind the Court now suggests, it's still hard to see how that would help the petitioner in this case. Why is someone's location when using a phone so much more sensitive than who he was talking to (*Smith*) or what financial transactions he engaged in (*Miller*)? I do not know and the Court does not say.

I cannot fault the Sixth Circuit for holding that *Smith* and *Miller* extinguish any *Katz*-based Fourth Amendment interest in third party cell-site data. That is the plain effect of their categorical holdings. Nor can I fault the Court today for its implicit but unmistakable conclusion that the rationale of *Smith* and *Miller* is wrong; indeed, I agree with that. The Sixth Circuit was powerless to say so, but this Court can and should. At the same time, I do not agree with the Court's decision today to keep *Smith* and *Miller* on life support and supplement them with a new and multilayered inquiry that seems to be only *Katz*-squared. Returning there, I worry, promises more trouble than help. Instead, I would look to a more traditional Fourth Amendment approach. Even if *Katz* may still supply one way to prove a Fourth Amendment interest, it has never been the only way. Neglecting more traditional approaches may mean failing to vindicate the full protections of the Fourth Amendment.

NOTES AND QUESTIONS

1.   *New versus traditional surveillance techniques.* The Supreme Court's *Carpenter* decision draws a distinction between new technologies that cause "seismic shifts" in the government's power and "traditional surveillance techniques" that are not called into question by the Court's reasoning. On one hand, *Carpenter* directs that use of "seismic shift" technologies can be a search to prevent the government from having too much surveillance power as a result of technological change. On the other hand, *Carpenter* suggests that traditional surveillance techniques that were not a search under traditional Fourth Amendment principles remain a non-search. How should courts apply this distinction to Internet surveillance?

2.   *Translating Carpenter's physical expectations to the Internet.* *Carpenter* is based on an understanding of traditional expectations in the physical world. In the past, the Court reasons, you wouldn't expect others to monitor your every single movement in physical space for a long period of time because it would be technologically impossible. New technology has changed that expectation, *Carpenter* explains. Technology has enabled perfect location surveillance that previously didn't exist. The law must declare that monitoring a search, the Court reasons, to restore the earlier balance of government power.

But how does that apply to Internet surveillance? There is likely no established past set of societal expectations about how much Internet surveillance power the government has. Given that, how can you tell if technological changes in Internet surveillance power have changed a previous expectation? Or is the idea that the entire Internet, viewed as a whole, works a "seismic shift" in the amount of surveillance power the government has relative to the pre-Internet age? If so, what were the old expectations about government power, and what is the new reality? And what legal rules are needed to restore the old reality of government power by changing Fourth Amendment doctrine?

3.   *Carpenter and collecting IP addresses.* The post-*Carpenter* cases on surveillance of IP addresses have so far concluded that collecting the IP address that an account is using to connect to the Internet is not a search. Consider the First Circuit's reasoning in United States v. Hood, 920 F.3d 87

(1st Cir. 2019). In *Hood*, the government had reason to believe that someone using a particular Kik account with the associated name "Rusty Hood" had recently used the account to commit a crime. In an effort to identify the suspect, investigators asked Kik to disclose the IP addresses used to log in to the account recently. Kik disclosed the IP addresses used over a four-day period, and that led to the identification and prosecution of the user, Mr. Rusty Hood. Hood argued that obtaining his IP addresses was a Fourth Amendment search under *Carpenter*. The First Circuit disagreed:

> An internet user generates the IP address data that the government acquired from Kik in this case only by making the affirmative decision to access a website or application. By contrast, as the Supreme Court noted in *Carpenter*, every time a cell phone receives a call, text message, or email, the cell phone pings CSLI to the nearest cell site tower without the cell phone user lifting a finger. In fact, those pings are recorded every time a cell phone application updates of its own accord, possibly to refresh a news feed or generate new weather data, such that even a cell phone sitting untouched in a suspect's pocket is continually chronicling that user's movements throughout the day.

> Moreover, the IP address data that the government acquired from Kik does not itself convey any location information. The IP address data is merely a string of numbers associated with a device that had, at one time, accessed a wireless network. By contrast, CSLI itself reveals—without any independent investigation—the (at least approximate) location of the cell phone user who generates that data simply by possessing the phone.

> Thus, the government's warrantless acquisition from Kik of the IP address data at issue here in no way gives rise to the unusual concern that the Supreme Court identified in *Carpenter* that, if the third-party doctrine were applied to the acquisition of months of Carpenter's CSLI, only the few without cell phones could escape tireless and absolute surveillance. Accordingly, we conclude that Hood did not have a reasonable expectation of privacy in the information that the government acquired from Kik without a warrant.

Id. at 91–92. *See also* United States v. Morel, 922 F.3d 1 (1st Cir. 2019); United States v. Wellbeloved-Stone, 777 Fed.Appx. 605 (4th Cir. 2019). Do you agree?

Also consider how *Carpenter* might apply to the facts of *United States v. Forrester* on pages 425–28 of your casebook. In *Forrester*, the government monitored a home Internet connection and obtained the IP addresses of the websites visited from the account. Note the key difference between the facts of *Forrester* and the facts of *Hood*. In *Hood*, the IP addresses collected were Hood's assigned IP addresses. In *Forrester*, the IP addresses collected were those visited from the home's account. Should that make a difference? Is the government's power to observe the address of every website a person visits over time a new power that has caused a "seismic shift" in government power? Or is IP address monitoring merely a "traditional" surveillance technique because IP addresses are just the Internet version of telephone numbers dialed?

4.   *Short-term vs. long-term surveillance.* Footnote 3 of *Carpenter* states that the Court "need not decide whether there is a limited period for which the Government may obtain an individual's historical CSLI free from Fourth Amendment scrutiny, and if so, how long that period might be." The distinction between long-term and short-term surveillance was the basis of Justice Alito's concurring opinion in *Jones,* on which the reasoning of *Carpenter* is based. In *Jones,* the government installed a physical GPS device on a car the suspect was driving and tracked the car's location for 28 days. Justice Alito reasoned that using the GPS device only briefly was not a search because that was the kind of government surveillance people have traditionally expected. Longer term surveillance became a search, Justice Alito reasoned, because it was the kind of surveillance that people wouldn't expect the government to be able to conduct. Here's the key language from Justice Alito's *Jones* concurrence:

> Relatively short-term monitoring of a person's movements on public streets accords with expectations of privacy that our society has recognized as reasonable. But the use of longer term GPS monitoring in investigations of most offenses impinges on expectations of privacy. For such offenses, society's expectation has been that law enforcement agents and others would not—and indeed, in the main, simply could not—secretly monitor and catalogue every single movement of an individual's car for a very long period. In this case, for four weeks, law enforcement agents tracked every movement that respondent made in the vehicle he was driving.

> We need not identify with precision the point at which the tracking of this vehicle became a search, for the line was surely crossed before the 4-week mark. Other cases may present more difficult questions. But where uncertainty exists with respect to whether a certain period of GPS surveillance is long enough to constitute a Fourth Amendment search, the police may always seek a warrant. We also need not consider whether prolonged GPS monitoring in the context of investigations involving extraordinary offenses would similarly intrude on a constitutionally protected sphere of privacy. In such cases, long-term tracking might have been mounted using previously available techniques.

> For these reasons, I conclude that the lengthy monitoring that occurred in this case constituted a search under the Fourth Amendment.

United States v. Jones, 565 U.S. 400, 430–31 (Alito, J., concurring in the judgment).

If *Carpenter* is based on the reasoning of Justice Alito's *Jones* concurrence, does that mean that some kind of short-term collection of CSLI is not a search?

If so, how short is short enough not to be a search? In Kinslow v. State, 2019 WL 2440229 (Ind. Ct. App. 2019), investigators placed a GPS device inside a package that Kinslow later picked up and placed in his car. The police tracked the location of Kinslow's car as it drove around for about six hours. The Indiana Court of Appeals held that no search occurred under *Carpenter*:

> While the United States Supreme Court found that tracking such information violated Carpenter's expectation of privacy, we read the Court's holding to apply to records, such as cellphone tracking data, that hold for many Americans the 'privacies of life.' Cell phone location data provides an intimate window into a person's life, revealing not only his particular movements, but through them his professional, political, religious, and sexual associations. Because the tracking of Kinslow lasted only approximately six hours and because the electronic devices used here do not provide an intimate window into a person's life, we find that *Carpenter* has no bearing on this case.

Id. at *3 n.6. *See also* Sims v. State, 569 S.W.3d 634 (Tex. Ct. Crim. App. 2019) (holding that *Carpenter* applies to real-time cell-site pinging, but that obtaining real-time location with five pings over less than three hours was insufficient to trigger a *Carpenter* search).

C. EXCEPTIONS TO THE WARRANT REQUIREMENT

2. EXIGENT CIRCUMSTANCES

At the top of page 477, before the beginning of Section 3, add the following new Notes 5 and 6:

5.   *When does seizing a computer for too long without a warrant justify suppression of the evidence found inside it?* In United States v. Jobe, 933 F.3d 1074 (9th Cir. 2019), the Ninth Circuit added a wrinkle to the question of how long an officer can seize a computer before obtaining a warrant to search it. Even if a computer was seized and held for an overly long period, the court reasoned, the good-faith exception to the exclusionary rule may apply if the extended period of the warrantless seizure was not particularly culpable and the officer reasonably believed the seizure was reasonable. In that setting, there may be no suppression remedy for the failure to obtain a warrant promptly. *Id.* at 1079–80.

If *Jobe* is correct that the good-faith exception can apply in these circumstances, how much more time should the good-faith exception add to the period over which a warrantless seizure of a computer is effectively allowed?

6.   *Exigent circumstances requires reason to believe digital evidence will be destroyed or concealed.* In Hupp v. Cook, 931 F.3d 307 (4th Cir. 2019), Trooper Cook testified that he had a regular practice of seizing any computer or cell phone that he believed might contain video of a crime he was

investigating. He did this, he claimed, because digital evidence can be easily deleted or destroyed. The Fourth Circuit concluded that Trooper Cook's regular practice was not permitted by the exigent circumstances exception:

> In an era in which cell phones are increasingly used to capture much of what happens in daily life, it is important to emphasize the limitations that the Fourth Amendment continues to place on a state's seizure of video evidence.
>
> The exigent circumstances exception does not permit police officers to do what Trooper Cook routinely does: seize video evidence without a warrant even when there is no reason to believe that the evidence will likely be destroyed or concealed. Such a rule would allow officers to seize as a matter of course video-recording devices from not just those involved in an incident, but also from neighbors and other curious bystanders who happen to record the events as they transpire. Under this view, police officers would lawfully be permitted to enter the home of every person living nearby who stands in her doorway or window recording an arrest, to seize her recording device, and to do so without a warrant or her consent—simply because video evidence, by its nature, can be easily deleted.
>
> Such a view finds no support in our Fourth Amendment jurisprudence. While video evidence contained in a cell phone can be easily deleted or concealed, it is not merely the ease with which evidence may be destroyed or concealed that dictates exigency. An officer must also have reason to believe that the evidence will be destroyed or concealed. In short, adopting the broad definition of exigency urged by Trooper Cook would remove the exigent circumstances exception to the warrant requirement from the class of narrow and well-delineated exceptions permissible under the Fourth Amendment. It would convert exigency from an exception to the rule.

Id. at 329–30.

4. BORDER SEARCHES

At the bottom of page 517, add the following new Notes 8, 9, and 10:

8.   *Federal circuits divide on applying the border search exception to computers.* Recent decisions from the Fourth Circuit and Eleventh Circuit have reached different conclusions on how to apply the border exception to computers. The new decisions create a clear disagreement among lower courts that may prompt review from the United States Supreme Court.

First, in United States v. Kolsuz, 890 F.3d 133 (4th Cir. 2018), the Fourth Circuit held that forensic searches of computers at the border require some kind of suspicion. The Fourth Circuit's decision, authored by Judge Pamela

Harris, did not resolve exactly how much suspicion was required—whether reasonable suspicion was sufficient as *Cotterman* had held, or if probable cause was needed, or even if the legal process of a warrant was necessary. But echoing the Ninth Circuit's decision in *Cotterman*, the Fourth Circuit in *Kolsuz* rejected the notion that forensic searches of computers could be allowed without any suspicion at all. Much of the reasoning in *Kolsuz* tracked the Ninth Circuit's reasoning in *Cotterman*, which the Fourth Circuit argued was bolstered by the Supreme Court's subsequent decision in *Riley v. California*, 573 U.S. 373 (2014):

> And then came *Riley*, in which the Supreme Court confirmed every particular of [the reasoning in *Cotterman*]. *Riley* holds that the search incident to arrest exception, which allows for automatic searches of personal effects in the possession of an arrestee, does not apply to manual searches of cell phones. The key to *Riley*'s reasoning is its express refusal to treat such phones as just another form of container, like the wallets, bags, address books, and diaries covered by the search incident exception. Instead, *Riley* insists, cell phones are fundamentally different in both a quantitative and a qualitative sense from other objects traditionally subject to government searches.
>
> And that is so, *Riley* explains, for precisely the reasons already identified by cases treating border searches of digital devices as nonroutine: the immense storage capacity of cell phones, putting a vastly larger array of information at risk of exposure; the special sensitivity of the kinds of information that may be stored on a phone, such as browsing history and historical location data; and, finally, the element of pervasiveness that characterizes cell phones, making them an "insistent part of daily life.
>
> After *Riley*, we think it is clear that a forensic search of a digital phone must be treated as a nonroutine border search, requiring some form of individualized suspicion.

Id. at 146. Notably, *Kolsuz* left open the possibility that there is also an individualized suspicion requirement for a manual search of a computer at the border. *See id.* at n.5 ("Because Kolsuz does not challenge the initial manual search of his phone at Dulles, we have no occasion here to consider whether *Riley* calls into question the permissibility of suspicionless manual searches of digital devices at the border.")

Two weeks after the Fourth Circuit handed down *Kolsuz*, the Eleventh Circuit adopted a very different approach in United States v. Touset, 890 F.3d 1227 (11th Cir. 2018). In a decision by Judge William Pryor, the Eleventh Circuit held that no suspicion is required for a border search of a computer whether it is a manual or forensic search:

> We see no reason why the Fourth Amendment would require suspicion for a forensic search of an electronic device when it imposes

no such requirement for a search of other personal property. Just as the United States is entitled to search a fuel tank for drugs, it is entitled to search a flash drive for child pornography. And it does not make sense to say that electronic devices should receive special treatment because so many people now own them or because they can store vast quantities of records or effects. The same could be said for a recreational vehicle filled with personal effects or a tractor-trailer loaded with boxes of documents. Border agents bear the same responsibility for preventing the importation of contraband in a traveler's possession regardless of advances in technology. Indeed, inspection of a traveler's property at the border is an old practice and is intimately associated with excluding illegal articles from the country.

In contrast with searches of property, we have required reasonable suspicion at the border only for highly intrusive searches of a person's body. Even though the Supreme Court has declined to decide what level of suspicion, if any, is required for such nonroutine border searches of a person, [our Eleventh Circuit caselaw has] required reasonable suspicion for a strip search or an x-ray examination. We have defined the intrusiveness of a search of a person's body that requires reasonable suspicion in terms of the indignity that will be suffered by the person being searched in contrast with whether one search will reveal more than another. And we have isolated three factors which contribute to the personal indignity endured by the person searched: (1) physical contact between the searcher and the person searched; (2) exposure of intimate body parts; and (3) use of force.

These factors are irrelevant to searches of electronic devices. A forensic search of an electronic device is not like a strip search or an x-ray; it does not require border agents to touch a traveler's body, to expose intimate body parts, or to use any physical force against him. Although it may intrude on the privacy of the owner, a forensic search of an electronic device is a search of property. And our precedents do not require suspicion for intrusive searches of any property at the border.

Id. at 1234. Judge Pryor's opinion in *Touset* recognizes the Eleventh Circuit disagreement with the Ninth Circuit in *Cotterman* and the Fourth Circuit's decision in *Kolsuz*.

Although the Supreme Court stressed in *Riley* that the search of a cell phone risks a significant intrusion on privacy, *Riley* does not apply to searches at the border. And our precedent considers only the personal indignity of a search, not its extensiveness. Again, we fail to see how the personal nature of data stored on electronic devices could trigger this kind of indignity when our precedent establishes that a suspicionless search of a home at the border does not. Property and persons are different.

We are also unpersuaded that a traveler's privacy interest should be given greater weight than the paramount interest of the sovereign in protecting its territorial integrity. The Ninth and Fourth Circuits stressed the former interest and asserted that travelers have no practical options to protect their privacy when traveling abroad. For example, the Ninth Circuit explained that it is "impractical, if not impossible, for individuals to make meaningful decisions regarding what digital content to expose to the scrutiny that accompanies international travel" and that "removing files unnecessary to an impending trip" is "a time-consuming task that may not even effectively erase the files." *Cotterman*, 709 F.3d at 965. The Fourth Circuit added that "it is neither realistic nor reasonable to expect the average traveler to leave his digital devices at home when traveling." *Kolsuz*, 890 F.3d at 145.

But a traveler's expectation of privacy is less at the border, and the Fourth Amendment does not guarantee the right to travel without great inconvenience, even within our borders. Anyone who has recently taken a domestic flight likely experienced inconvenient screening procedures that require passengers to unpack electronic devices, separate and limit liquids, gels, and creams, remove their shoes, and walk through a full-body scanner. Travelers crossing a border are on notice that a search may be made, and they are free to leave any property they do not want searched—unlike their bodies— at home.

In contrast with the diminished privacy interests of travelers, the government's interest in preventing the entry of unwanted persons and effects is at its zenith at the international border. Nothing in *Riley* undermines this interest. In *Riley*, the Supreme Court explained that the rationales that support the search-incident-to-arrest exception—namely the concerns of harm to officers and destruction of evidence—did not have much force with respect to digital content on cell phones, because digital data does not pose comparable risks. But digital child pornography [involved in *Touset*] poses the same exact risk of unlawful entry at the border as its physical counterpart. If anything, the advent of sophisticated technological means for concealing contraband only heightens the need of the government to search property at the border unencumbered by judicial second-guessing.

Indeed, if we were to require reasonable suspicion for searches of electronic devices, we would create special protection for the property most often used to store and disseminate child pornography. With the advent of the internet, child pornography offenses overwhelmingly involve the use of electronic devices for the receipt, storage, and distribution of unlawful images. And law enforcement officers routinely investigate child-pornography offenses by forensically searching an individual's electronic devices. We see no reason why we would permit traditional, invasive searches of all other kinds of property, but create a special rule that will benefit offenders who now conceal contraband in a new kind of property.

Id. at 1234–35.

Where does that leave us? After *Cotterman, Kolsuz,* and *Touset,* the law of computer border searches in the Ninth, Fourth, and Eleventh Circuits can be summarized by the following chart:

	Ninth Circuit (Cotterman)	*Fourth Circuit (Kolsuz)*	*Eleventh Circuit (Touset)*
Manual Search at the Border	No suspicion required	Undecided	No suspicion required
Forensic Search at the Border	Reasonable suspicion required	Some individualized suspicion required, although undecided how much	No suspicion required

If the Supreme Court agrees to decide how the Fourth Amendment applies to border searches, how should the Supreme Court rule? Should there be a different answer for manual searches and forensic searches? Or should there be one answer for all computer searches—and if so, what should it be?

9. *More on the distinction between manual and forensic searches.* The Fourth Circuit offered additional clarification on the distinction between "manual" and "forensic" searches in United States v. Kolsuz, 890 F.3d 133 (4th Cir. 2018). Recall from Note 2 on page 514 of your casebook that *Kolsuz* involved the use of a Cellebrite Universal Forensic Extraction Device Physical Analyzer to extract 896 printed pages of data from a cell phone. The Fourth Circuit agreed with the district court that this was a forensic search. The Fourth Circuit further explained the distinction by reference to a computer border search policy enacted by the Department of Homeland Security:

> Shortly after argument in this case, the Department of Homeland Security adopted a policy that treats forensic searches of digital devices as nonroutine border searches, insofar as such searches now may be conducted only with reasonable suspicion of activity that violates the customs laws or in cases raising national security

concerns. U.S. Customs and Border Prot., CBP Directive No. 3340–049A, Border Search of Electronic Devices 5 (2018).

> The new policy does not use the "routine" and "nonroutine" terminology of Supreme Court case law, distinguishing instead between "basic" and "advanced" searches. But the import is the same. "Basic" searches (like those we term "manual") are examinations of an electronic device that do not entail the use of external equipment or software and may be conducted without suspicion. "Advanced" searches (like "forensic" searches) involve the connection of external equipment to a device—such as the Cellebrite Physical Analyzer used on Kolsuz's phone—in order to review, copy, or analyze its contents, and are subject to the restrictions noted above.

Id. at 146, 146 n.6. At least in the Fourth Circuit, then, the distinction between manual and forensic searches appears to hinge on whether the search involves the use of external equipment or software.

10. *What is the permitted scope of a border search of an electronic device?* Most of the caselaw applying the border search exception to computers considers how much cause the government must establish for such a search to start. In United States v. Cano, 934 F.3d 1002 (9th Cir. 2019), the Ninth Circuit focused on the next question: Assuming there is a lawful basis to begin a border search of an electronic storage device, how comprehensive can the search be? In other words, how far can such a search extend?

Manuel Cano attempted to cross the border from Mexico to the United States at the San Ysidro Port of Entry in Southern California. A drug-sniffing dog alerted to the presence of drugs in Cano's car. A search of the car's spare tire revealed 14 kilograms of cocaine stored inside it. Cano was arrested, and an officer conducted three searches of the cell phone he was carrying. First, an officer briefly conducted a manual search of the phone that revealed a "lengthy call log" but no text messages. Second, an officer conducted a second manual search that revealed additional information in the call log and uncovered two text messages on the phone that had arrived after Cano had arrived at the border. The officer also wrote down some of the numbers in the call log and took photos of the text messages. Third, an official then used Cellebrite software to conduct a search of the phone that revealed extensive information including its call history.

The Ninth Circuit ruled that the first search was constitutional but that the second and third searches violated the Fourth Amendment. According to Judge Bybee, writing for the panel, the animating purpose of the border search exception is "interdicting foreign contraband," not merely searching "for evidence that would aid in prosecuting past and preventing future border-related crimes." *Id.* at 1017. To keep the scope of searches within that purpose, the border search exception must be interpreted to "authorize[ ] warrantless searches of a cell phone only to determine whether the phone contains contraband." *Id.* at 1018. This meant that "border officials are limited to searching for contraband only," and "they may not search in a manner untethered to the search for contraband." *Id.* at 1019.

The Ninth Circuit recognized that its approach conflicted with the Fourth Circuit's opinion in United States v. Kolsuz, 890 F.3d 133 (4th Cir. 2018). *Kolsuz* had concluded that "the justification behind the border search exception is broad enough to accommodate not only the direct interception of contraband as it crosses the border, but also the prevention and disruption of ongoing efforts to export contraband illegally." *Id.* at 143. In the Ninth Circuit's view, however, the Fourth Circuit was wrong. The Ninth Circuit's border search exception only permitted a warrantless search for contraband itself, and it did not permit "a warrantless search for evidence of past or future border-related crimes." *Cano*, 934 F.3d at 1018.

Applying its narrow test, the Ninth Circuit concluded that the first manual search was constitutional:

> Once Cano was arrested, [an officer] briefly searched Cano's phone and observed that there were no text messages. The observation that the phone contained no text messages falls comfortably within the scope of a search for digital contraband. Child pornography may be sent via text message, so the officers acted within the scope of a permissible border search in accessing the phone's text messages.

Id. at 1019. The court next ruled that the second manual search was unconstitutional. Although no reasonable suspicion was required for a manual search under Ninth Circuit precedent, the scope of the second manual search violated the Fourth Amendment because it "went beyond a verification that the phone lacked digital contraband." *Id.*

> [The officer] did more than thumb through the phone consistent with a search for contraband. He also recorded phone numbers found in the call log, and he photographed two messages received after Cano had reached the border. Those actions have no connection whatsoever to digital contraband. Criminals may hide contraband in unexpected places, so it was reasonable for the two HSI officers to open the phone's call log to verify that the log contained a list of phone numbers and not surreptitious images or videos. But the border search exception does not justify [the officer's] recording of the phone numbers and text messages for further processing, because that action has no connection to ensuring that the phone lacks digital contraband.

Id. at 1019.

Finally, the Cellebrite search was also unconstitutional. Notably, the court did not decide if the Cellebrite search was a manual search that did not require cause or a forensic search that required reasonable suspicion under Ninth Circuit caselaw. *See id.* at 1021 n.21. Either way, Judge Bybee concluded, the Cellebrite search was unlawful. If the Cellebrite search was a manual search, it was unlawful because it went beyond a verification that the phone lacked digital contraband. And if it was a forensic search, it was unlawful because the relevant kind of reasonable suspicion was lacking:

> We have held that a "highly intrusive" search—such as a forensic cell phone search—requires some level of particularized suspicion. But that just begs the question: Particularized suspicion of what? Contraband? Or evidence of future border-related crimes? Having concluded above that border searches are limited in scope to searches for contraband and do not encompass searches for evidence of past or future border-related crimes, we think the answer here is clear: to conduct a more intrusive, forensic cell phone search border officials must reasonably suspect that the cell phone to be searched itself contains contraband.
>
> Were we to rule otherwise, the government could conduct a full forensic search of every electronic device of anyone arrested at the border, for the probable cause required to justify an arrest at the border will always satisfy the lesser reasonable suspicion standard needed to justify a forensic search. As the Court pointed out in *Riley v. California*, modern cell phones are "minicomputers" with "immense storage capacity." Such phones "carry a cache of sensitive personal information"—"the sum of an individual's private life"—such that a search of a cell phone may give the government not only "sensitive records previously found in the home," but a "broad array of private information never found in a home in any form—unless the phone is." Were we to give the government unfettered access to cell phones, we would enable the government to evade the protections laid out in *Riley* on the mere basis that the searches occurred at the border.
>
> Moreover, in cases such as this, where the individual suspected of committing the border-related crime has already been arrested, there is no reason why border officials cannot obtain a warrant before conducting their forensic search. This is particularly true in light of advances in technology that now permit the more expeditious processing of warrant applications. Indeed, in most cases the time required to obtain a warrant would seem trivial compared to the hours, days, and weeks needed to complete a forensic electronic search. We therefore conclude that border officials may conduct a forensic cell phone search only when they reasonably suspect that the cell phone to be searched itself contains contraband.

Id. at 1019–20. Under this standard, a forensic search of the phone was unlawful: "Although [the officers] had reason to suspect that Cano's phone would contain evidence leading to additional drugs, the record does not give rise to any objectively reasonable suspicion that the digital data in the phone contained contraband." *Id.* at 1021.

Do you agree that border searches of digital storage devices must be limited to searches for contraband such as child pornography, and that they cannot be conducted to collect non-contraband evidence of criminal activity? If so, how can you tell whether a digital search is sufficiently limited? Is the test a subjective inquiry into what the officer was looking for? Or is it an objective inquiry into whether the search was consistent with that of a reasonable officer looking for contraband? Further, imagine an officer searches a phone by making ten different queries through the search function of its operating system over a period of ten minutes. Should that count as ten different searches, with each query individually evaluated for whether it is a lawful search for contraband? Or should all ten queries count as a single search that is collectively evaluated for its lawfulness?

D. SEARCHING AND SEIZING COMPUTERS WITH A WARRANT

1. PROBABLE CAUSE

On page 541, at the bottom, add the following new Note 7:

7. *Probable cause based on clicking on a website address from an unknown source.* In United States v. Bosyk, 933 F.3d 319 (4th Cir. 2019), the Fourth Circuit divided on whether a magistrate judge had a substantial basis for finding probable cause to search a home based on a single click of a website link.

Here are the basic facts. Investigators were monitoring an online message board dedicated to child pornography referred to in the opinion as Bulletin Board A. Bulletin Board A was hosted on the Internet's "dark web," which consists of websites that are available only through anonymizing services that hide the location of the webserver and its users. On a particular day, an unknown user of Bulletin Board A posted a link to a website address on a file-sharing website. The file-sharing site was typically used for lawful content, and it permitted anyone to upload and share various media. The posting on Bulletin Board A indicated that child pornography videos were available at the specific link on the file-sharing website, and it included the password that was needed to access and view the videos.

The government could not obtain any records from Bulletin Board A about who had posted or accessed the files. Because Bulletin Board A was on the dark web, the location of its server was unknown and it was effectively unreachable. Instead, the government issued a subpoena to the file-sharing website asking for any IP addresses that had been used to visit the address at which the child pornography videos had been available on the file-sharing website. In response to the subpoena, the file-sharing website disclosed that one of the requests for files at that address that was made on the same day as the posting on Bulletin Board A was from an IP address assigned to a particular home.

Investigators obtained a warrant to search the home for child pornography. The police then executed the search, which belonged to Bosyk. The search revealed thousands of images and videos of child pornography—

including the videos that were available from the link posted on Bulletin Board A.

The Fourth Circuit divided on whether the magistrate judge had a substantial basis to find probable cause to issue the warrant to search Bosyk's home. Writing for the majority, Judge Diaz concluded that probable cause existed:

> The facts in the affidavit support a reasonable inference that someone using Bosyk's IP address clicked the link knowing that it contained child pornography. This in turn makes it fairly probable that criminal evidence would have been found at Bosyk's address.

> The critical fact in this case is the timing. On the very day that someone clicked the link, it appeared on a website whose purpose was to advertise and distribute child pornography to its limited membership. And it appeared in a post containing text and images that unequivocally identified its contents as child pornography. The close timing between the link's appearance on Bulletin Board A and the click by a user's IP address is highly relevant: because the link was accessed on the same day it appeared on Bulletin Board A, it is at least reasonably probable that the user clicked the link having encountered it on that website.

> With this fair assumption, several inferences drop into place to support the magistrate judge's decision to issue the warrant. If one assumes, given the close timing, that the user accessed the link after seeing it on Bulletin Board A, it's fair to conclude that the user also knew it contained child pornography, as that much was explicit from the posting. On top of that, one can fairly conclude that the same person typed the password posted on Bulletin Board A, downloaded the content, and viewed the video contained at that URL. For why else would someone who had seen the pornographic stills and read the description on Bulletin Board A click the link if not to access its contents? Thus, if we suppose that someone accessed the link through Bulletin Board A, it's fairly probable that the same person downloaded or viewed child-pornographic images.

> Recall that the magistrate judge knew someone using Bosyk's home IP address had clicked the link. Given that fact—and the permissible inferences described above—we think it was fairly probable that child pornography would be found on computers or other devices within Bosyk's property. And because child pornography constitutes contraband or evidence of a crime, this is all that was needed for probable cause to search Bosyk's house.

Id. at 325–26.

Judge Wynn dissented. According to Judge Wynn, probable cause was lacking because there was no reason to think that the click on the file-sharing website had come from Bulletin Board A. That click could have come from anywhere. And without knowing where the click had come from, there was no reason to think that whoever clicked on the link had sufficient reason to realize that the link contained child pornography that would then be found on the computer in the home searched:

> Users can *encounter* URLs, or hyperlinks to URLs, in myriad ways—including through websites, emails, chats, text messages, comment threads, discussion boards, File Sharing Sites (such as DropBox, Google Drive, or Apple iCloud), tweets, Facebook posts, Instagram captions, Snapchat messages, embedded images or videos, unwanted pop-up windows, any combination thereof, or by any other digital means. And because a URL, or a hyperlink to a URL, can be copied with only a click of a button, a single URL can be copied and further disseminated through any or all of these ways millions of additional times, often in a matter of seconds.

> Thus, it is no exaggeration to state that URLs, or hyperlinks to URLs, can be posted and disseminated millions of times anywhere by anyone. Take for example, the trailer for the movie *Avengers: Endgame*—which was shared through multiple online platforms such as YouTube, Facebook, and Twitter—was viewed 289 million times in the first 24 hours after it was posted online. Todd Spangler, *'Avengers: Endgame' Trailer Smashes 24-Hour Video Views Record*, Variety (Dec. 8, 2018, 11:02 a.m.). In this matter, none of the facts alleged in the affidavit rule out any of these potentially millions of alternative paths—wholly unconnected to the Bulletin Board A post—through which someone using Defendant's IP address could have encountered the URL navigating to the child pornography on File Sharing Site.

> Additionally, users can *navigate* to a URL in numerous ways beyond clicking on a link included in a post on a particular webpage, like Bulletin Board A. For example, a user could click on a copy of the URL posted to another website, click on a bookmark, type the URL directly into a browser's navigation bar, or click a hyperlink in an email or a news article, to name only a few. That is particularly true when the URL navigates to a site on the normal Internet, like File Sharing Site, as opposed to a site, like Bulletin Board A, that can only be reached using a specialty browser, like Tor.

> Importantly, users can *unintentionally navigate* to URLs because—as is the case with the URL clicked by someone using Defendant's IP address—URLs frequently do not provide any external indication of the content to which they navigate. For example, services like YouTube and DropBox generate random URLs that provide no information about their underlying content. Other services, like Bitly, TinyURL, and Perma shorten URLs, which may otherwise provide external indicators of their content, to generic URLs that include a standard URL base, such as "https://bit.ly/,"

"https://tinyurl.com/," or "https://perma.cc/," followed by a random string of alphanumeric characters. Such generic URLs offer no indication of the content to which they navigate.

Link shortening and disguising often serve beneficial purposes by, for example, permitting distribution of password-protected files, facilitating the sharing of less clunky links, or permitting simpler citation styles. And link shortening and disguising can serve other innocuous purposes. URL spoofing, for example, permits one user to disguise a hyperlink as directing to specific content or a particular website, while in reality directing the unwitting user to a distinct website altogether.

One humorous form of URL spoofing is "rickrolling," one of the Internet's oldest memes, in which individuals click on a link expecting one thing but are instead led to a video of Rick Astley singing 'Never Gonna Give You Up.' The unsuspecting individual who follows the disguised URL is said to be "rickrolled."

Thus, with a few clicks, anyone—even users with no advanced computational skills—can disguise a link and lure an unsuspecting user to click that link. In such circumstances, the user would learn of the content to which the URL navigates only *after* clicking on the link.

In sum, there are myriad ways users can encounter and navigate to a URL—including unintentionally, particularly when, as here, the text of the URL provides no indication as to the nature of the content to which it navigates. Accordingly, even if the Bulletin Board A post preceded the attempt by someone using Defendant's IP address to download child pornography from File Sharing Site—a fact not established by the affidavit—there are potentially millions of paths through which someone using Defendant's IP address could have encountered and navigated to the File Sharing Site URL hosting the child pornography other than through Bulletin Board A.

Put simply, the affidavit does not establish the probability of the single sequence of events upon which the majority opinion relies— that someone using Defendant's IP address navigated to the File Sharing Site URL after encountering it on Bulletin Board A.

Id. at 342–46 (Wynn, J., dissenting).

Can the disagreement between Judge Diaz and Judge Wynn be resolved by understanding the nature of the probable cause standard? Importantly, the relevant legal question is whether probable cause was shown that child pornography would be found in the home, not whether probable cause was shown that someone had intentionally looked for child pornography. Given that, how much does it matter whether the person who visited the specific address where child pornography would be obtained had done so intending to find child pornography?

5.   EX ANTE RESTRICTIONS ON COMPUTER WARRANTS

On page 596 at the top, add the following new Note 10 before the beginning of Section 6:

10. *Varying ex ante restrictions based on probable cause?* In United States v. Stetkiw, 2019 WL 2866516 (E.D. Mich. 2019), Judge Victoria Roberts suggested that whether magistrate judges impose ex ante search restrictions should be decided on a case-by-case basis based in part on how much probable cause exists:

> Ex ante review is a flexible system where the magistrate judge can balance the needs of an investigation and the demands of the Fourth Amendment. Certain procedures may be found inappropriate in certain contexts depending on the extent of probable cause the Government has, but that is distinct from mandating that the Government follow a specific procedure.

> Ex ante review is flexible enough that the Government can opt to apply for a warrant with no procedures or minimization and still be approved. However, in such cases the Government should demonstrate that the level of probable cause to search ESI is high enough to justify a search without minimization. Additionally, even if a no-protocol approach is appropriate at the outset, it is recommended the Government return to the reviewing judge to confirm that searching the ESI without a protocol is appropriate after the investigation proceeds far enough for that information to become available.

> The Court recommends that the Government submit the procedural steps it will take to minimize searching non-responsive ESI in its warrant applications. It is also recommended that magistrate judges deny applications if they find the Government has not proposed sufficient means to minimize the search of non-responsive ESI, given the extent of probable cause shown. If the Government needs to change its procedures mid-investigation, it is encouraged to return to the magistrate judge for approval.

Id. at *5–*6. *See also* Emily Berman, *Digital Searches, the Fourth Amendment, and the Magistrates' Revolt*, 68 Emory L.J. 49, 55 (2018) (advocating the use of ex ante search restrictions).

According to Judge Roberts, magistrate judges can impose ex ante restrictions to "balance the needs of an investigation and the demands of the Fourth Amendment" on a flexible case-by-case basis. Consider what this means. Traditionally, investigators identify the needs of an investigation. Investigators determine which steps they will pursue to collect evidence subject to legal restrictions such as the Fourth Amendment. Does Judge Roberts envision a different system, in which magistrate judges manage criminal investigations and decide what the government's needs are and whether particular investigative tools are proper on a flexible case-by-case basis? If so, why should magistrate judges have that power?

6. ENCRYPTION

b) Fifth Amendment Issues

On page 609, after Note 1, add the following new Note 1.1:

1.1 The Massachusetts Supreme Judicial Court adopted the analysis proposed in Note 1 in Commonwealth v. Jones, 481 Mass. 540 (2019). The government had obtained a warrant to search Jones's locked LG cell phone. The government also obtained an order requiring Jones to unlock the phone. When Jones asserted his privilege against self-incrimination under both the Fifth Amendment and its state equivalent, Article 12 of the Massachusetts Declaration of Rights, the court offered the following explanation of how the foregone conclusion doctrine should apply:

> For the foregone conclusion exception to apply, the Commonwealth must establish that it already knows the testimony that is implicit in the act of the required production. In the context of compelled decryption, the only fact conveyed by compelling a defendant to enter the password to an encrypted electronic device is that the defendant knows the password, and can therefore access the device. The Commonwealth must therefore establish that a defendant knows the password to decrypt an electronic device before his or her knowledge of the password can be deemed a foregone conclusion under the Fifth Amendment or art. 12.

> We clarify that the evidence at issue in the compelled decryption here is the password itself, not the contents of the phone. The only testimony that would be conveyed by compelling the defendant to enter the password is the fact that the defendant knows the password, and therefore has the ability to access the phone. The entry would convey no information about the contents of the LG phone.

> The analysis would be different had the Commonwealth sought to compel the defendant to produce specific files located in the contents of the LG phone. If that had been the case, the production of the files would implicitly convey far more information than just the fact that the defendant knows the password. The defendant's production of specific files would implicitly testify to the existence of the files, his control over them, and their authenticity. Accordingly, the Commonwealth would be required to prove its prior knowledge of those facts.

Id. at 548, 538 n.10.

Justice Lenk argued separately in a concurrence that the majority had misapplied the foregone conclusion doctrine. Echoing the Eleventh Circuit's reasoning in *In re Subpoena Duces Tecum*, on page 601 of your casebook, Justice Lenk argued that the government should also be required to demonstrate that the defendant "already knows, with reasonable particularity, the existence and location of relevant, incriminating evidence it expects to find on that device." But the majority disagreed:

> This is not correct. It is well established that under the Fourth Amendment to the United States Constitution and art. 14 of the Massachusetts Declaration of Rights, the police are ordinarily required to obtain a search warrant before a search of the contents of an electronic device may take place. Accordingly, in this case, the police were required to obtain a warrant before they could seek to search the contents of the LG phone, and they did so. The full protections against improper searches—probable cause to believe that a crime had been committed and that evidence of the crime would be found on the device—were required and, in the opinion of the clerk-magistrate who issued the search warrant, were satisfied here.
>
> The standard proposed by the concurrence conflates these protections with the protections afforded by art. 12 of the Massachusetts Declaration of Rights. Our task under art. 12 in this context is to determine only what facts are conveyed to the government when a defendant is compelled to enter a password to decrypt an electronic device. As we have explained, the only fact conveyed by the physical act of entering the password into an electronic device is that the defendant knows the password. Such an act says nothing about the contents of the device. Nor does the act alone "produce" any evidence to the Commonwealth. Accordingly, under these circumstances, the Commonwealth was required to abide by two sets of constitutional protections.
>
> Requiring this dual protection does not, as the concurrence contends, sound a "death knell" for constitutional protection in the digital age. Nor do we read the two constitutional protections in "splendid isolation." Each has its own purpose, function, and requirements, and they work together to form a double protection of digital privacy before particular files on the phone can be accessed

Id. at 549 n.11. *See also* State v. Pittman, 300 Or. App. 147 (2019) (adopting the same reasoning).

Are you more persuaded by the reasoning of the Eleventh Circuit or the reasoning of the Massachusetts Supreme Judicial Court?

On page 611, after Note 5, add the following new Note 5.1:

5.1 *A different view of applying the Fifth Amendment to compelled biometric access.* A majority of judges have concluded that compelling biometric access does not implicate the Fifth Amendment privilege against self-incrimination. They reason that compelling biometric access, such as placing a finger on a keypad, is not testimonial for Fifth Amendment purposes. *See, e.g.,* Note 4 on pages 610–11. A few judges have taken a different view, however. Consider the argument of Magistrate Judge Westmore that compelling biometric access is testimonial under the Fifth Amendment:

> The Court finds that utilizing a biometric feature to unlock an electronic device is not akin to submitting to fingerprinting or a DNA swab, because it differs in two fundamental ways. First, the Government concedes that a finger, thumb, or other biometric feature may be used to unlock a device in lieu of a passcode. In this context, biometric features serve the same purpose of a passcode, which is to secure the owner's content, pragmatically rendering them functionally equivalent.
>
> As the Government acknowledges, there are times when the device will not accept the biometric feature and require the user to type in the passcode to unlock the device. For example, a passcode is generally required when a device has been restarted, inactive, or has not been unlocked for a certain period of time. This is, no doubt, a security feature to ensure that someone without the passcode cannot readily access the contents of the phone. Indeed, the Government expresses some urgency with the need to compel the use of the biometric features to bypass the need to enter a passcode.
>
> This urgency appears to be rooted in the Government's inability to compel the production of the passcode under the current jurisprudence. It follows, however, that if a person cannot be compelled to provide a passcode because it is a testimonial communication, a person cannot be compelled to provide one's finger, thumb, iris, face, or other biometric feature to unlock that same device.
>
> Second, requiring someone to affix their finger or thumb to a digital device is fundamentally different than requiring a suspect to submit to fingerprinting. A finger or thumb scan used to unlock a device indicates that the device belongs to a particular individual. In other words, the act concedes that the phone was in the possession and control of the suspect, and authenticates ownership or access to the phone and all of its digital contents. Thus, the act of unlocking a phone with a finger or thumb scan far exceeds the "physical evidence" created when a suspect submits to fingerprinting to merely compare his fingerprints to existing physical evidence (another fingerprint) found at a crime scene, because there is no comparison or witness corroboration required to confirm a positive match.
>
> Instead, a successful finger or thumb scan confirms ownership or control of the device, and, unlike fingerprints, the authentication of its contents cannot be reasonably refuted. In a similar situation, the court in *In re Application for a Search Warrant* observed that "with a touch of a finger, a suspect is testifying that he or she has accessed

the phone before, at a minimum, to set up the fingerprint password capabilities, and that he or she currently has some level of control over or relatively significant connection to the phone and its contents." 236 F.Supp.3d 1066, 1073 (N.D. Ill. 2017).

It is also noteworthy that many smartphone applications providing access to personal, private information—including medical records and financial accounts—now allow users to utilize biometric features in lieu of passcodes to access those records. As Judge Weisman astutely observed, using a fingerprint to place someone at a particular location is a starkly different scenario than using a finger scan to access a database of someone's most private information. Thus, the undersigned finds that a biometric feature is analogous to the nonverbal, physiological responses elicited during a polygraph test, which are used to determine guilt or innocence, and are considered testimonial.

While the Court sympathizes with the Government's interest in accessing the contents of any electronic devices it might lawfully seize, there are other ways that the Government might access the content that do not trample on the Fifth Amendment. In the instant matter, the Government may obtain any Facebook Messenger communications from Facebook under the Stored Communications Act or warrant based on probable cause. While it may be more expedient to circumvent Facebook, and attempt to gain access by infringing on the Fifth Amendment's privilege against self-incrimination, it is an abuse of power and is unconstitutional.

In the Matter of the Search of a Residence in Oakland, Cal., 354 F. Supp. 3d 1010, 1015–16 (N.D. Cal. 2019) (Westmore, M.J.).

Are you persuaded by Magistrate Judge Westmore's analysis? Consider her argument that biometric access must be testimonial because it is "functionally equivalent" to compelling the disclosure of the passcode. Does this functional equivalence test make sense? Imagine a person sets up his phone so that there are two ways of unlocking it. The first way requires making a testimonial statement, and the second way does not. Why should the functional equivalence of these two methods from the standpoint of access to evidence mean that the Fifth Amendment must apply in the same way to both methods? And if the same standard must apply, does which standard applies depend which issue is decided first? Most courts have held that compelling biometric access is not testimonial. If courts apply a functional equivalence test, does this mean that forcing a suspect to state his passcode must now be deemed non-testimonial because it is the functional equivalent of the non-testimonial act of compelling biometric access?

CHAPTER 6

STATUTORY PRIVACY PROTECTIONS

...

D. THE STORED COMMUNICATIONS ACT

1. THE BASIC STRUCTURE

On page 691 at the top, add the following new Note 8 before the beginning of Section 2:

8. *Applying the SCA to websites with messaging services.* Modern websites often permit users to create accounts that allow users to send and receive messages with other users. The dual functionality of such websites raises a question: Does the SCA treat the messages sent and received like e-mails that are covered by the SCA, or does it treat them like other website records not covered by the SCA?

This issue arose in Casillas v. Cypress Ins. Co., 770 Fed. Appx. 329 (9th Cir. 2019). Casillas had an account at a website operated by HQ Sign-Up Services ("HQSU"). According to Casillas, agents of the Cypress Insurance Company hacked into his account and stole electronic case files that Casillas had stored in his account. Casillas sued Cypress under the civil provision of the SCA, which applies only to unauthorized access to providers of ECS. The district court ruled that the stolen files were being held by HQSU acting as a provider of RCS, not a provider of ECS, and therefore that the civil SCA suit could not proceed. *See* Casillas v. Berkshire Hathaway Homestate Cos., 2017 WL 2813145 (C.D. Cal. 2017).

On appeal, the Ninth Circuit affirmed in an unpublished opinion using a different and broader rationale. According to the Ninth Circuit, the suit could not proceed because HQSU was not configured properly to provide ECS even though it enabled users to send and receive messages:

> It is evident that HQSU does not permit users to communicate directly with each other. The documents and accompanying comments do not travel directly from the sender to the recipient; instead, the recipient of any message would have to *retrieve* it by downloading it from HQSU's server.

> Because Plaintiffs do not allege that any direct communication takes place, the district court correctly determined that Plaintiffs fail to plead that HQSU constitutes an ECS provider. Plaintiffs argue that the district court drew a false dichotomy between an RCS and an ECS

when it determined that HQSU can be characterized only as an RCS. This argument lacks merit. An RCS is an off-site provider that processes and stores data, such as physicians and hospitals maintaining medical files in offsite data banks. In other words, an RCS is a virtual filing cabinet.

Plaintiffs correctly point out that, in some cases, a single entity may be both an ECS and an RCS. But such a duality will exist only when the service provider fulfills both of the provided definitions; separate analyses are required. Here, even if HQSU's website, database, and servers constitute an RCS, the inability to communicate directly with users leaves HQSU outside of the SCA's definition of an ECS.

Id. at 331.

Does this distinction make sense? What is the difference between messaging services that send messages "directly" from sender to recipient and those that require the recipient to "retrieve" the message from the server? Consider a web-based e-mail provider. On one hand, it is a classic example of an ECS provider. On the other hand, users have to log in to their accounts and retrieve their web-based e-mails from the server. Can the Ninth Circuit's reasoning be correct?

3. VOLUNTARY DISCLOSURE UNDER § 2702

On page 716, add the following citation at the end of Note 10:

See also Facebook v. Superior Court, 4 Cal.5th 1245, 1282–85 (Cal. 2018) (agreeing with the reasoning of *Negro*).

On page 718, add the following new Note 15:

15. *The consent exception and public postings.* Imagine a private party issues a subpoena to Facebook directing Facebook to disclose status updates that the user had posted on his Facebook wall. Imagine some of the status updates were configured to be visible to the general public, while other status updates were configured so that they could be viewed only by the person's Facebook friends. Must Facebook comply with the subpoena, or is compliance blocked by the Stored Communications Act?

In Facebook v. Superior Court, 4 Cal.5th 1245 (Cal. 2018), the Supreme Court of California held that the answer depends on the privacy settings of the status update. If the privacy settings are set to public, the court reasoned, then the posting of the contents in a way available to the public amounts to consent to disclosure that is permitted by the implied consent provision of 18 U.S.C. 2702(b)(3). *See id.* at 1274–7. On the other hand, if the posting is restricted, then there is no implied consent. That is true, the court held, even if "a communication was configured by the user to be accessible to a large group of friends or followers." *Id.* at 1281.

Do you agree that a user's privacy settings can create implied consent to disclose communications? If so, what is the relevant timeframe for consent? Users can change the privacy settings for particular communications at any time. Imagine a user posts a public status update in 2018. Two years later, in 2020, the user is embroiled in litigation and restricts the status update to friends only. Does the 2020 restriction amount to a withdrawal of consent?

CHAPTER 7

JURISDICTION

■ ■ ■

B. STATE POWER

2. PROCEDURAL LIMITS

On page 774, at the top, add the following new Note 12:

12. *A warrant requirement for IP addresses?* In State v. Mixton, 447 P.3d 829 (Az. Ct. App. 2019), the Arizona Court of Appeals ruled that the Arizona Constitution requires the state government to obtain a search warrant to collect IP addresses associated with a pseudonymous online account. The court relied in part on the implications of permitting the government to unmask anonymous users with a lower standard:

> We are especially troubled that the third-party doctrine grants the government unfettered ability to learn the identity behind anonymous speech, even without any showing or even suspicion of unlawful activity. An author's decision to remain anonymous, whether "motivated by fear of economic or official retaliation, by concern about social ostracism, or merely by a desire to preserve as much of one's privacy as possible," "is an aspect of the freedom of speech protected by the First Amendment." McIntyre v. Ohio Elections Comm'n, 514 U.S. 334, 341–42 (1995) (striking down state statute outlawing anonymous political leaflets). Even in benign exercise, the government's ability to identify anonymous speakers, if not meaningfully limited, intrudes on the speaker's desire to remain anonymous and may discourage valuable speech. At worst, the power may be wielded to silence dissent.

> Even if the government obtains nothing more without a warrant than basic identifying information connected to specific internet activity, other cherished rights are endangered. The right of free association, for example, is hollow when the government can identify an association's members through subscriber information matched with particular internet activity. To allow the government to obtain without a warrant information showing who a person communicates with and what websites he or she visits may reveal a person's associations and therefore intrude on a person's right to privacy in those associations.

Id. at 842–3.

C. INTERNATIONAL COMPUTER CRIMES

2. STATUTORY PRIVACY LAWS

On page 791, replace Notes 1–3 with the following new Note on the CLOUD Act:

1. *Congress resolves the Microsoft issue by enacting the CLOUD Act.* Congress passed a new law in March 2018 to resolve the question in the *Microsoft* case. The new law, the Clarifying Lawful Overseas Use of Data Act ("CLOUD") Act, was enacted as part of the Consolidated Appropriations Act of 2018, Pub. L. 115–141. The CLOUD Act requires a provider to disclose contents or records "regardless of whether such communication, record, or other information is located within or outside the United States." 18 U.S.C. § 2713. In that sense, the new statute reflects the government's goal in the *Microsoft* litigation. Providers now cannot refuse to comply with domestic legal process based on the foreign location of stored data.

At the same time, the CLOUD Act gives providers a limited statutory basis on which to challenge domestic legal process that involves a conflict with foreign law. The provider has 14 days to file a motion to quash or modify the legal process on the grounds of a perceived conflict of law. The circumstances in which this challenge can succeed are very narrow, however. Under 18 U.S.C. § 2703(h)(2)(A), a provider can file a challenge to domestic legal process only when the following five conditions are all met:

(1) the domestic legal process is seeking the contents of communications;

(2) the provider reasonably believes that the customer or subscriber is not a United States person;

(3) the provider reasonably believes that the customer or subscriber does not reside in the United States; and

(4) the disclosure implicates the law of a foreign government that has been designated a "qualifying foreign government"; and

(5) the provider reasonably believes that the required disclosure would create a material risk that the provider would violate the law of the qualifying foreign government.

The concept of a "qualifying foreign government" is explained in the new Note below. As the new Note explains, a "qualifying foreign government" essentially refers to a foreign government with U.S.-like privacy laws that has been pre-approved as having sufficient privacy protection to permit mutual legal compliance.

After hearing a response from the government, the court can modify or quash (that is, annul) legal process under this provision only if the court makes three findings:

(i)   the required disclosure would cause the provider to violate the laws of a qualifying foreign government;

(ii)   based on the totality of the circumstances, the interests of justice dictate that the legal process should be modified or quashed; and

(iii) the customer or subscriber is not a United States person and does not reside in the United States.

18 U.S.C. § 2703(h)(2)(B).

The "interests of justice" factors are detailed in 18 U.S.C. § 2703(h)(3). Courts should consider, "as appropriate," the following eight factors:

(A)   the interests of the United States, including the investigative interests of the governmental entity seeking to require the disclosure;

(B)   the interests of the qualifying foreign government in preventing any prohibited disclosure;

(C)   the likelihood, extent, and nature of penalties to the provider or any employees of the provider as a result of inconsistent legal requirements imposed on the provider;

(D)   the location and nationality of the subscriber or customer whose communications are being sought, if known, and the nature and extent of the subscriber or customer's connection to the United States, or if the legal process has been sought on behalf of a foreign authority pursuant to section 3512, the nature and extent of the subscriber or customer's connection to the foreign authority's country;

(E)   the nature and extent of the provider's ties to and presence in the United States;

(F)   the importance to the investigation of the information required to be disclosed;

(G)   the likelihood of timely and effective access to the information required to be disclosed through means that would cause less serious negative consequences; and

(H)   if the legal process has been sought on behalf of a foreign authority pursuant to section 3512, the investigative interests of the foreign authority making the request for assistance.

Note that the basis for challenging domestic legal process under the CLOUD Act is exceedingly narrow. The provider must take the initiative and file the challenge. The disclosure must be unlawful under the law of a government that has been designated a "qualifying foreign government." The interests of justice must favor quashing or modifying the legal process. And the account holder must be a non-U.S. person who does not reside in the United States. If any of these requirements has not been met, the domestic legal process is binding on the provider despite the foreign law implications of the process.

How often is that likely to happen?

4. MUTUAL LEGAL ASSISTANCE AND INTERNATIONAL TREATIES

On page 817, replace Note 6 with the following new Notes 6, 6.1, and 6.2:

6. *Congress creates a new regime for cross-border data requests.* In March 2018, Congress created a new legal framework for cross-border data requests with pre-approved foreign governments as part of the Clarifying Lawful Overseas Use of Data Act ("CLOUD") Act. Under the new statute, the United States government can determine that a foreign government is a "qualifying foreign government." *See* 18 U.S.C. § 2523 (establishing the process). When a U.S. provider receives foreign legal process from a qualifying foreign government, new exceptions to the U.S. surveillance laws permit the provider to comply with the foreign legal process without violating U.S. law.

Importantly, the CLOUD Act does not require the provider to comply with foreign legal process. The legal burden to comply with the foreign legal process comes, if at all, from the law of the foreign government. Instead, the CLOUD Act removes the federal legal prohibition on compliance with the foreign legal process so long as the foreign government has been declared a "qualifying foreign government" under the process provided by 18 U.S.C. § 2523.

To achieve this result, the CLOUD Act adds new exceptions to each of three major federal statutory surveillance laws for conduct in response to foreign legal process. *See, e.g.,* 18 U.S.C. § 2702(b)(9) (new exception to the Stored Communications Act permits disclosure of contents "to a foreign government pursuant to an order from a foreign government that is subject to an executive agreement that the Attorney General has determined and certified to Congress satisfies section 2523"); 18 U.S.C. § 2702(b)(9) (new exception to the Stored Communications Act permits disclosure of non-content records "to a foreign government pursuant to an order from a foreign government that is subject to an executive agreement that the Attorney General has determined and certified to Congress satisfies section 2523"); 18 U.S.C. § 2511(j) (new exception to the Wiretap Act permitting "a provider of electronic communication service to the public or remote computing service to intercept or disclose the contents of a wire or electronic communication in response to an order from a foreign government that is subject to an executive agreement that the Attorney General has determined and certified to Congress satisfies section 2523."); 18 U.S.C. § 3121(a) (new exception to the Pen Register statute permits installation of a pen register and trap and trace device pursuant to "an order from a foreign government that is subject to an executive agreement that the Attorney General has determined and certified to Congress satisfies section 2523.").

The effect of the CLOUD Act is to create an "insider's club" among countries in terms of legal process. When a foreign government is admitted into the club by being designated a "qualifying foreign government," evidence collection using foreign legal process becomes relatively easy. Domestic providers can follow foreign court orders—the foreign equivalent of their Wiretap orders, 2703(a) warrants, and pen/trap orders—just like they follow domestic legal process. And under the reciprocity requirements that are part of being a "qualifying foreign government"—as explained in Note 6.1 below—domestic legal process can be followed by foreign providers just like they now comply with foreign legal process.

6.1. *Becoming a "qualifying foreign government" under 18 U.S.C. § 2523.* The CLOUD Act's regime for cross-border data requests hinges on designation of a foreign government as a "qualifying foreign government." The procedure for this designation is detailed in 18 U.S.C. § 2523. The procedure is complex, but the basics can be readily understood here. First, the foreign government must enter into an executive agreement with the United States concerning mutual legal assistance that satisfies a long list of statutory requirements. When the executive agreement is made, the Attorney General, with the concurrence of the Secretary of State, submits a written certification to Congress that a foreign government is properly qualifying. Congress then has an opportunity to reject the agreement. If Congress does not act after 180 days, the executive agreement goes into effect and the foreign government is a "qualifying foreign government" for five years.

The terms of the executive agreement are explained in § 2523(b). First, "the domestic law of the foreign government, including the implementation of that law," must afford "robust substantive and procedural protections for privacy and civil liberties in light of the data collection and activities of the foreign government that will be subject to the agreement." § 2523(b)(1). Factors to be considered to determine if the foreign government's laws and practices are adequate include whether the government demonstrates respect for the rule of law and principles of nondiscrimination; whether it adheres to applicable international human rights obligations and commitments or demonstrates respect for international universal human rights; and whether it has sufficient mechanisms to provide accountability and appropriate transparency regarding the collection and use of electronic data. *See id.* at § 2523(b)(1)(B).

The executive agreements must also be mutual. Just as the United States will permit U.S.-based providers to comply with foreign legal process, so must the foreign governments permit their providers to comply with U.S. legal process. *See* § 2523(b)(4)(I) ("[T]he foreign government shall afford reciprocal rights of data access, to include, where applicable, removing restrictions on communications service providers, including providers subject to United States jurisdiction, and thereby allow them to respond to valid legal process sought by a governmental entity (as defined in section 2711) if foreign law would otherwise prohibit communications-service providers from disclosing the data.").

After the Attorney General certifies that a valid executive agreement exists, the Attorney General must submit the certification to Congress. Congress then has 180 days in which to consider the executive agreement. If Congress has not acted in 180 days, the agreement goes into effect. *See* § 2523(d). On the other hand, if Congress enters a joint resolution in the 180-day period disapproving of the executive agreement, then the executive agreement does not go into effect. *See* § 2523(d)(4)(B). Executive agreements are valid for five years and can be renewed for additional five-year periods. If revisions are made to the executive agreements as part of their proposed renewal, the Attorney General must resubmit the revised executive agreement to Congress to give Congress a 90-day window in which to consider the agreement. *See* § 2523(h).

6.2. *The first certification of an executive agreement under the CLOUD Act—with more coming soon.* On October 3, 2019, the Attorney General of the United States and the Home Secretary of the United Kingdom announced that they had signed the first CLOUD Act agreement. *See* U.S. Department of Justice, *U.S. And UK Sign Landmark Cross-Border Data Access Agreement to Combat Criminals and Terrorists Online,* October 3, 2019. The text of the proposed agreement is 17 pages long, and it is available online. *See* https://tiny url.com/yyt7ddpd (link created October 16, 2019). The agreement will go into effect in 180 days if Congress does not disapprove it.

The US/UK agreement includes a number of transparency and civil liberties protections not found in the CLOUD Act itself. First, a designated authority in the issuing country must certify in writing that the order complies with both the agreement and any applicable law. Second, if a provider in Country A objects to an order served on it from Country B, the provider can file an objection with the government of Country B. If that objection it is not resolved to the satisfaction of the provider, the provider can file its objection before Country A, which then has veto power over whether the provider must comply with Country B's order. Third, each government must file an annual report on how often the CLOUD Act was used. *See generally* Jennifer Daskal & Peter Swire, *The U.K.-U.S. CLOUD Act Agreement Is Finally Here, Containing New Safeguards,* Lawfare Blog, October 8, 2019, available at https://www.lawfareblog.com/uk-us-cloud-act-agreement-finally-here-containing-new-safeguards.

Additional negotiations are ongoing. For example, on October 7, 2019, the Attorney General of the United States and the Minister for Home Affairs of Australia announced that the United States and Australia had entered into formal negotiations over the terms of a bilateral agreement between the United States and Australia under the CLOUD Act. *See* https://www.justice.gov/opa/pr/joint-statement-announcing-united-states-and-australian-negotiation-cloud-act-agreement-us.

PART B

STATUTORY SUPPLEMENT

■ ■ ■

18 U.S.C. § 641. PUBLIC MONEY, PROPERTY OR RECORDS

Whoever embezzles, steals, purloins, or knowingly converts to his use or the use of another, or without authority, sells, conveys or disposes of any record, voucher, money, or thing of value of the United States or of any department or agency thereof, or any property made or being made under contract for the United States or any department or agency thereof; or

Whoever receives, conceals, or retains the same with intent to convert it to his use or gain, knowing it to have been embezzled, stolen, purloined or converted—

Shall be fined under this title or imprisoned not more than ten years, or both; but if the value of such property in the aggregate, combining amounts from all the counts for which the defendant is convicted in a single case, does not exceed the sum of $1,000, he shall be fined under this title or imprisoned not more than one year, or both.

The word "value" means face, par, or market value, or cost price, either wholesale or retail, whichever is greater.

18 U.S.C. § 875. INTERSTATE COMMUNICATIONS

(a) Whoever transmits in interstate or foreign commerce any communication containing any demand or request for a ransom or reward for the release of any kidnapped person, shall be fined under this title or imprisoned not more than twenty years, or both.

(b) Whoever, with intent to extort from any person, firm, association, or corporation, any money or other thing of value, transmits in interstate or foreign commerce any communication containing any threat to kidnap any person or any threat to injure the person of another, shall be fined under this title or imprisoned not more than twenty years, or both.

(c) Whoever transmits in interstate or foreign commerce any communication containing any threat to kidnap any person or any threat to injure the person of another, shall be fined under this title or imprisoned not more than five years, or both.

(d) Whoever, with intent to extort from any person, firm, association, or corporation, any money or other thing of value, transmits in interstate or foreign commerce any communication containing any threat to injure the property or reputation of the addressee or of another or the reputation of a deceased person or any threat to accuse the addressee or any other person of a crime, shall be fined under this title or imprisoned not more than two years, or both.

18 U.S.C. § 1028. FRAUD AND RELATED ACTIVITY IN CONNECTION WITH IDENTIFICATION DOCUMENTS, AUTHENTICATION FEATURES, AND INFORMATION

(a) Whoever, in a circumstance described in subsection (c) of this section—

(1) knowingly and without lawful authority produces an identification document, authentication feature, or a false identification document;

(2) knowingly transfers an identification document, authentication feature, or a false identification document knowing that such document or feature was stolen or produced without lawful authority;

(3) knowingly possesses with intent to use unlawfully or transfer unlawfully five or more identification documents (other than those issued lawfully for the use of the possessor), authentication features, or false identification documents;

(4) knowingly possesses an identification document (other than one issued lawfully for the use of the possessor), authentication feature, or a false identification document, with the intent such document or feature be used to defraud the United States;

(5) knowingly produces, transfers, or possesses a document-making implement or authentication feature with the intent such document-making implement or authentication feature will be used in the production of a false identification document or another document-making implement or authentication feature which will be so used;

(6) knowingly possesses an identification document or authentication feature that is or appears to be an identification document or authentication feature of the United States or a sponsoring entity of an event designated as a special event of national significance which is stolen or produced without lawful authority knowing that such document or feature was stolen or produced without such authority;

(7) knowingly transfers, possesses, or uses, without lawful authority, a means of identification of another person with the intent to commit, or to aid or abet, or in connection with, any unlawful activity that constitutes a violation of Federal law, or that constitutes a felony under any applicable State or local law; or

(8) knowingly traffics in false or actual authentication features for use in false identification documents, document-making implements, or means of identification; shall be punished * * *.

* * *

(c) The circumstance referred to in subsection (a) of this section is that—

(1) the identification document, authentication feature, or false identification document is or appears to be issued by or under the authority of the United States or a sponsoring entity of an event designated as a special event of national significance or the document-making implement is designed or suited for making such an identification document, authentication feature, or false identification document;

(2) the offense is an offense under subsection (a) (4) of this section; or

(3) either—

(A) the production, transfer, possession, or use prohibited by this section is in or affects interstate or foreign commerce, including the transfer of a document by electronic means; or

(B) the means of identification, identification document, false identification document, or document-making implement is transported in the mail in the course of the production, transfer, possession, or use prohibited by this section.

(d) In this section and section 1028A—

(1) the term "authentication feature" means any hologram, watermark, certification, symbol, code, image, sequence of numbers or letters, or other feature that either individually or in combination with another feature is used by the issuing authority on an identification document, document-making implement, or means of identification to determine if the document is counterfeit, altered, or otherwise falsified;

(2) the term "document-making implement" means any implement, impression, template, computer file, computer disc, electronic device, or computer hardware or software, that is specifically configured or primarily used for making an identification document, a false identification document, or another document-making implement;

(3) the term "identification document" means a document made or issued by or under the authority of the United States Government, a State, political subdivision of a State, a sponsoring entity of an event designated as a special event of national significance, a foreign

government, political subdivision of a foreign government, an international governmental or an international quasi-governmental organization which, when completed with information concerning a particular individual, is of a type intended or commonly accepted for the purpose of identification of individuals;

(4) the term "false identification document" means a document of a type intended or commonly accepted for the purposes of identification of individuals that—

(A) is not issued by or under the authority of a governmental entity or was issued under the authority of a governmental entity but was subsequently altered for purposes of deceit; and

(B) appears to be issued by or under the authority of the United States Government, a State, a political subdivision of a State, a sponsoring entity of an event designated by the President as a special event of national significance, a foreign government, a political subdivision of a foreign government, or an international governmental or quasi-governmental organization;

(5) the term "false authentication feature" means an authentication feature that—

(A) is genuine in origin, but, without the authorization of the issuing authority, has been tampered with or altered for purposes of deceit;

(B) is genuine, but has been distributed, or is intended for distribution, without the authorization of the issuing authority and not in connection with a lawfully made identification document, document-making implement, or means of identification to which such authentication feature is intended to be affixed or embedded by the respective issuing authority; or

(C) appears to be genuine, but is not;

(6) the term "issuing authority"—

(A) means any governmental entity or agency that is authorized to issue identification documents, means of identification, or authentication features; and

(B) includes the United States Government, a State, a political subdivision of a State, a sponsoring entity of an event designated by the President as a special event of national significance, a foreign government, a political subdivision of a foreign government, or an international government or quasi-governmental organization;

(7) the term "means of identification" means any name or number that may be used, alone or in conjunction with any other information, to identify a specific individual, including any—

(A) name, social security number, date of birth, official State or government issued driver's license or identification number, alien registration number, government passport number, employer or taxpayer identification number;

(B) unique biometric data, such as fingerprint, voice print, retina or iris image, or other unique physical representation;

(C) unique electronic identification number, address, or routing code; or

(D) telecommunication identifying information or access device (as defined in section 1029(e));

(8) the term "personal identification card" means an identification document issued by a State or local government solely for the purpose of identification;

(9) the term "produce" includes alter, authenticate, or assemble;

(10) the term "transfer" includes selecting an identification document, false identification document, or document-making implement and placing or directing the placement of such identification document, false identification document, or document-making implement on an online location where it is available to others;

(11) the term "State" includes any State of the United States, the District of Columbia, the Commonwealth of Puerto Rico, and any other commonwealth, possession, or territory of the United States; and

(12) the term "traffic" means—

(A) to transport, transfer, or otherwise dispose of, to another, as consideration for anything of value; or

(B) to make or obtain control of with intent to so transport, transfer, or otherwise dispose of.

(e) This section does not prohibit any lawfully authorized investigative, protective, or intelligence activity of a law enforcement agency of the United States, a State, or a political subdivision of a State, or of an intelligence agency of the United States, or any activity authorized under chapter 224 of this title.

(f) **Attempt and conspiracy.**—Any person who attempts or conspires to commit any offense under this section shall be subject to the same penalties as those prescribed for the offense, the commission of which was the object of the attempt or conspiracy.

18 U.S.C. § 1028A. AGGRAVATED IDENTITY THEFT

(a) Offenses.

(1) In general. Whoever, during and in relation to any felony violation enumerated in subsection (c), knowingly transfers, possesses, or uses, without lawful authority, a means of identification of another person shall, in addition to the punishment provided for such felony, be sentenced to a term of imprisonment of 2 years.

(2) Terrorism offense. Whoever, during and in relation to any felony violation enumerated in section 2332b(g)(5)(B), knowingly transfers, possesses, or uses, without lawful authority, a means of identification of another person or a false identification document shall, in addition to the punishment provided for such felony, be sentenced to a term of imprisonment of 5 years.

* * *

(c) Definition. For purposes of this section, the term "felony violation enumerated in subsection (c)" means any offense that is a felony violation of—

(1) section 641 (relating to theft of public money, property, or records), section 656 (relating to theft, embezzlement, or misapplication by bank officer or employee), or section 664 (relating to theft from employee benefit plans);

(2) section 911 (relating to false personation of citizenship);

(3) section 922(a)(6) (relating to false statements in connection with the acquisition of a firearm);

(4) any provision contained in this chapter (relating to fraud and false statements), other than this section or section 1028(a)(7);

(5) any provision contained in chapter 63 (relating to mail, bank, and wire fraud);

(6) any provision contained in chapter 69 (relating to nationality and citizenship);

(7) any provision contained in chapter 75 (relating to passports and visas);

(8) section 523 of the Gramm-Leach-Bliley Act (15 U.S.C. 6823) (relating to obtaining customer information by false pretenses);

(9) section 243 or 266 of the Immigration and Nationality Act (8 U.S.C. 1253 and 1306) (relating to willfully failing to leave the United States after deportation and creating a counterfeit alien registration card);

(10) any provision contained in chapter 8 of title II of the Immigration and Nationality Act (8 U.S.C. 1321 et seq.) (relating to various immigration offenses); or

(11) section 208, 811, 1107(b), 1128B(a), or 1632 of the Social Security Act (42 U.S.C. 408, 1011, 1307(b), 1320a–7b(a), and 1383a) (relating to false statements relating to programs under the Act).

18 U.S.C. § 1029. FRAUD AND RELATED ACTIVITY IN CONNECTION WITH ACCESS DEVICES

(a) Whoever—

(1) knowingly and with intent to defraud produces, uses, or traffics in one or more counterfeit access devices;

(2) knowingly and with intent to defraud traffics in or uses one or more unauthorized access devices during any one-year period, and by such conduct obtains anything of value aggregating $1,000 or more during that period;

(3) knowingly and with intent to defraud possesses fifteen or more devices which are counterfeit or unauthorized access devices;

(4) knowingly, and with intent to defraud, produces, traffics in, has control or custody of, or possesses device-making equipment;

(5) knowingly and with intent to defraud effects transactions, with 1 or more access devices issued to another person or persons, to receive payment or any other thing of value during any 1-year period the aggregate value of which is equal to or greater than $1,000;

(6) without the authorization of the issuer of the access device, knowingly and with intent to defraud solicits a person for the purpose of—

(A) offering an access device; or

(B) selling information regarding or an application to obtain an access device;

(7) knowingly and with intent to defraud uses, produces, traffics in, has control or custody of, or possesses a telecommunications instrument that has been modified or altered to obtain unauthorized use of telecommunications services;

(8) knowingly and with intent to defraud uses, produces, traffics in, has control or custody of, or possesses a scanning receiver;

(9) knowingly uses, produces, traffics in, has control or custody of, or possesses hardware or software, knowing it has been configured to insert or modify telecommunication identifying information associated with or contained in a telecommunications instrument so that such instrument may be used to obtain telecommunications service without authorization; or

(10) without the authorization of the credit card system member or its agent, knowingly and with intent to defraud causes or arranges for another person to present to the member or its agent, for payment, 1 or more evidences or records of transactions made by an access device;

shall, if the offense affects interstate or foreign commerce, be punished as provided in subsection (c) of this section.

(b)(1)   Whoever attempts to commit an offense under subsection (a) of this section shall be subject to the same penalties as those prescribed for the offense attempted.

(2)   Whoever is a party to a conspiracy of two or more persons to commit an offense under subsection (a) of this section, if any of the parties engages in any conduct in furtherance of such offense, shall be fined an amount not greater than the amount provided as the maximum fine for such offense under subsection (c) of this section or imprisoned not longer than one-half the period provided as the maximum imprisonment for such offense under subsection (c) of this section, or both.

* * *

(e) As used in this section—

(1) the term "access device" means any card, plate, code, account number, electronic serial number, mobile identification number, personal identification number, or other telecommunications service, equipment, or instrument identifier, or other means of account access that can be used, alone or in conjunction with another access device, to obtain money, goods, services, or any other thing of value, or that can be used to initiate a transfer of funds (other than a transfer originated solely by paper instrument);

(2) the term "counterfeit access device" means any access device that is counterfeit, fictitious, altered, or forged, or an identifiable component of an access device or a counterfeit access device;

(3) the term "unauthorized access device" means any access device that is lost, stolen, expired, revoked, canceled, or obtained with intent to defraud;

(4) the term "produce" includes design, alter, authenticate, duplicate, or assemble;

(5) the term "traffic" means transfer, or otherwise dispose of, to another, or obtain control of with intent to transfer or dispose of;

(6) the term "device-making equipment" means any equipment, mechanism, or impression designed or primarily used for making an access device or a counterfeit access device;

(7) The term "credit card system member" means a financial institution or other entity that is a member of a credit card system, including an entity, whether affiliated with or identical to the credit card issuer, that is the sole member of a credit card system;

(8) the term "scanning receiver" means a device or apparatus that can be used to intercept a wire or electronic communication in violation of chapter 119 or to intercept an electronic serial number, mobile identification number, or other identifier of any telecommunications service, equipment, or instrument;

(9) the term "telecommunications service" has the meaning given such term in section 3 of title I of the Communications Act of 1934 (47 U.S.C. § 153);

(10) the term "facilities-based carrier" means an entity that owns communications transmission facilities, is responsible for the operation and maintenance of those facilities, and holds an operating license issued by the Federal Communications Commission under the authority of title III of the Communications Act of 1934; and

(11) the term "telecommunication identifying information" means electronic serial number or any other number or signal that identifies a specific telecommunications instrument or account, or a specific communication transmitted from a telecommunications instrument.

(f) This section does not prohibit any lawfully authorized investigative, protective, or intelligence activity of a law enforcement agency of the United States, a State, or a political subdivision of a State, or of an intelligence agency of the United States, or any activity authorized under chapter 224 of this title. For purposes of this subsection, the term "State" includes a State of the United States, the District of Columbia, and any commonwealth, territory, or possession of the United States.

(g)(1) It is not a violation of subsection (a)(9) for an officer, employee, or agent of, or a person engaged in business with, a facilities-based carrier, to engage in conduct (other than trafficking) otherwise prohibited by that subsection for the purpose of protecting the property or legal rights of that carrier, unless such conduct is for the purpose of obtaining telecommunications service provided by another facilities-based carrier without the authorization of such carrier.

(2) In a prosecution for a violation of subsection (a)(9), (other than a violation consisting of producing or trafficking) it is an affirmative defense (which the defendant must establish by a preponderance of the evidence) that the conduct charged was engaged in for research or development in connection with a lawful purpose.

(h) Any person who, outside the jurisdiction of the United States, engages in any act that, if committed within the jurisdiction of the United States, would constitute an offense under subsection (a) or (b) of this section, shall be subject to the fines, penalties, imprisonment, and forfeiture provided in this title if—

(1) the offense involves an access device issued, owned, managed, or controlled by a financial institution, account issuer, credit card system member, or other entity within the jurisdiction of the United States; and

(2) the person transports, delivers, conveys, transfers to or through, or otherwise stores, secrets, or holds within the jurisdiction of the United States, any article used to assist in the commission of the offense or the proceeds of such offense or property derived therefrom.

18 U.S.C. § 1030. FRAUD AND RELATED ACTIVITY IN CONNECTION WITH COMPUTERS

(a) Whoever—

(1) having knowingly accessed a computer without authorization or exceeding authorized access, and by means of such conduct having obtained information that has been determined by the United States Government pursuant to an Executive order or statute to require protection against unauthorized disclosure for reasons of national defense or foreign relations, or any restricted data, as defined in paragraph y. of section 11 of the Atomic Energy Act of 1954, with reason to believe that such information so obtained could be used to the injury of the United States, or to the advantage of any foreign nation willfully communicates, delivers, transmits, or causes to be communicated, delivered, or transmitted, or attempts to communicate, deliver, transmit or cause to be communicated, delivered, or transmitted the same to any person not entitled to receive it, or willfully retains the same and fails to deliver it to the officer or employee of the United States entitled to receive it;

(2) intentionally accesses a computer without authorization or exceeds authorized access, and thereby obtains—

(A) information contained in a financial record of a financial institution, or of a card issuer as defined in section 1602(n) of title 15, or contained in a file of a consumer reporting agency on a consumer, as such terms are defined in the Fair Credit Reporting Act (15 U.S.C. 1681 et seq.);

(B) information from any department or agency of the United States; or

(C) information from any protected computer;

(3) intentionally, without authorization to access any nonpublic computer of a department or agency of the United States, accesses such a computer of that department or agency that is exclusively for the use of the Government of the United States or, in the case of a computer not exclusively for such use, is used by or for the Government of the United States and such conduct affects that use by or for the Government of the United States;

(4) knowingly and with intent to defraud, accesses a protected computer without authorization, or exceeds authorized access, and by means of such conduct furthers the intended fraud and obtains anything of value, unless the object of the fraud and the thing obtained consists only of the use of the computer and the value of such use is not more than $5,000 in any 1-year period;

(5) (A) knowingly causes the transmission of a program, information, code, or command, and as a result of such conduct, intentionally causes damage without authorization, to a protected computer;

(B) intentionally accesses a protected computer without authorization, and as a result of such conduct, recklessly causes damage; or

(C) intentionally accesses a protected computer without authorization, and as a result of such conduct, causes damage and loss.

(6) knowingly and with intent to defraud traffics (as defined in section 1029) in any password or similar information through which a computer may be accessed without authorization, if—

(A) such trafficking affects interstate or foreign commerce; or

(B) such computer is used by or for the Government of the United States;

(7) with intent to extort from any person any money or other thing of value, transmits in interstate or foreign commerce any communication containing any—

(A) threat to cause damage to a protected computer;

(B) threat to obtain information from a protected computer without authorization or in excess of authorization or to impair the confidentiality of information obtained from a protected computer without authorization or by exceeding authorized access; or

(C) demand or request for money or other thing of value in relation to damage to a protected computer, where such damage was caused to facilitate the extortion;

shall be punished as provided in subsection (c) of this section.

(b) Whoever conspires to commit or attempts to commit an offense under subsection (a) of this section shall be punished as provided in subsection (c) of this section.

(c) The punishment for an offense under subsection (a) or (b) of this section is—

(1)(A)   a fine under this title or imprisonment for not more than ten years, or both, in the case of an offense under subsection (a)(1) of this section which does not occur after a conviction for another offense under this section, or an attempt to commit an offense punishable under this subparagraph; and

(B) a fine under this title or imprisonment for not more than twenty years, or both, in the case of an offense under subsection (a)(1) of this section which occurs after a conviction for another offense under this section, or an attempt to commit an offense punishable under this subparagraph;

(2)(A)   except as provided in subparagraph (B), a fine under this title or imprisonment for not more than one year, or both, in the case of an offense under subsection (a)(2), (a)(3), or (a)(6) of this section which does not occur after a conviction for another offense under this section, or an attempt to commit an offense punishable under this subparagraph;

(B) a fine under this title or imprisonment for not more than 5 years, or both, in the case of an offense under subsection (a)(2), or an attempt to commit an offense punishable under this subparagraph, if—

(i) the offense was committed for purposes of commercial advantage or private financial gain;

(ii) the offense was committed in furtherance of any criminal or tortious act in violation of the Constitution or laws of the United States or of any State; or

(iii) the value of the information obtained exceeds $5,000; and

(C) a fine under this title or imprisonment for not more than ten years, or both, in the case of an offense under subsection (a)(2), (a)(3) or (a)(6) of this section which occurs after a conviction for another offense under this section, or an attempt to commit an offense punishable under this subparagraph;

(3)(A)   a fine under this title or imprisonment for not more than five years, or both, in the case of an offense under subsection (a)(4) or (a)(7) of this section which does not occur after a conviction for another offense under this section, or an attempt to commit an offense punishable under this subparagraph; and

(B) a fine under this title or imprisonment for not more than ten years, or both, in the case of an offense under subsection (a)(4) or (a)(7) of this section which occurs after a conviction for another offense under this section, or an attempt to commit an offense punishable under this subparagraph;

(4)(A)   except as provided in subparagraphs (E) and (F), a fine under this title, imprisonment for not more than 5 years, or both, in the case of—

(i)   an offense under subsection (a)(5)(B), which does not occur after a conviction for another offense under this section, if the offense caused (or, in the case of an attempted offense, would, if completed, have caused)—

(I)   loss to 1 or more persons during any 1-year period (and, for purposes of an investigation, prosecution, or other proceeding brought by the United States only, loss resulting from a related course of conduct affecting 1 or more other protected computers) aggregating at least $5,000 in value;

(II)   the modification or impairment, or potential modification or impairment, of the medical examination, diagnosis, treatment, or care of 1 or more individuals;

(III) physical injury to any person;

(IV) a threat to public health or safety;

(V)   damage affecting a computer used by or for an entity of the United States Government in furtherance of the administration of justice, national defense, or national security; or

(VI) damage affecting 10 or more protected computers during any 1-year period; or

(ii) an attempt to commit an offense punishable under this subparagraph;

(B) except as provided in subparagraphs (E) and (F), a fine under this title, imprisonment for not more than 10 years, or both, in the case of—

    (i) an offense under subsection (a)(5)(A), which does not occur after a conviction for another offense under this section, if the offense caused (or, in the case of an attempted offense, would, if completed, have caused) a harm provided in subclauses (I) through (VI) of subparagraph (A)(i); or

    (ii) an attempt to commit an offense punishable under this subparagraph;

(C) except as provided in subparagraphs (E) and (F), a fine under this title, imprisonment for not more than 20 years, or both, in the case of—

    (i) an offense or an attempt to commit an offense under subparagraphs (A) or (B) of subsection (a)(5) that occurs after a conviction for another offense under this section; or

    (ii) an attempt to commit an offense punishable under this subparagraph;

(D) a fine under this title, imprisonment for not more than 10 years, or both, in the case of—

    (i) an offense or an attempt to commit an offense under subsection (a)(5)(C) that occurs after a conviction for another offense under this section; or

    (ii) an attempt to commit an offense punishable under this subparagraph;

(E) if the offender attempts to cause or knowingly or recklessly causes serious bodily injury from conduct in violation of subsection (a)(5)(A), a fine under this title, imprisonment for not more than 20 years, or both;

(F) if the offender attempts to cause or knowingly or recklessly causes death from conduct in violation of subsection (a)(5)(A), a fine under this title, imprisonment for any term of years or for life, or both; or

(G) a fine under this title, imprisonment for not more than 1 year, or both, for—

    (i) any other offense under subsection (a)(5); or

    (ii) an attempt to commit an offense punishable under this subparagraph.

(d)(1) The United States Secret Service shall, in addition to any other agency having such authority, have the authority to investigate offenses under this section.

(2) The Federal Bureau of Investigation shall have primary authority to investigate offenses under subsection (a)(1) for any cases involving espionage, foreign counterintelligence, information protected against unauthorized disclosure for reasons of national defense or foreign relations, or Restricted Data (as that term is defined in section 11y of the Atomic Energy Act of 1954 (42 U.S.C. 2014(y)), except for offenses affecting the duties of the United States Secret Service pursuant to section 3056(a) of this title.

(3) Such authority shall be exercised in accordance with an agreement which shall be entered into by the Secretary of the Treasury and the Attorney General.

(e) As used in this section—

(1) the term "computer" means an electronic, magnetic, optical, electrochemical, or other high speed data processing device performing logical, arithmetic, or storage functions, and includes any data storage facility or communications facility directly related to or operating in conjunction with such device, but such term does not include an automated typewriter or typesetter, a portable hand held calculator, or other similar device;

(2) the term "protected computer" means a computer—

(A) exclusively for the use of a financial institution or the United States Government, or, in the case of a computer not exclusively for such use, used by or for a financial institution or the United States Government and the conduct constituting the offense affects that use by or for the financial institution or the Government; or

(B) which is used in or affecting interstate or foreign commerce or communication, including a computer located outside the United States that is used in a manner that affects interstate or foreign commerce or communication of the United States;

(3) the term "State" includes the District of Columbia, the Commonwealth of Puerto Rico, and any other commonwealth, possession or territory of the United States;

(4) the term "financial institution" means—

(A) an institution, with deposits insured by the Federal Deposit Insurance Corporation;

(B) the Federal Reserve or a member of the Federal Reserve including any Federal Reserve Bank;

(C) a credit union with accounts insured by the National Credit Union Administration;

(D) a member of the Federal home loan bank system and any home loan bank;

(E) any institution of the Farm Credit System under the Farm Credit Act of 1971;

(F) a broker-dealer registered with the Securities and Exchange Commission pursuant to section 15 of the Securities Exchange Act of 1934;

(G) the Securities Investor Protection Corporation;

(H) a branch or agency of a foreign bank (as such terms are defined in paragraphs (1) and (3) of section 1(b) of the International Banking Act of 1978); and

(I) an organization operating under section 25 or section 25(a) of the Federal Reserve Act;

(5) the term "financial record" means information derived from any record held by a financial institution pertaining to a customer's relationship with the financial institution;

(6) the term "exceeds authorized access" means to access a computer with authorization and to use such access to obtain or alter information in the computer that the accesser is not entitled so to obtain or alter;

(7) the term "department of the United States" means the legislative or judicial branch of the Government or one of the executive departments enumerated in section 101 of title 5;

(8) the term "damage" means any impairment to the integrity or availability of data, a program, a system, or information;

(9) the term "government entity" includes the Government of the United States, any State or political subdivision of the United States, any foreign country, and any state, province, municipality, or other political subdivision of a foreign country;

(10) the term "conviction" shall include a conviction under the law of any State for a crime punishable by imprisonment for more than 1 year, an element of which is unauthorized access, or exceeding authorized access, to a computer;

(11) the term "loss" means any reasonable cost to any victim, including the cost of responding to an offense, conducting a damage assessment, and restoring the data, program, system, or information to its condition prior to the offense, and any revenue lost, cost incurred, or other consequential damages incurred because of interruption of service; and

(12) the term "person" means any individual, firm, corporation, educational institution, financial institution, governmental entity, or legal or other entity.

(f) This section does not prohibit any lawfully authorized investigative, protective, or intelligence activity of a law enforcement agency of the United States, a State, or a political subdivision of a State, or of an intelligence agency of the United States.

(g) Any person who suffers damage or loss by reason of a violation of this section may maintain a civil action against the violator to obtain compensatory damages and injunctive relief or other equitable relief. A civil action for a violation of this section may be brought only if the conduct involves 1 of the factors set forth in subclauses (I), (II), (III), (IV), or (V) of subsection (c)(4)(A)(i). Damages for a violation involving only conduct described in subsection (c)(4)(A)(i)(I) are limited to economic damages. No action may be brought under this subsection unless such action is begun within 2 years of the date of the act complained of or the date of the discovery of the damage. No action may be brought under this subsection for the negligent design or manufacture of computer hardware, computer software, or firmware.

(h) The Attorney General and the Secretary of the Treasury shall report to the Congress annually, during the first 3 years following the date of the enactment of this subsection, concerning investigations and prosecutions under subsection (a)(5).

(i)(1) The court, in imposing sentence on any person convicted of a violation of this section, or convicted of conspiracy to violate this section, shall order, in addition to any other sentence imposed and irrespective of any provision of State law, that such person forfeit to the United States—

(A) such person's interest in any personal property that was used or intended to be used to commit or to facilitate the commission of such violation; and

(B) any property, real or personal, constituting or derived from, any proceeds that such person obtained, directly or indirectly, as a result of such violation.

(2) The criminal forfeiture of property under this subsection, any seizure and disposition thereof, and any judicial proceeding in relation thereto, shall be governed by the provisions of section 413 of the Comprehensive Drug Abuse Prevention and Control Act of 1970 (21 U.S.C. 853), except subsection (d) of that section.

(j) For purposes of subsection (i), the following shall be subject to forfeiture to the United States and no property right shall exist in them:

(1) Any personal property used or intended to be used to commit or to facilitate the commission of any violation of this section, or a conspiracy to violate this section.

(2) Any property, real or personal, which constitutes or is derived from proceeds traceable to any violation of this section, or a conspiracy to violate this section.

18 U.S.C. § 1084. TRANSMISSION OF WAGERING INFORMATION; PENALTIES

(a) Whoever being engaged in the business of betting or wagering knowingly uses a wire communication facility for the transmission in interstate or foreign commerce of bets or wagers or information assisting in the placing of bets or wagers on any sporting event or contest, or for the transmission of a wire communication which entitles the recipient to receive money or credit as a result of bets or wagers, or for information assisting in the placing of bets or wagers, shall be fined under this title or imprisoned not more than two years, or both.

(b) Nothing in this section shall be construed to prevent the transmission in interstate or foreign commerce of information for use in news reporting of sporting events or contests, or for the transmission of information assisting in the placing of bets or wagers on a sporting event or contest from a State or foreign country where betting on that sporting event or contest is legal into a State or foreign country in which such betting is legal.

(c) Nothing contained in this section shall create immunity from criminal prosecution under any laws of any State.

(d) When any common carrier, subject to the jurisdiction of the Federal Communications Commission, is notified in writing by a Federal, State, or local law enforcement agency, acting within its jurisdiction, that any facility furnished by it is being used or will be used for the purpose of transmitting or receiving gambling information in interstate or foreign commerce in violation of Federal, State or local law, it shall discontinue or refuse, the leasing, furnishing, or maintaining of such facility, after reasonable notice to the subscriber, but no damages, penalty or forfeiture, civil or criminal, shall be found against any common carrier for any act done in compliance with any notice received from a law enforcement agency. Nothing in this section shall be deemed to prejudice the right of any person affected thereby to secure an appropriate determination, as otherwise provided by law, in a Federal court or in a State or local tribunal or agency, that such facility should not be discontinued or removed, or should be restored.

(e) As used in this section, the term "State" means a State of the United States, the District of Columbia, the Commonwealth of Puerto Rico, or a commonwealth, territory or possession of the United States.

18 U.S.C. § 1343. FRAUD BY WIRE, RADIO, OR TELEVISION

Whoever, having devised or intending to devise any scheme or artifice to defraud, or for obtaining money or property by means of false or fraudulent pretenses, representations, or promises, transmits or causes to be transmitted by means of wire, radio, or television communication in interstate or foreign commerce, any writings, signs, signals, pictures, or sounds for the purpose of executing such scheme or artifice, shall be fined under this title or imprisoned not more than 20 years, or both. If the violation occurs in relation to, or involving any benefit authorized, transported, transmitted, transferred, disbursed, or paid in connection with, a presidentially declared major disaster or emergency (as those terms are defined in section 102 of the Robert T. Stafford Disaster Relief and Emergency Assistance Act (42 U.S.C. 5122)), or affects a financial institution, such person shall be fined not more than $1,000,000 or imprisoned not more than 30 years, or both.

18 U.S.C. § 1462. IMPORTATION OR TRANSPORTATION OF OBSCENE MATTERS

Whoever brings into the United States, or any place subject to the jurisdiction thereof, or knowingly uses any express company or other common carrier or interactive computer service (as defined in section 230(e)(2) of the Communications Act of 1934), for carriage in interstate or foreign commerce—

(a) any obscene, lewd, lascivious, or filthy book, pamphlet, picture, motion-picture film, paper, letter, writing, print, or other matter of indecent character; or

(b) any obscene, lewd, lascivious, or filthy phonograph recording, electrical transcription, or other article or thing capable of producing sound; or

(c) any drug, medicine, article, or thing designed, adapted, or intended for producing abortion, or for any indecent or immoral use; or any written or printed card, letter, circular, book, pamphlet, advertisement, or notice of any kind giving information, directly or indirectly, where, how, or of whom, or by what means any of such mentioned articles, matters, or things may be obtained or made; or

Whoever knowingly takes or receives, from such express company or other common carrier or interactive computer service (as defined in section 230(e)(2) of the Communications Act of 1934) any matter or thing the carriage or importation of which is herein made unlawful—

Shall be fined under this title or imprisoned not more than five years, or both, for the first such offense and shall be fined under this title or imprisoned not more than ten years, or both, for each such offense thereafter.

18 U.S.C. § 1465. PRODUCTION AND TRANSPORTATION OF OBSCENE MATTERS FOR SALE OR DISTRIBUTION

Whoever knowingly produces with the intent to transport, distribute, or transmit in interstate or foreign commerce, or whoever knowingly transports or travels in, or uses a facility or means of, interstate or foreign commerce or an interactive computer service (as defined in section 230(e)(2) of the Communications Act of 1934) in or affecting such commerce, for the purpose of sale or distribution of any obscene, lewd, lascivious, or filthy book, pamphlet, picture, film, paper, letter, writing, print, silhouette, drawing, figure, image, cast, phonograph recording, electrical transcription or other article capable of producing sound or any other matter of indecent or immoral character, shall be fined under this title or imprisoned not more than five years, or both.

The transportation as aforesaid of two or more copies of any publication or two or more of any article of the character described above, or a combined total of five such publications and articles, shall create a presumption that such publications or articles are intended for sale or distribution, but such presumption shall be rebuttable.

18 U.S.C. § 1831. ECONOMIC ESPIONAGE

(a) In general.—Whoever, intending or knowing that the offense will benefit any foreign government, foreign instrumentality, or foreign agent, knowingly—

(1) steals, or without authorization appropriates, takes, carries away, or conceals, or by fraud, artifice, or deception obtains a trade secret;

(2) without authorization copies, duplicates, sketches, draws, photographs, downloads, uploads, alters, destroys, photocopies, replicates, transmits, delivers, sends, mails, communicates, or conveys a trade secret;

(3) receives, buys, or possesses a trade secret, knowing the same to have been stolen or appropriated, obtained, or converted without authorization;

(4) attempts to commit any offense described in any of paragraphs (1) through (3); or

(5) conspires with one or more other persons to commit any offense described in any of paragraphs (1) through (3), and one or more of such persons do any act to effect the object of the conspiracy,

shall, except as provided in subsection (b), be fined not more than $500,000 or imprisoned not more than 15 years, or both.

(b) Organizations.—Any organization that commits any offense described in subsection (a) shall be fined not more than $10,000,000.

18 U.S.C. § 1832. THEFT OF TRADE SECRETS

(a) Whoever, with intent to convert a trade secret, that is related to a product or service used in or intended for use in interstate or foreign commerce, to the economic benefit of anyone other than the owner thereof, and intending or knowing that the offense will, injure any owner of that trade secret, knowingly—

(1) steals, or without authorization appropriates, takes, carries away, or conceals, or by fraud, artifice, or deception obtains such information;

(2) without authorization copies, duplicates, sketches, draws, photographs, downloads, uploads, alters, destroys, photocopies, replicates, transmits, delivers, sends, mails, communicates, or conveys such information;

(3) receives, buys, or possesses such information, knowing the same to have been stolen or appropriated, obtained, or converted without authorization;

(4) attempts to commit any offense described in paragraphs (1) through (3); or

(5) conspires with one or more other persons to commit any offense described in paragraphs (1) through (3), and one or more of such persons do any act to effect the object of the conspiracy,

shall, except as provided in subsection (b), be fined under this title or imprisoned not more than 10 years, or both.

(b) Any organization that commits any offense described in subsection (a) shall be fined not more than the greater of $5,000,000 or 3 times the value of the stolen trade secret to the organization, including expenses for research and design and other costs of reproducing the trade secret that the organization has thereby avoided.

18 U.S.C. § 1839. DEFINITIONS

As used in this chapter—

(1) the term "foreign instrumentality" means any agency, bureau, ministry, component, institution, association, or any legal, commercial, or business organization, corporation, firm, or entity that is substantially owned, controlled, sponsored, commanded, managed, or dominated by a foreign government;

(2) the term "foreign agent" means any officer, employee, proxy, servant, delegate, or representative of a foreign government;

(3) the term "trade secret" means all forms and types of financial, business, scientific, technical, economic, or engineering information, including patterns, plans, compilations, program devices, formulas, designs, prototypes, methods, techniques, processes, procedures, programs, or codes, whether tangible or intangible, and whether or how stored, compiled, or memorialized physically, electronically, graphically, photographically, or in writing if—

> **(A)** the owner thereof has taken reasonable measures to keep such information secret; and

> **(B)** the information derives independent economic value, actual or potential, from not being generally known to, and not being readily ascertainable through proper means by, the public; and

(4) the term "owner", with respect to a trade secret, means the person or entity in whom or in which rightful legal or equitable title to, or license in, the trade secret is reposed.

18 U.S.C. § 2251. SEXUAL EXPLOITATION OF CHILDREN

(a) Any person who employs, uses, persuades, induces, entices, or coerces any minor to engage in, or who has a minor assist any other person to engage in, or who transports any minor in or affecting interstate or foreign commerce, or in any Territory or Possession of the United States, with the intent that such minor engage in, any sexually explicit conduct for the purpose of producing any visual depiction of such conduct or for the purpose of transmitting a live visual depiction of such conduct, shall be punished as provided under subsection (e), if such person knows or has reason to know that such visual depiction will be transported or transmitted using any means or facility of interstate or foreign commerce or in or affecting interstate or foreign commerce or mailed, if that visual depiction was produced or transmitted using materials that have been mailed, shipped, or transported in or affecting interstate or foreign commerce by any means, including by computer, or if such visual depiction has actually been transported or transmitted using any means or facility of interstate or foreign commerce or in or affecting interstate or foreign commerce or mailed.

(b) Any parent, legal guardian, or person having custody or control of a minor who knowingly permits such minor to engage in, or to assist any other person to engage in, sexually explicit conduct for the purpose of producing any visual depiction of such conduct or for the purpose of transmitting a live visual depiction of such conduct shall be punished as provided under subsection (e) of this section, if such parent, legal guardian, or person knows or has reason to know that such visual depiction will be transported or transmitted using any means or facility of interstate or foreign commerce or in or affecting interstate or foreign commerce or mailed, if that visual depiction was produced or transmitted using materials that have been mailed, shipped, or transported in or affecting interstate or foreign commerce by any means, including by computer, or if such visual depiction has actually been transported or transmitted using any means or facility of interstate or foreign commerce or in or affecting interstate or foreign commerce or mailed.

(c)(1)   Any person who, in a circumstance described in paragraph (2), employs, uses, persuades, induces, entices, or coerces any minor to engage in, or who has a minor assist any other person to engage in, any sexually explicit conduct outside of the United States, its territories or possessions, for the purpose of producing any visual depiction of such conduct, shall be punished as provided under subsection (e).

(2)   The circumstance referred to in paragraph (1) is that—

(A) the person intends such visual depiction to be transported to the United States, its territories or possessions, by any means, including by using any means or facility of interstate or foreign commerce or mail; or

(B) the person transports such visual depiction to the United States, its territories or possessions, by any means, including by using any means or facility of interstate or foreign commerce or mail.

(d)(1)   Any person who, in a circumstance described in paragraph (2), knowingly makes, prints, or publishes, or causes to be made, printed, or published, any notice or advertisement seeking or offering—

(A) to receive, exchange, buy, produce, display, distribute, or reproduce, any visual depiction, if the production of such visual depiction involves the use of a minor engaging in sexually explicit conduct and such visual depiction is of such conduct; or

(B) participation in any act of sexually explicit conduct by or with any minor for the purpose of producing a visual depiction of such conduct:

shall be punished as provided under subsection (e).

(2)   The circumstance referred to in paragraph (1) is that—

(A) such person knows or has reason to know that such notice or advertisement will be transported using any means or facility of interstate or foreign commerce or in or affecting interstate or foreign commerce by any means including by computer or mailed; or

(B) such notice or advertisement is transported using any means or facility of interstate or foreign commerce or in or affecting interstate or foreign commerce by any means including by computer or mailed.

(e) Any individual who violates, or attempts or conspires to violate, this section shall be fined under this title and imprisoned not less than 15 years nor more than 30 years, but if such person has one prior conviction under this chapter, section 1591, chapter 71, chapter 109A, or chapter 117, or under section 920 of title 10 (article 120 of the Uniform Code of Military Justice), or under the laws of any State relating to aggravated sexual abuse, sexual abuse, abusive sexual contact involving a minor or ward, or sex trafficking of children, or the production, possession, receipt, mailing, sale, distribution, shipment, or transportation of child pornography, such person shall be fined under this title and imprisoned for not less than 25 years nor more than 50 years, but if such person has 2 or more prior convictions under this chapter, chapter 71, chapter 109A, or chapter 117, or under section 920 of title 10 (article 120 of the Uniform Code of Military Justice), or under the laws of any State relating to the sexual exploitation of children, such person shall be fined under this title and imprisoned not less than 35 years nor more than life. Any organization that violates, or attempts or conspires to violate, this section shall be fined under this title. Whoever, in the course of an offense under this section, engages in conduct that results in the death of a person, shall be punished by death or imprisoned for not less than 30 years or for life.

18 U.S.C. § 2252. CERTAIN ACTIVITIES RELATING TO MATERIAL INVOLVING THE SEXUAL EXPLOITATION OF MINORS

(a) Any person who—

(1) knowingly transports or ships using any means or facility of interstate or foreign commerce or in or affecting interstate or foreign commerce by any means including by computer or mails, any visual depiction, if—

(A) the producing of such visual depiction involves the use of a minor engaging in sexually explicit conduct; and

(B) such visual depiction is of such conduct;

(2) knowingly receives, or distributes, any visual depiction using any means or facility of interstate or foreign commerce or that has been mailed, or has been shipped or transported in or affecting interstate or foreign commerce, or which contains materials which have been mailed or so shipped or transported, by any means including by computer, or knowingly reproduces any visual depiction for distribution using any means or facility of interstate or foreign commerce or in or affecting interstate or foreign commerce or through the mails, if—

 (A) the producing of such visual depiction involves the use of a minor engaging in sexually explicit conduct; and

 (B) such visual depiction is of such conduct;

(3) either—

 (A) in the special maritime and territorial jurisdiction of the United States, or on any land or building owned by, leased to, or otherwise used by or under the control of the Government of the United States, or in the Indian country as defined in section 1151 of this title, knowingly sells or possesses with intent to sell any visual depiction; or

 (B) knowingly sells or possesses with intent to sell any visual depiction that has been mailed, shipped, or transported using any means or facility of interstate or foreign commerce, or has been shipped or transported in or affecting interstate or foreign commerce, or which was produced using materials which have been mailed or so shipped or transported using any means or facility of interstate or foreign commerce, including by computer, if—

  (i) the producing of such visual depiction involves the use of a minor engaging in sexually explicit conduct; and

  (ii) such visual depiction is of such conduct; or

(4) either—

 (A) in the special maritime and territorial jurisdiction of the United States, or on any land or building owned by, leased to, or otherwise used by or under the control of the Government of the United States, or in the Indian country as defined in section 1151 of this title, knowingly possesses, or knowingly accesses with intent to view, 1 or more books, magazines, periodicals, films, video tapes, or other matter which contain any visual depiction; or

 (B) knowingly possesses, or knowingly accesses with intent to view, 1 or more books, magazines, periodicals, films, video tapes, or other matter which contain any visual depiction that has been mailed, or has been shipped or transported using any means or facility of interstate or foreign commerce or in or affecting interstate or foreign commerce, or which was produced using materials which have been mailed or so shipped or transported, by any means including by computer, if—

> **(i)** the producing of such visual depiction involves the use of a minor engaging in sexually explicit conduct; and

> **(ii)** such visual depiction is of such conduct;

shall be punished as provided in subsection (b) of this section.

(b)(1) Whoever violates, or attempts or conspires to violate, paragraph (1), (2), or (3) of subsection (a) shall be fined under this title and imprisoned not less than 5 years and not more than 20 years, but if such person has a prior conviction under this chapter, section 1591, chapter 71, chapter 109A, chapter 117, or under section 920 of title 10 (article 120 of the Uniform Code of Military Justice), or under the laws of any State relating to aggravated sexual abuse, sexual abuse, or abusive sexual conduct involving a minor or ward, or the production, possession, receipt, mailing, sale, distribution, shipment, or transportation of child pornography, or sex trafficking of children, such person shall be fined under this title and imprisoned for not less than 15 years nor more than 40 years.

(2) Whoever violates, or attempts or conspires to violate, paragraph (4) of subsection (a) shall be fined under this title or imprisoned not more than 10 years, or both, but if such person has a prior conviction under this chapter, chapter 71, chapter 109A, or chapter 117, or under section 920 of Title 10 (article 120 of the Uniform Code of Military Justice), or under the laws of any State relating to aggravated sexual abuse, sexual abuse, or abusive sexual conduct involving a minor or ward, or the production, possession, receipt, mailing, sale, distribution, shipment, or transportation of child pornography, such person shall be fined under this title and imprisoned for not less than 10 years nor more than 20 years.

(c) Affirmative defense.—It shall be an affirmative defense to a charge of violating paragraph (4) of subsection (a) that the defendant—

> **(1)** possessed less than three matters containing any visual depiction proscribed by that paragraph; and

> **(2)** promptly and in good faith, and without retaining or allowing any person, other than a law enforcement agency, to access any visual depiction or copy thereof—

>> **(A)** took reasonable steps to destroy each such visual depiction; or

>> **(B)** reported the matter to a law enforcement agency and afforded that agency access to each such visual depiction.

18 U.S.C. § 2252A. CERTAIN ACTIVITIES RELATING TO MATERIAL CONSTITUTING OR CONTAINING CHILD PORNOGRAPHY

(a) Any person who—

(1) knowingly mails, or transports or ships using any means or facility of interstate or foreign commerce or in or affecting interstate or foreign commerce by any means, including by computer, any child pornography;

(2) knowingly receives or distributes—

(A) any child pornography using any means or facility of interstate or foreign commerce or that has been mailed, or has been shipped or transported in or affecting interstate or foreign commerce by any means, including by computer; or

(B) any material that contains child pornography using any means or facility of interstate or foreign commerce or that has been mailed, or has been shipped or transported in or affecting interstate or foreign commerce by any means, including by computer;

(3) knowingly—

(A) reproduces any child pornography for distribution through the mails, or using any means or facility of interstate or foreign commerce or in or affecting interstate or foreign commerce by any means, including by computer; or

(B) advertises, promotes, presents, distributes, or solicits through the mails, or using any means or facility of interstate or foreign commerce or in or affecting interstate or foreign commerce by any means, including by computer, any material or purported material in a manner that reflects the belief, or that is intended to cause another to believe, that the material or purported material is, or contains—

(i) an obscene visual depiction of a minor engaging in sexually explicit conduct; or

(ii) a visual depiction of an actual minor engaging in sexually explicit conduct;

(4) either—

(A) in the special maritime and territorial jurisdiction of the United States, or on any land or building owned by, leased to, or otherwise used by or under the control of the United States Government, or in the Indian country (as defined in section 1151), knowingly sells or possesses with the intent to sell any child pornography; or

(B) knowingly sells or possesses with the intent to sell any child pornography that has been mailed, or shipped or transported using any means or facility of interstate or foreign commerce or in or affecting interstate or foreign commerce by any means, including by computer, or that was produced using materials that have been mailed, or shipped or transported in or affecting interstate or foreign commerce by any means, including by computer;

(5) either—

(A) in the special maritime and territorial jurisdiction of the United States, or on any land or building owned by, leased to, or otherwise used by or under the control of the United States Government, or in the Indian country (as defined in section 1151), knowingly possesses, or knowingly accesses with intent to view, any book, magazine, periodical, film, videotape, computer disk, or any other material that contains an image of child pornography; or

(B) knowingly possesses, or knowingly accesses with intent to view, any book, magazine, periodical, film, videotape, computer disk, or any other material that contains an image of child pornography that has been mailed, or shipped or transported using any means or facility of interstate or foreign commerce or in or affecting interstate or foreign commerce by any means, including by computer, or that was produced using materials that have been mailed, or shipped or transported in or affecting interstate or foreign commerce by any means, including by computer;

(6) knowingly distributes, offers, sends, or provides to a minor any visual depiction, including any photograph, film, video, picture, or computer generated image or picture, whether made or produced by electronic, mechanical, or other means, where such visual depiction is, or appears to be, of a minor engaging in sexually explicit conduct—

(A) that has been mailed, shipped, or transported using any means or facility of interstate or foreign commerce or in or affecting interstate or foreign commerce by any means, including by computer;

(B) that was produced using materials that have been mailed, shipped, or transported in or affecting interstate or foreign commerce by any means, including by computer; or

(C) which distribution, offer, sending, or provision is accomplished using the mails or any means or facility of interstate or foreign commerce,

for purposes of inducing or persuading a minor to participate in any activity that is illegal; or

(7) knowingly produces with intent to distribute, or distributes, by any means, including a computer, in or affecting interstate or foreign commerce, child pornography that is an adapted or modified depiction of an identifiable minor.

shall be punished as provided in subsection (b).

(b)(1) Whoever violates, or attempts or conspires to violate, paragraph (1), (2), (3), (4), or (6) of subsection (a) shall be fined under this title and imprisoned not less than 5 years and not more than 20 years, but, if such person has a prior conviction under this chapter, section 1591, chapter 71, chapter 109A, chapter 117, or under section 920 of title 10 (article 120 of the Uniform Code of Military Justice), or under the laws of any State relating to aggravated sexual abuse, sexual abuse, or abusive sexual conduct involving a minor or ward, or the production, possession, receipt, mailing, sale, distribution, shipment, or transportation of child pornography, or sex trafficking of children, such person shall be fined under this title and imprisoned for not less than 15 years nor more than 40 years.

(2) Whoever violates, or attempts or conspires to violate, subsection (a)(5) shall be fined under this title or imprisoned not more than 10 years, or both, but, if such person has a prior conviction under this chapter, chapter 71, chapter 109A, or chapter 117, or under section 920 of title 10 (article 120 of the Uniform Code of Military Justice), or under the laws of any State relating to aggravated sexual abuse, sexual abuse, or abusive sexual conduct involving a minor or ward, or the production, possession, receipt, mailing, sale, distribution, shipment, or transportation of child pornography, such person shall be fined under this title and imprisoned for not less than 10 years nor more than 20 years.

(3) Whoever violates, or attempts or conspires to violate, subsection (a)(7) shall be fined under this title or imprisoned not more than 15 years, or both.

(c) It shall be an affirmative defense to a charge of violating paragraph (1), (2), (3)(A), (4), or (5) of subsection (a) that—

(1)(A) the alleged child pornography was produced using an actual person or persons engaging in sexually explicit conduct; and

(B) each such person was an adult at the time the material was produced; or

(2) the alleged child pornography was not produced using any actual minor or minors.

No affirmative defense under subsection (c)(2) shall be available in any prosecution that involves child pornography as described in section

2256(8)(C). A defendant may not assert an affirmative defense to a charge of violating paragraph (1), (2), (3)(A), (4), or (5) of subsection (a) unless, within the time provided for filing pretrial motions or at such time prior to trial as the judge may direct, but in no event later than 10 days before the commencement of the trial, the defendant provides the court and the United States with notice of the intent to assert such defense and the substance of any expert or other specialized testimony or evidence upon which the defendant intends to rely. If the defendant fails to comply with this subsection, the court shall, absent a finding of extraordinary circumstances that prevented timely compliance, prohibit the defendant from asserting such defense to a charge of violating paragraph (1), (2), (3)(A), (4), or (5) of subsection (a) or presenting any evidence for which the defendant has failed to provide proper and timely notice.

   (d) Affirmative defense. It shall be an affirmative defense to a charge of violating subsection (a)(5) that the defendant—

   (1) possessed less than three images of child pornography; and

   (2) promptly and in good faith, and without retaining or allowing any person, other than a law enforcement agency, to access any image or copy thereof—

   (A) took reasonable steps to destroy each such image; or

   (B) reported the matter to a law enforcement agency and afforded that agency access to each such image.

   (e) Admissibility of evidence. On motion of the government, in any prosecution under this chapter or section 1466A, except for good cause shown, the name, address, social security number, or other nonphysical identifying information, other than the age or approximate age, of any minor who is depicted in any child pornography shall not be admissible and may be redacted from any otherwise admissible evidence, and the jury shall be instructed, upon request of the United States, that it can draw no inference from the absence of such evidence in deciding whether the child pornography depicts an actual minor.

   (f) Civil remedies.—

   (1) In general. Any person aggrieved by reason of the conduct prohibited under subsection (a) or (b) or section 1466A may commence a civil action for the relief set forth in paragraph (2).

   (2) Relief. In any action commenced in accordance with paragraph (1), the court may award appropriate relief, including—

   (A) temporary, preliminary, or permanent injunctive relief;

   (B) compensatory and punitive damages; and

(C) the costs of the civil action and reasonable fees for attorneys and expert witnesses.

(g) Child exploitation enterprises.—

(1) Whoever engages in a child exploitation enterprise shall be fined under this title and imprisoned for any term of years not less than 20 or for life.

(2) A person engages in a child exploitation enterprise for the purposes of this section if the person violates section 1591, section 1201 if the victim is a minor, or chapter 109A (involving a minor victim), 110 (except for sections 2257 and 2257A), or 117 (involving a minor victim), as a part of a series of felony violations constituting three or more separate incidents and involving more than one victim, and commits those offenses in concert with three or more other persons.

18 U.S.C. § 2256. DEFINITIONS FOR CHAPTER

For the purposes of this chapter, the term—

(1) "minor" means any person under the age of eighteen years;

(2)(A) Except as provided in subparagraph (B), "sexually explicit conduct" means actual or simulated—

> **(i)** sexual intercourse, including genital-genital, oral-genital, anal-genital, or oral-anal, whether between persons of the same or opposite sex;
>
> **(ii)** bestiality;
>
> **(iii)** masturbation;
>
> **(iv)** sadistic or masochistic abuse; or
>
> **(v)** lascivious exhibition of the anus, genitals or pubic area of any person;

(B) For purposes of subsection 8(B) of this section, "sexually explicit conduct" means—

> **(i)** graphic sexual intercourse, including genital-genital, oral-genital, anal-genital, or oral-anal, whether between persons of the same or opposite sex, or lascivious simulated sexual intercourse where the genitals, breast, or pubic area of any person is exhibited;
>
> **(ii)** graphic or lascivious simulated;
>
> > **(I)** bestiality;
> >
> > **(II)** masturbation; or
> >
> > **(III)** sadistic or masochistic abuse; or

(iii) graphic or simulated lascivious exhibition of the anus, genitals or pubic area of any person;

(3) "producing" means producing, directing, manufacturing, issuing, publishing, or advertising;

(4) "organization" means a person other than an individual;

(5) "visual depiction" includes undeveloped film and videotape, data stored on computer disk or by electronic means which is capable of conversion into a visual image, and data which is capable of conversion into a visual image that has been transmitted by any means, whether or not stored in a permanent format;

(6) "computer" has the meaning given that term in section 1030 of this title;

(7) "custody or control" includes temporary supervision over or responsibility for a minor whether legally or illegally obtained;

(8) "child pornography" means any visual depiction, including any photograph, film, video, picture, or computer or computer-generated image or picture, whether made or produced by electronic, mechanical, or other means, of sexually explicit conduct, where—

(A) the production of such visual depiction involves the use of a minor engaging in sexually explicit conduct;

(B) such visual depiction is a digital image, computer image, or computer-generated image that is, or is indistinguishable from, that of a minor engaging in sexually explicit conduct; or

(C) such visual depiction has been created, adapted, or modified to appear that an identifiable minor is engaging in sexually explicit conduct.

(9) "identifiable minor"—

(A) means a person—

(i)(I) who was a minor at the time the visual depiction was created, adapted, or modified; or

(II) whose image as a minor was used in creating, adapting, or modifying the visual depiction; and

(ii) who is recognizable as an actual person by the person's face, likeness, or other distinguishing characteristic, such as a unique birthmark or other recognizable feature; and

(B) shall not be construed to require proof of the actual identity of the identifiable minor.

(10) "graphic", when used with respect to a depiction of sexually explicit conduct, means that a viewer can observe any part of the genitals or pubic area of any depicted person or animal during any part of the time that the sexually explicit conduct is being depicted; and

(11) the term "indistinguishable" used with respect to a depiction, means virtually indistinguishable, in that the depiction is such that an ordinary person viewing the depiction would conclude that the depiction is of an actual minor engaged in sexually explicit conduct. This definition does not apply to depictions that are drawings, cartoons, sculptures, or paintings depicting minors or adults.

18 U.S.C. § 2258A. Reporting Requirements of Electronic Communication Service Providers and Remote Computing Service Providers

(a) Duty to report.—

(1) In general.—

(A) Duty.—In order to reduce the proliferation of online child sexual exploitation and to prevent the online sexual exploitation of children, a provider—

(i) shall, as soon as reasonably possible after obtaining actual knowledge of any facts or circumstances described in paragraph (2)(A), take the actions described in subparagraph (B); and

(ii) may, after obtaining actual knowledge of any facts or circumstances described in paragraph (2)(B), take the actions described in subparagraph (B).

(B) Actions described.—The actions described in this subparagraph are—

(i) providing to the CyberTipline of NCMEC, or any successor to the CyberTipline operated by NCMEC, the mailing address, telephone number, facsimile number, electronic mailing address of, and individual point of contact for, such provider; and **(ii)** making a report of such facts or circumstances to the CyberTipline, or any successor to the CyberTipline operated by NCMEC.

(2) Facts or circumstances.—

(A) Apparent violations.—The facts or circumstances described in this subparagraph are any facts or circumstances from which there is an apparent violation of section 2251, 2251A, 2252, 2252A, 2252B, or 2260 that involves child pornography.

(B) Imminent violations.—The facts or circumstances described in this subparagraph are any facts or circumstances which indicate a violation of any of the sections described in subparagraph (A) involving child pornography may be planned or imminent.

(b) Contents of report.—In an effort to prevent the future sexual victimization of children, and to the extent the information is within the custody or control of a provider, the facts and circumstances included in each report under subsection (a)(1) may, at the sole discretion of the provider, include the following information:

(1) Information about the involved individual.—Information relating to the identity of any individual who appears to have violated or plans to violate a Federal law described in subsection (a)(2), which may, to the extent reasonably practicable, include the electronic mail address, Internet Protocol address, uniform resource locator, payment information (excluding personally identifiable information), or any other identifying information, including self-reported identifying information.

(2) Historical reference.—Information relating to when and how a customer or subscriber of a provider uploaded, transmitted, or received content relating to the report or when and how content relating to the report was reported to, or discovered by the provider, including a date and time stamp and time zone.

(3) Geographic location information.—Information relating to the geographic location of the involved individual or website, which may include the Internet Protocol address or verified address, or, if not reasonably available, at least one form of geographic identifying information, including area code or zip code, provided by the customer or subscriber, or stored or obtained by the provider.

(4) Visual depictions of apparent child pornography.—Any visual depiction of apparent child pornography or other content relating to the incident such report is regarding.

(5) Complete communication.—The complete communication containing any visual depiction of apparent child pornography or other content, including—

   (A) any data or information regarding the transmission of the communication; and

   (B) any visual depictions, data, or other digital files contained in, or attached to, the communication.

(c) Forwarding of report to law enforcement.—Pursuant to its clearinghouse role as a private, nonprofit organization, and at the conclusion of its review in furtherance of its nonprofit mission, NCMEC shall make available each report made under subsection (a)(1) to one or more of the following law enforcement agencies:

(1) Any Federal law enforcement agency that is involved in the investigation of child sexual exploitation, kidnapping, or enticement crimes.

(2) Any State or local law enforcement agency that is involved in the investigation of child sexual exploitation.

(3) A foreign law enforcement agency designated by the Attorney General under subsection (d)(3) or a foreign law enforcement agency that has an established relationship with the Federal Bureau of Investigation, Immigration and Customs Enforcement, or INTERPOL, and is involved in the investigation of child sexual exploitation, kidnapping, or enticement crimes.

(d) Attorney General responsibilities.—

(1) In general.—The Attorney General shall enforce this section.

(2) Designation of Federal agencies.—The Attorney General may designate a Federal law enforcement agency or agencies to which a report shall be forwarded under subsection (c)(1).

(3) Designation of foreign agencies.—The Attorney General may—

(A) in consultation with the Secretary of State, designate foreign law enforcement agencies to which a report may be forwarded under subsection (c)(3);

(B) establish the conditions under which such a report may be forwarded to such agencies; and

(C) develop a process for foreign law enforcement agencies to request assistance from Federal law enforcement agencies in obtaining evidence related to a report referred under subsection (c)(3).

(4) Reporting designated foreign agencies.—The Attorney General may maintain and make available to the Department of State, NCMEC, providers, the Committee on the Judiciary of the Senate, and the Committee on the Judiciary of the House of Representatives a list of the foreign law enforcement agencies designated under paragraph (3).

(5) Notification to providers.—

(A) In general.—NCMEC may notify a provider of the information described in subparagraph (B), if—

(i) a provider notifies NCMEC that the provider is making a report under this section as the result of a request by a foreign law enforcement agency; and

(ii) NCMEC forwards the report described in clause (i) to—

(I) the requesting foreign law enforcement agency; or

(II) another agency in the same country designated by the Attorney General under paragraph (3) or that has an established relationship with the Federal Bureau of Investigation, U.S. Immigration and Customs Enforcement, or INTERPOL and is involved in the investigation of child sexual exploitation, kidnapping, or enticement crimes.

(B) **Information described.**—The information described in this subparagraph is—

(i) the identity of the foreign law enforcement agency to which the report was forwarded; and

(ii) the date on which the report was forwarded.

(C) **Notification of inability to forward report.**—If a provider notifies NCMEC that the provider is making a report under this section as the result of a request by a foreign law enforcement agency and NCMEC is unable to forward the report as described in subparagraph (A)(ii), NCMEC shall notify the provider that NCMEC was unable to forward the report.

(6) Redesignated (5)

(e) **Failure to report.**—A provider that knowingly and willfully fails to make a report required under subsection (a)(1) shall be fined—

(1) in the case of an initial knowing and willful failure to make a report, not more than $150,000; and

(2) in the case of any second or subsequent knowing and willful failure to make a report, not more than $300,000.

(f) **Protection of privacy.**—Nothing in this section shall be construed to require a provider to—

(1) monitor any user, subscriber, or customer of that provider;

(2) monitor the content of any communication of any person described in paragraph (1); or

(3) affirmatively search, screen, or scan for facts or circumstances described in sections (a) and (b).

(g) **Conditions of disclosure information contained within report.**—

(1) In general.—Except as provided in paragraph (2), a law enforcement agency that receives a report under subsection (c) shall not disclose any information contained in that report.

(2) Permitted disclosures by law enforcement.—

(A) In general.—A law enforcement agency may disclose information in a report received under subsection (c)—

(i) to an attorney for the government for use in the performance of the official duties of that attorney;

(ii) to such officers and employees of that law enforcement agency, as may be necessary in the performance of their investigative and recordkeeping functions;

(iii) to such other government personnel (including personnel of a State or subdivision of a State) as are determined to be necessary by an attorney for the government to assist the attorney in the performance of the official duties of the attorney in enforcing Federal criminal law;

(iv) if the report discloses a violation of State criminal law, to an appropriate official of a State or subdivision of a State for the purpose of enforcing such State law;

(v) to a defendant in a criminal case or the attorney for that defendant, subject to the terms and limitations under section 3509(m) or a similar State law, to the extent the information relates to a criminal charge pending against that defendant;

(vi) subject to subparagraph (B), to a provider if necessary to facilitate response to legal process issued in connection to a criminal investigation, prosecution, or post-conviction remedy relating to that report; and

(vii) as ordered by a court upon a showing of good cause and pursuant to any protective orders or other conditions that the court may impose.

(B) Limitation.—Nothing in subparagraph (A)(vi) authorizes a law enforcement agency to provide visual depictions of apparent child pornography to a provider.

(3) Permitted disclosures by NCMEC.—NCMEC may disclose by mail, electronic transmission, or other reasonable means, information received in a report under subsection (a) only to—

(A) any Federal law enforcement agency designated by the Attorney General under subsection (d)(2) or that is involved in the investigation of child sexual exploitation, kidnapping, or enticement crimes;

(B) any State, local, or tribal law enforcement agency involved in the investigation of child sexual exploitation, kidnapping, or enticement crimes;

(C) any foreign law enforcement agency designated by the Attorney General under subsection (d)(3) or that has an established relationship with the Federal Bureau of Investigation, Immigration and Customs Enforcement, or INTERPOL, and is involved in the investigation of child sexual exploitation, kidnapping, or enticement crimes;

(D) a provider as described in section 2258C; and

(E) respond to legal process, as necessary.

(4) Permitted disclosure by a provider.—A provider that submits a report under subsection (a)(1) may disclose by mail, electronic transmission, or other reasonable means, information, including visual depictions contained in the report, in a manner consistent with permitted disclosures under paragraphs (3) through (8) of section 2702(b) only to a law enforcement agency described in subparagraph (A), (B), or (C) of paragraph (3), to NCMEC, or as necessary to respond to legal process.

(h) Preservation.—

(1) In general.—For the purposes of this section, a completed submission by a provider of a report to the CyberTipline under subsection (a)(1) shall be treated as a request to preserve the contents provided in the report for 90 days after the submission to the CyberTipline.

(2) Preservation of commingled content.—Pursuant to paragraph (1), a provider shall preserve any visual depictions, data, or other digital files that are reasonably accessible and may provide context or additional information about the reported material or person.

(3) Protection of preserved materials.—A provider preserving materials under this section shall maintain the materials in a secure location and take appropriate steps to limit access by agents or employees of the service to the materials to that access necessary to comply with the requirements of this subsection.

(4) Authorities and duties not affected.—Nothing in this section shall be construed as replacing, amending, or otherwise interfering with the authorities and duties under section 2703.

(5) Redesignated (4).

18 U.S.C. § 2261A. STALKING

Whoever—

(1) travels in interstate or foreign commerce or is present within the special maritime and territorial jurisdiction of the United States, or enters or leaves Indian country, with the intent to kill, injure, harass, intimidate, or place under surveillance with intent to kill, injure, harass, or intimidate another person, and in the course of, or as a result of, such travel or presence engages in conduct that—

(A) places that person in reasonable fear of the death of, or serious bodily injury to—

(i) that person;

(ii) an immediate family member (as defined in section 115) of that person;

(iii) a spouse or intimate partner of that person;

(iv) the pet, service animal, emotional support animal, or horse of that person; or

(B) causes, attempts to cause, or would be reasonably expected to cause substantial emotional distress to a person described in clause (i), (ii), or (iii) of subparagraph (A); or

(2) with the intent to kill, injure, harass, intimidate, or place under surveillance with intent to kill, injure, harass, or intimidate another person, uses the mail, any interactive computer service or electronic communication service or electronic communication system of interstate commerce, or any other facility of interstate or foreign commerce to engage in a course of conduct that—

(A) places that person in reasonable fear of the death of or serious bodily injury to a person, a pet, a service animal, an emotional support animal, or a horse described in clause (i), (ii), (iii), or (iv) of paragraph (1)(A); or

(B) causes, attempts to cause, or would be reasonably expected to cause substantial emotional distress to a person described in clause (i), (ii), or (iii) of paragraph (1)(A),

shall be punished as provided in section 2261(b) of this title.

18 U.S.C. § 2314. TRANSPORTATION OF STOLEN GOODS, SECURITIES, MONEYS, FRAUDULENT STATE TAX STAMPS, OR ARTICLES USED IN COUNTERFEITING

Whoever transports, transmits, or transfers in interstate or foreign commerce any goods, wares, merchandise, securities or money, of the value of \$5,000 or more, knowing the same to have been stolen, converted or taken by fraud; or

Whoever, having devised or intending to devise any scheme or artifice to defraud, or for obtaining money or property by means of false or fraudulent pretenses, representations, or promises, transports or causes to be transported, or induces any person or persons to travel in, or to be transported in interstate or foreign commerce in the execution or concealment of a scheme or artifice to defraud that person or those persons of money or property having a value of \$5,000 or more; or

Whoever, with unlawful or fraudulent intent, transports in interstate or foreign commerce any falsely made, forged, altered, or counterfeited securities or tax stamps, knowing the same to have been falsely made, forged, altered, or counterfeited; or

Whoever, with unlawful or fraudulent intent, transports in interstate or foreign commerce any traveler's check bearing a forged countersignature; or

Whoever, with unlawful or fraudulent intent, transports in interstate or foreign commerce, any tool, implement, or thing used or fitted to be used in falsely making, forging, altering, or counterfeiting any security or tax stamps, or any part thereof—

Shall be fined under this title or imprisoned not more than ten years, or both.

This section shall not apply to any falsely made, forged, altered, counterfeited or spurious representation of an obligation or other security of the United States, or of an obligation, bond, certificate, security, treasury note, bill, promise to pay or bank note issued by any foreign government. This section also shall not apply to any falsely made, forged, altered, counterfeited, or spurious representation of any bank note or bill issued by a bank or corporation of any foreign country which is intended by the laws or usage of such country to circulate as money.

18 U.S.C. § 2319. CRIMINAL INFRINGEMENT OF A COPYRIGHT

(a) Any person who violates section 506(a) (relating to criminal offenses) of title 17 shall be punished as provided in subsections (b), (c), and (d) and such penalties shall be in addition to any other provisions of title 17 or any other law.

(b) Any person who commits an offense under section 506(a)(1)(A) of title 17—

（1) shall be imprisoned not more than 5 years, or fined in the amount set forth in this title, or both, if the offense consists of the reproduction or distribution, including by electronic means, during any 180-day period, of at least 10 copies or phonorecords, of 1 or more copyrighted works, which have a total retail value of more than $2,500;

(2) shall be imprisoned not more than 10 years, or fined in the amount set forth in this title, or both, if the offense is a felony and is a second or subsequent offense under subsection (a); and

(3) shall be imprisoned not more than 1 year, or fined in the amount set forth in this title, or both, in any other case.

(c) Any person who commits an offense under section 506(a)(1)(B) of title 17—

(1) shall be imprisoned not more than 3 years, or fined in the amount set forth in this title, or both, if the offense consists of the reproduction or distribution of 10 or more copies or phonorecords of 1 or more copyrighted works, which have a total retail value of $2,500 or more;

(2) shall be imprisoned not more than 6 years, or fined in the amount set forth in this title, or both, if the offense is a felony and is a second or subsequent offense under subsection (a); and

(3) shall be imprisoned not more than 1 year, or fined in the amount set forth in this title, or both, if the offense consists of the reproduction or distribution of 1 or more copies or phonorecords of 1 or more copyrighted works, which have a total retail value of more than $1,000.

(d) Any person who commits an offense under section 506(a)(1)(C) of title 17—

(1) shall be imprisoned not more than 3 years, fined under this title, or both;

(2) shall be imprisoned not more than 5 years, fined under this title, or both, if the offense was committed for purposes of commercial advantage or private financial gain;

(3) shall be imprisoned not more than 6 years, fined under this title, or both, if the offense is a felony and is a second or subsequent offense under subsection (a); and

(4) shall be imprisoned not more than 10 years, fined under this title, or both, if the offense is a felony and is a second or subsequent offense under paragraph (2).

(e)(1) During preparation of the presentence report pursuant to Rule 32(c) of the Federal Rules of Criminal Procedure, victims of the offense shall be permitted to submit, and the probation officer shall receive, a victim impact statement that identifies the victim of the offense and the extent and scope of the injury and loss suffered by the victim, including the estimated economic impact of the offense on that victim.

(2) Persons permitted to submit victim impact statements shall include—

(A) producers and sellers of legitimate works affected by conduct involved in the offense;

(B) holders of intellectual property rights in such works; and

(C) the legal representatives of such producers, sellers, and holders.

(f) As used in this section—

(1) the terms "phonorecord" and "copies" have, respectively, the meanings set forth in section 101 (relating to definitions) of title 17;

(2) the terms "reproduction" and "distribution" refer to the exclusive rights of a copyright owner under clauses (1) and (3) respectively of section 106 (relating to exclusive rights in copyrighted works), as limited by sections 107 through 122, of title 17;

(3) the term "financial gain" has the meaning given the term in section 101 of title 17; and

(4) the term "work being prepared for commercial distribution" has the meaning given the term in section 506(a) of title 17.

17 U.S.C. § 506. CRIMINAL OFFENSES

(a) Criminal infringement.

(1) In general. Any person who willfully infringes a copyright shall be punished as provided under section 2319 of title 18, if the infringement was committed—

(A) for purposes of commercial advantage or private financial gain;

(B) by the reproduction or distribution, including by electronic means, during any 180-day period, of 1 or more copies or phonorecords of 1 or more copyrighted works, which have a total retail value of more than $1,000; or

(C) by the distribution of a work being prepared for commercial distribution, by making it available on a computer network accessible to members of the public, if such person knew or should have known that the work was intended for commercial distribution.

(2) Evidence. For purposes of this subsection, evidence of reproduction or distribution of a copyrighted work, by itself, shall not be sufficient to establish willful infringement of a copyright.

(3) **Definition.** In this subsection, the term "work being prepared for commercial distribution" means—

(A) a computer program, a musical work, a motion picture or other audiovisual work, or a sound recording, if, at the time of unauthorized distribution—

(i) the copyright owner has a reasonable expectation of commercial distribution; and

(ii) the copies or phonorecords of the work have not been commercially distributed; or

(B) a motion picture, if, at the time of unauthorized distribution, the motion picture—

(i) has been made available for viewing in a motion picture exhibition facility; and

(ii) has not been made available in copies for sale to the general public in the United States in a format intended to permit viewing outside a motion picture exhibition facility.

(b) **Forfeiture, destruction, and restitution.** Forfeiture, destruction, and restitution relating to this section shall be subject to section 2323 of title 18, to the extent provided in that section, in addition to any other similar remedies provided by law.

(c) **Fraudulent Copyright Notice.** Any person who, with fraudulent intent, places on any article a notice of copyright or words of the same purport that such person knows to be false, or who, with fraudulent intent, publicly distributes or imports for public distribution any article bearing such notice or words that such person knows to be false, shall be fined not more than $2,500.

(d) **Fraudulent Removal of Copyright Notice.** Any person who, with fraudulent intent, removes or alters any notice of copyright appearing on a copy of a copyrighted work shall be fined not more than $2,500.

(e) **False Representation.** Any person who knowingly makes a false representation of a material fact in the application for copyright registration provided for by section 409, or in any written statement filed in connection with the application, shall be fined not more than $2,500.

(f) **Rights of Attribution and Integrity.** Nothing in this section applies to infringement of the rights conferred by section 106A(a).

18 U.S.C. § 2422. COERCION AND ENTICEMENT

(a) Whoever knowingly persuades, induces, entices, or coerces any individual to travel in interstate or foreign commerce, or in any Territory or Possession of the United States, to engage in prostitution, or in any sexual activity for which any person can be charged with a criminal offense, or attempts to do so, shall be fined under this title or imprisoned not more than 20 years, or both.

(b) Whoever, using the mail or any facility or means of interstate or foreign commerce, or within the special maritime and territorial jurisdiction of the United States knowingly persuades, induces, entices, or coerces any individual who has not attained the age of 18 years, to engage in prostitution or any sexual activity for which any person can be charged with a criminal offense, or attempts to do so, shall be fined under this title and imprisoned not less than 10 years or for life.

18 U.S.C. § 2423. TRANSPORTATION OF MINORS

(a) Transportation with intent to engage in criminal sexual activity. A person who knowingly transports an individual who has not attained the age of 18 years in interstate or foreign commerce, or in any commonwealth, territory or possession of the United States, with intent that the individual engage in prostitution, or in any sexual activity for which any person can be charged with a criminal offense, shall be fined under this title and imprisoned not less than 10 years or for life.

(b) Travel with intent to engage in illicit sexual conduct. A person who travels in interstate commerce or travels into the United States, or a United States citizen or an alien admitted for permanent residence in the United States who travels in foreign commerce, with a motivating purpose of engaging in any illicit sexual conduct with another person shall be fined under this title or imprisoned not more than 30 years, or both.

(c) Engaging in illicit sexual conduct in foreign places. Any United States citizen or alien admitted for permanent residence who travels in foreign commerce, and engages in any illicit sexual conduct with another person shall be fined under this title or imprisoned not more than 30 years, or both.

(d) Ancillary offenses. Whoever, for the purpose of commercial advantage or private financial gain, arranges, induces, procures, or facilitates the travel of a person knowing that such a person is traveling in interstate commerce or foreign commerce with a motivating purpose of engaging in illicit sexual conduct shall be fined under this title, imprisoned not more than 30 years, or both.

(e) Attempt and conspiracy. Whoever attempts or conspires to violate subsection (a), (b), (c), or (d) shall be punishable in the same manner as a completed violation of that subsection.

(f) Definition. As used in this section, the term "illicit sexual conduct" means (1) a sexual act (as defined in section 2246) with a person under 18 years of age that would be in violation of chapter 109A if the sexual act occurred in the special maritime and territorial jurisdiction of the United States; or (2) any commercial sex act (as defined in section 1591) with a person under 18 years of age.

(g) Defense. In a prosecution under this section based on illicit sexual conduct as defined in subsection (f)(2), it is a defense, which the defendant must establish by a preponderance of the evidence, that the defendant reasonably believed that the person with whom the defendant engaged in the commercial sex act had attained the age of 18 years.

18 U.S.C. § 2510. DEFINITIONS

As used in this chapter—

(1) "wire communication" means any aural transfer made in whole or in part through the use of facilities for the transmission of communications by the aid of wire, cable, or other like connection between the point of origin and the point of reception (including the use of such connection in a switching station) furnished or operated by any person engaged in providing or operating such facilities for the transmission of interstate or foreign communications or communications affecting interstate or foreign commerce;

(2) "oral communication" means any oral communication uttered by a person exhibiting an expectation that such communication is not subject to interception under circumstances justifying such expectation, but such term does not include any electronic communication;

(3) "State" means any State of the United States, the District of Columbia, the Commonwealth of Puerto Rico, and any territory or possession of the United States;

(4) "intercept" means the aural or other acquisition of the contents of any wire, electronic, or oral communication through the use of any electronic, mechanical, or other device.

(5) "electronic, mechanical, or other device" means any device or apparatus which can be used to intercept a wire, oral, or electronic communication other than—

(A) any telephone or telegraph instrument, equipment or facility, or any component thereof, (i) furnished to the subscriber or user by a provider of wire or electronic communication service in the ordinary course of its business and being used by the subscriber or user in the ordinary course of its business or furnished by such subscriber or user for connection to the facilities of such service and used in the ordinary course of its business; or (ii) being used by a provider of wire or electronic communication service in the ordinary course of its business, or by an investigative or law enforcement officer in the ordinary course of his duties;

(B) a hearing aid or similar device being used to correct subnormal hearing to not better than normal;

(6) "person" means any employee, or agent of the United States or any State or political subdivision thereof, and any individual, partnership, association, joint stock company, trust, or corporation;

(7) "Investigative or law enforcement officer" means any officer of the United States or of a State or political subdivision thereof, who is empowered by law to conduct investigations of or to make arrests for offenses enumerated in this chapter, and any attorney authorized by law to prosecute or participate in the prosecution of such offenses;

(8) "contents", when used with respect to any wire, oral, or electronic communication, includes any information concerning the substance, purport, or meaning of that communication;

(9) "Judge of competent jurisdiction" means—

(A) a judge of a United States district court or a United States court of appeals; and

(B) a judge of any court of general criminal jurisdiction of a State who is authorized by a statute of that State to enter orders authorizing interceptions of wire, oral, or electronic communications;

(10) "communication common carrier" has the meaning given that term in section 3 of the Communications Act of 1934;

(11) "aggrieved person" means a person who was a party to any intercepted wire, oral, or electronic communication or a person against whom the interception was directed;

(12) "electronic communication" means any transfer of signs, signals, writing, images, sounds, data, or intelligence of any nature transmitted in whole or in part by a wire, radio, electromagnetic, photoelectronic or photooptical system that affects interstate or foreign commerce, but does not include—

(A) any wire or oral communication;

(B) any communication made through a tone-only paging device;

(C) any communication from a tracking device (as defined in section 3117 of this title); or

(D) electronic funds transfer information stored by a financial institution in a communications system used for the electronic storage and transfer of funds;

(13) "user" means any person or entity who—

(A) uses an electronic communication service; and

(B) is duly authorized by the provider of such service to engage in such use;

(14) "electronic communications system" means any wire, radio, electromagnetic, photooptical or photoelectronic facilities for the transmission of wire or electronic communications, and any computer facilities or related electronic equipment for the electronic storage of such communications;

(15) "electronic communication service" means any service which provides to users thereof the ability to send or receive wire or electronic communications;

(16) "readily accessible to the general public" means, with respect to a radio communication, that such communication is not—

(A) scrambled or encrypted;

(B) transmitted using modulation techniques whose essential parameters have been withheld from the public with the intention of preserving the privacy of such communication;

(C) carried on a subcarrier or other signal subsidiary to a radio transmission;

(D) transmitted over a communication system provided by a common carrier, unless the communication is a tone only paging system communication; or

(E) transmitted on frequencies allocated under part 25, subpart D, E, or F of part 74, or part 94 of the Rules of the Federal Communications Commission, unless, in the case of a communication transmitted on a frequency allocated under part 74 that is not exclusively allocated to broadcast auxiliary services, the communication is a two-way voice communication by radio;

(17) "electronic storage" means—

(A) any temporary, intermediate storage of a wire or electronic communication incidental to the electronic transmission thereof; and

(B) any storage of such communication by an electronic communication service for purposes of backup protection of such communication;

(18) "aural transfer" means a transfer containing the human voice at any point between and including the point of origin and the point of reception;

(19) "foreign intelligence information", for purposes of section 2517(6) of this title, means—

(A) information, whether or not concerning a United States person, that relates to the ability of the United States to protect against—

(i) actual or potential attack or other grave hostile acts of a foreign power or an agent of a foreign power;

(ii) sabotage or international terrorism by a foreign power or an agent of a foreign power; or

(iii) clandestine intelligence activities by an intelligence service or network of a foreign power or by an agent of a foreign power; or

(B) information, whether or not concerning a United States person, with respect to a foreign power or foreign territory that relates to—

(i) the national defense or the security of the United States; or

(ii) the conduct of the foreign affairs of the United States;

(20) "protected computer" has the meaning set forth in section 1030; and

(21) "computer trespasser"—

(A) means a person who accesses a protected computer without authorization and thus has no reasonable expectation of privacy in any communication transmitted to, through, or from the protected computer; and

(B) does not include a person known by the owner or operator of the protected computer to have an existing contractual relationship with the owner or operator of the protected computer for access to all or part of the protected computer.

18 U.S.C. § 2511. INTERCEPTION AND DISCLOSURE OF WIRE, ORAL, OR ELECTRONIC COMMUNICATIONS PROHIBITED

(1) Except as otherwise specifically provided in this chapter any person who—

(a) intentionally intercepts, endeavors to intercept, or procures any other person to intercept or endeavor to intercept, any wire, oral, or electronic communication;

(b) intentionally uses, endeavors to use, or procures any other person to use or endeavor to use any electronic, mechanical, or other device to intercept any oral communication when—

    (i) such device is affixed to, or otherwise transmits a signal through, a wire, cable, or other like connection used in wire communication; or

    (ii) such device transmits communications by radio, or interferes with the transmission of such communication; or

    (iii) such person knows, or has reason to know, that such device or any component thereof has been sent through the mail or transported in interstate or foreign commerce; or

    (iv) such use or endeavor to use (A) takes place on the premises of any business or other commercial establishment the operations of which affect interstate or foreign commerce; or (B) obtains or is for the purpose of obtaining information relating to the operations of any business or other commercial establishment the operations of which affect interstate or foreign commerce; or

    (v) such person acts in the District of Columbia, the Commonwealth of Puerto Rico, or any territory or possession of the United States;

(c) intentionally discloses, or endeavors to disclose, to any other person the contents of any wire, oral, or electronic communication, knowing or having reason to know that the information was obtained through the interception of a wire, oral, or electronic communication in violation of this subsection;

(d) intentionally uses, or endeavors to use, the contents of any wire, oral, or electronic communication, knowing or having reason to know that the information was obtained through the interception of a wire, oral, or electronic communication in violation of this subsection; or

(e)(i) intentionally discloses, or endeavors to disclose, to any other person the contents of any wire, oral, or electronic communication, intercepted by means authorized by sections 2511(2)(a)(ii), 2511(2)(b)–(c), 2511(2)(e), 2516, and 2518 of this chapter, (ii) knowing or having reason to know that the information was obtained through the interception of such a communication in connection with a criminal investigation, (iii) having obtained or received the information in connection with a criminal investigation, and (iv) with intent to improperly obstruct, impede, or interfere with a duly authorized criminal investigation,

shall be punished as provided in subsection (4) or shall be subject to suit as provided in subsection (5).

(2)(a)(i) It shall not be unlawful under this chapter for an operator of a switchboard, or an officer, employee, or agent of a provider of wire or electronic communication service, whose facilities are used in the transmission of a wire or electronic communication, to intercept, disclose, or use that communication in the normal course of his employment while engaged in any activity which is a necessary incident to the rendition of his service or to the protection of the rights or property of the provider of that service, except that a provider of wire communication service to the public shall not utilize service observing or random monitoring except for mechanical or service quality control checks.

(ii) Notwithstanding any other law, providers of wire or electronic communication service, their officers, employees, and agents, landlords, custodians, or other persons, are authorized to provide information, facilities, or technical assistance to persons authorized by law to intercept wire, oral, or electronic communications or to conduct electronic surveillance, as defined in section 101 of the Foreign Intelligence Surveillance Act of 1978, if such provider, its officers, employees, or agents, landlord, custodian, or other specified person, has been provided with—

(A) a court order directing such assistance or a court order pursuant to section 704 of the Foreign Intelligence Surveillance Act of 1978 signed by the authorizing judge, or

(B) a certification in writing by a person specified in section 2518(7) of this title or the Attorney General of the United States that no warrant or court order is required by law, that all statutory requirements have been met, and that the specified assistance is required,

setting forth period of time during which the provision of the information, facilities, or technical assistance is authorized and specifying the information, facilities, or technical assistance required. No provider of wire or electronic communication service, officer, employee, or agent thereof, or landlord, custodian, or other specified person shall disclose the existence of any interception or surveillance or the device used to accomplish the interception or surveillance with respect to which the person has been furnished a court order or certification under this chapter, except as may otherwise be required by legal process and then only after prior notification to the Attorney General or to the principal prosecuting attorney of a State or any political subdivision of a

State, as may be appropriate. Any such disclosure, shall render such person liable for the civil damages provided for in section 2520. No cause of action shall lie in any court against any provider of wire or electronic communication service, its officers, employees, or agents, landlord, custodian, or other specified person for providing information, facilities, or assistance in accordance with the terms of a court order, statutory authorization, or certification under this chapter.

(iii) If a certification under subparagraph (ii)(B) for assistance to obtain foreign intelligence information is based on statutory authority, the certification shall identify the specific statutory provision and shall certify that the statutory requirements have been met.

(b) It shall not be unlawful under this chapter for an officer, employee, or agent of the Federal Communications Commission, in the normal course of his employment and in discharge of the monitoring responsibilities exercised by the Commission in the enforcement of chapter 5 of title 47 of the United States Code, to intercept a wire or electronic communication, or oral communication transmitted by radio, or to disclose or use the information thereby obtained.

(c) It shall not be unlawful under this chapter for a person acting under color of law to intercept a wire, oral, or electronic communication, where such person is a party to the communication or one of the parties to the communication has given prior consent to such interception.

(d) It shall not be unlawful under this chapter for a person not acting under color of law to intercept a wire, oral, or electronic communication where such person is a party to the communication or where one of the parties to the communication has given prior consent to such interception unless such communication is intercepted for the purpose of committing any criminal or tortious act in violation of the Constitution or laws of the United States or of any State.

(e) Notwithstanding any other provision of this title or section 705 or 706 of the Communications Act of 1934, it shall not be unlawful for an officer, employee, or agent of the United States in the normal course of his official duty to conduct electronic surveillance, as defined in section 101 of the Foreign Intelligence Surveillance Act of 1978, as authorized by that Act.

(f) Nothing contained in this chapter or chapter 121 or 206 of this title, or section 705 of the Communications Act of 1934, shall be deemed to affect the acquisition by the United States Government of foreign intelligence information from international or foreign communications, or foreign intelligence activities conducted in accordance with otherwise applicable Federal law involving a foreign electronic communications system, utilizing a means other than electronic surveillance as defined in section 101 of the Foreign Intelligence Surveillance Act of 1978, and procedures in this chapter or chapter 121 and the Foreign Intelligence Surveillance Act of 1978 shall be the exclusive means by which electronic surveillance, as defined in section 101 of such Act, and the interception of domestic wire, oral, and electronic communications may be conducted.

(g) It shall not be unlawful under this chapter or chapter 121 of this title for any person—

(i) to intercept or access an electronic communication made through an electronic communication system that is configured so that such electronic communication is readily accessible to the general public;

(ii) to intercept any radio communication which is transmitted—

(I) by any station for the use of the general public, or that relates to ships, aircraft, vehicles, or persons in distress;

(II) by any governmental, law enforcement, civil defense, private land mobile, or public safety communications system, including police and fire, readily accessible to the general public;

(III) by a station operating on an authorized frequency within the bands allocated to the amateur, citizens band, or general mobile radio services; or

(IV) by any marine or aeronautical communications system;

(iii) to engage in any conduct which—

(I) is prohibited by section 633 of the Communications Act of 1934; or

(II) is excepted from the application of section 705(a) of the Communications Act of 1934 by section 705(b) of that Act;

(iv) to intercept any wire or electronic communication the transmission of which is causing harmful interference to any lawfully operating station or consumer electronic equipment, to the extent necessary to identify the source of such interference; or

(v) for other users of the same frequency to intercept any radio communication made through a system that utilizes frequencies monitored by individuals engaged in the provision or the use of such system, if such communication is not scrambled or encrypted.

(h) It shall not be unlawful under this chapter—

(i) to use a pen register or a trap and trace device (as those terms are defined for the purposes of chapter 206 (relating to pen registers and trap and trace devices) of this title); or

(ii) for a provider of electronic communication service to record the fact that a wire or electronic communication was initiated or completed in order to protect such provider, another provider furnishing service toward the completion of the wire or electronic communication, or a user of that service, from fraudulent, unlawful or abusive use of such service.

(i) It shall not be unlawful under this chapter for a person acting under color of law to intercept the wire or electronic communications of a computer trespasser transmitted to, through, or from the protected computer, if—

(I) the owner or operator of the protected computer authorizes the interception of the computer trespasser's communications on the protected computer;

(II) the person acting under color of law is lawfully engaged in an investigation;

(III) the person acting under color of law has reasonable grounds to believe that the contents of the computer trespasser's communications will be relevant to the investigation; and

(IV) such interception does not acquire communications other than those transmitted to or from the computer trespasser.

(j) It shall not be unlawful under this chapter for a provider of electronic communication service to the public or remote computing service to intercept or disclose the contents of a wire or electronic communication in response to an order from a foreign government that is subject to an executive agreement that the Attorney General has determined and certified to Congress satisfies section 2523.

(3)(a) Except as provided in paragraph (b) of this subsection, a person or entity providing an electronic communication service to the public shall not intentionally divulge the contents of any communication (other than one to such person or entity, or an agent thereof) while in transmission on that service to any person or entity other than an addressee or intended recipient of such communication or an agent of such addressee or intended recipient.

(b) A person or entity providing electronic communication service to the public may divulge the contents of any such communication—

(i) as otherwise authorized in section 2511(2)(a) or 2517 of this title;

(ii) with the lawful consent of the originator or any addressee or intended recipient of such communication;

(iii) to a person employed or authorized, or whose facilities are used, to forward such communication to its destination; or

(iv) which were inadvertently obtained by the service provider and which appear to pertain to the commission of a crime, if such divulgence is made to a law enforcement agency.

(4)(a) Except as provided in paragraph (b) of this subsection or in subsection (5), whoever violates subsection (1) of this section shall be fined under this title or imprisoned not more than five years, or both.

(b) Conduct otherwise an offense under this subsection that consists of or relates to the interception of a satellite transmission that is not encrypted or scrambled and that is transmitted—

(i) to a broadcasting station for purposes of retransmission to the general public; or

(ii) as an audio subcarrier intended for redistribution to facilities open to the public, but not including data transmissions or telephone calls,

is not an offense under this subsection unless the conduct is for the purposes of direct or indirect commercial advantage or private financial gain.

(5)(a)(i) If the communication is—

(A) a private satellite video communication that is not scrambled or encrypted and the conduct in violation of this chapter is the private viewing of that communication and is not for a tortious or illegal purpose or for purposes of direct or indirect commercial advantage or private commercial gain; or

(B) a radio communication that is transmitted on frequencies allocated under subpart D of part 74 of the rules of the Federal Communications Commission that is not scrambled or encrypted and the conduct in violation of this chapter is not for a tortious or illegal purpose or for purposes of direct or indirect commercial advantage or private commercial gain,

then the person who engages in such conduct shall be subject to suit by the Federal Government in a court of competent jurisdiction.

(ii) In an action under this subsection—

(A) if the violation of this chapter is a first offense for the person under paragraph (a) of subsection (4) and such person has not been found liable in a civil action under section 2520 of this title, the Federal Government shall be entitled to appropriate injunctive relief; and

(B) if the violation of this chapter is a second or subsequent offense under paragraph (a) of subsection (4) or such person has been found liable in any prior civil action under section 2520, the person shall be subject to a mandatory $500 civil fine.

(b) The court may use any means within its authority to enforce an injunction issued under paragraph (ii)(A), and shall impose a civil fine of not less than $500 for each violation of such an injunction.

18 U.S.C. § 2512. MANUFACTURE, DISTRIBUTION, POSSESSION, AND ADVERTISING OF WIRE, ORAL, OR ELECTRONIC COMMUNICATION INTERCEPTING DEVICES PROHIBITED

(1) Except as otherwise specifically provided in this chapter, any person who intentionally—

(a) sends through the mail, or sends or carries in interstate or foreign commerce, any electronic, mechanical, or other device, knowing or having reason to know that the design of such device renders it primarily useful for the purpose of the surreptitious interception of wire, oral, or electronic communications;

(b) manufactures, assembles, possesses, or sells any electronic, mechanical, or other device, knowing or having reason to know that the design of such device renders it primarily useful for the purpose of the surreptitious interception of wire, oral, or electronic communications, and that such device or any component thereof has been or will be sent through the mail or transported in interstate or foreign commerce; or

(c) places in any newspaper, magazine, handbill, or other publication or disseminates by electronic means any advertisement of—

(i) any electronic, mechanical, or other device knowing the content of the advertisement and knowing or having reason to know that the design of such device renders it primarily useful for the purpose of the surreptitious interception of wire, oral, or electronic communications; or

(ii) any other electronic, mechanical, or other device, where such advertisement promotes the use of such device for the purpose of the surreptitious interception of wire, oral, or electronic communications,

knowing the content of the advertisement and knowing or having reason to know that such advertisement will be sent through the mail or transported in interstate or foreign commerce,

shall be fined under this title or imprisoned not more than five years, or both.

(2) It shall not be unlawful under this section for—

(a) a provider of wire or electronic communication service or an officer, agent, or employee of, or a person under contract with, such a provider, in the normal course of the business of providing that wire or electronic communication service, or

(b) an officer, agent, or employee of, or a person under contract with, the United States, a State, or a political subdivision thereof, in the normal course of the activities of the United States, a State, or a political subdivision thereof,

to send through the mail, send or carry in interstate or foreign commerce, or manufacture, assemble, possess, or sell any electronic, mechanical, or other device knowing or having reason to know that the design of such device renders it primarily useful for the purpose of the surreptitious interception of wire, oral, or electronic communications.

(3) It shall not be unlawful under this section to advertise for sale a device described in subsection (1) of this section if the advertisement is mailed, sent, or carried in interstate or foreign commerce solely to a domestic provider of wire or electronic communication service or to an agency of the United States, a State, or a political subdivision thereof which is duly authorized to use such device.

18 U.S.C. § 2513. CONFISCATION OF WIRE, ORAL, OR ELECTRONIC COMMUNICATION INTERCEPTING DEVICES

Any electronic, mechanical, or other device used, sent, carried, manufactured, assembled, possessed, sold, or advertised in violation of section 2511 or section 2512 of this chapter may be seized and forfeited to the United States. All provisions of law relating to (1) the seizure, summary and judicial forfeiture, and condemnation of vessels, vehicles, merchandise, and baggage for violations of the customs laws contained in title 19 of the United States Code, (2) the disposition of such vessels, vehicles, merchandise, and baggage or the proceeds from the sale thereof, (3) the remission or mitigation of such forfeiture, (4) the compromise of claims, and (5) the award of compensation to informers in respect of such forfeitures, shall apply to seizures and forfeitures incurred, or alleged to have been incurred, under the provisions of this section, insofar as applicable and not inconsistent with the provisions of this section; except that such duties as are imposed upon the collector of customs or any other person with respect to the seizure and forfeiture of vessels, vehicles, merchandise, and baggage under the provisions of the customs laws contained in title 19 of the United States Code shall be performed with respect to seizure and forfeiture of electronic, mechanical, or other intercepting devices under this section by such officers, agents, or other persons as may be authorized or designated for that purpose by the Attorney General.

18 U.S.C. § 2515. PROHIBITION OF USE AS EVIDENCE OF INTERCEPTED WIRE OR ORAL COMMUNICATIONS

Whenever any wire or oral communication has been intercepted, no part of the contents of such communication and no evidence derived therefrom may be received in evidence in any trial, hearing, or other proceeding in or before any court, grand jury, department, officer, agency, regulatory body, legislative committee, or other authority of the United States, a State, or a political subdivision thereof if the disclosure of that information would be in violation of this chapter.

18 U.S.C. § 2516. AUTHORIZATION FOR INTERCEPTION OF WIRE, ORAL, OR ELECTRONIC COMMUNICATIONS

(1) The Attorney General, Deputy Attorney General, Associate Attorney General, or any Assistant Attorney General, any acting Assistant Attorney General, or any Deputy Assistant Attorney General or acting Deputy Assistant Attorney General in the Criminal Division or National Security Division specially designated by the Attorney General, may authorize an application to a Federal judge of competent jurisdiction for, and such judge may grant in conformity with section 2518 of this chapter an order authorizing or approving the interception of wire or oral communications by the Federal Bureau of Investigation, or a Federal agency having responsibility for the investigation of the offense as to which the application is made, when such interception may provide or has provided evidence of—

(a) any offense punishable by death or by imprisonment for more than one year under sections 2122 and 2274 through 2277 of title 42 of the United States Code (relating to the enforcement of the Atomic Energy Act of 1954), section 2284 of title 42 of the United States Code (relating to sabotage of nuclear facilities or fuel), or under the following chapters of this title: chapter 10 (relating to biological weapons), chapter 37 (relating to espionage), chapter 55 (relating to kidnapping), chapter 90 (relating to protection of trade secrets), chapter 105 (relating to sabotage), chapter 115 (relating to treason), chapter 102 (relating to riots), chapter 65 (relating to malicious mischief), chapter 111 (relating to destruction of vessels), or chapter 81 (relating to piracy);

(b) a violation of section 186 or section 501(c) of title 29, United States Code (dealing with restrictions on payments and loans to labor organizations), or any offense which involves murder, kidnapping, robbery, or extortion, and which is punishable under this title;

(c) any offense which is punishable under the following sections of this title: section 37 (relating to violence at international airports), section 43 (relating to animal enterprise terrorism), section 81 (arson within special maritime and territorial jurisdiction), section 201 (bribery of public officials and witnesses), section 215 (relating to bribery of bank officials), section 224 (bribery in sporting contests), subsection (d), (e), (f), (g), (h), or (i) of section 844 (unlawful use of explosives), section 1032 (relating to concealment of assets), section 1084 (transmission of wagering information), section 751 (relating to escape), section 832 (relating to nuclear and weapons of mass destruction threats), section 842 (relating to explosive materials), section 930 (relating to possession of weapons in Federal facilities), section 1014 (relating to loans and credit applications generally; renewals and discounts), section 1114 (relating to officers and employees of the United States), section 1116 (relating to protection of foreign officials), sections 1503, 1512, and 1513 (influencing or injuring an officer, juror, or witness generally), section 1510 (obstruction of criminal investigations), section 1511 (obstruction of State or local law enforcement), section 1591 (sex trafficking of children by force, fraud, or coercion), section 1751 (Presidential and Presidential staff assassination, kidnapping, and assault), section 1951 (interference with commerce by threats or violence), section 1952 (interstate and foreign travel or transportation in aid of racketeering enterprises), section 1958 (relating to use of interstate commerce facilities in the commission of murder for hire), section 1959 (relating to violent crimes in aid of racketeering activity), section 1954 (offer, acceptance, or solicitation to influence operations of employee benefit plan), section 1955 (prohibition of business enterprises of gambling), section 1956 (laundering of monetary instruments), section 1957 (relating to engaging in monetary transactions in property derived from specified unlawful activity), section 659 (theft from interstate shipment), section 664 (embezzlement from pension and welfare funds), section 1343 (fraud by wire, radio, or television), section 1344 (relating to bank fraud), section 1992 (relating to terrorist attacks against mass transportation), sections 2251 and 2252 (sexual exploitation of children), section 2251A (selling or buying of children), section 2252A (relating to material constituting or containing child pornography), section 1466A (relating to child obscenity), section 2260 (production of sexually explicit depictions of a minor for importation into the United States), sections 2421, 2422, 2423, and 2425 (relating to transportation for illegal sexual activity and related crimes), sections 2312, 2313,

2314, and 2315 (interstate transportation of stolen property), section 2321 (relating to trafficking in certain motor vehicles or motor vehicle parts), section 2340A (relating to torture), section 1203 (relating to hostage taking), section 1029 (relating to fraud and related activity in connection with access devices), section 3146 (relating to penalty for failure to appear), section 3521(b)(3) (relating to witness relocation and assistance), section 32 (relating to destruction of aircraft or aircraft facilities), section 38 (relating to aircraft parts fraud), section 1963 (violations with respect to racketeer influenced and corrupt organizations), section 115 (relating to threatening or retaliating against a Federal official), section 1341 (relating to mail fraud), a felony violation of section 1030 (relating to computer fraud and abuse), section 351 (violations with respect to congressional, Cabinet, or Supreme Court assassinations, kidnapping, and assault), section 831 (relating to prohibited transactions involving nuclear materials), section 33 (relating to destruction of motor vehicles or motor vehicle facilities), section 175 (relating to biological weapons), section 175c (relating to variola virus), section 956 (conspiracy to harm persons or property overseas), a felony violation of section 1028 (relating to production of false identification documentation), section 1425 (relating to the procurement of citizenship or nationalization unlawfully), section 1426 (relating to the reproduction of naturalization or citizenship papers), section 1427 (relating to the sale of naturalization or citizenship papers), section 1541 (relating to passport issuance without authority), section 1542 (relating to false statements in passport applications), section 1543 (relating to forgery or false use of passports), section 1544 (relating to misuse of passports), or section 1546 (relating to fraud and misuse of visas, permits, and other documents);

(d) any offense involving counterfeiting punishable under section 471, 472, or 473 of this title;

(e) any offense involving fraud connected with a case under title 11 or the manufacture, importation, receiving, concealment, buying, selling, or otherwise dealing in narcotic drugs, marihuana, or other dangerous drugs, punishable under any law of the United States;

(f) any offense including extortionate credit transactions under sections 892, 893, or 894 of this title;

(g) a violation of section 5322 of title 31, United States Code (dealing with the reporting of currency transactions), or section 5324 of title 31, United States Code (relating to structuring transactions to evade reporting requirement prohibited);

(h) any felony violation of sections 2511 and 2512 (relating to interception and disclosure of certain communications and to certain intercepting devices) of this title;

(i) any felony violation of chapter 71 (relating to obscenity) of this title;

(j) any violation of section 60123(b) (relating to destruction of a natural gas pipeline), section 46502 (relating to aircraft piracy), the second sentence of section 46504 (relating to assault on a flight crew with dangerous weapon), or section 46505(b)(3) or (c) (relating to explosive or incendiary devices, or endangerment of human life, by means of weapons on aircraft) of title 49;

(k) any criminal violation of section 2778 of title 22 (relating to the Arms Export Control Act);

(l) the location of any fugitive from justice from an offense described in this section;

(m) a violation of section 274, 277, or 278 of the Immigration and Nationality Act (8 U.S.C. 1324, 1327, or 1328) (relating to the smuggling of aliens);

(n) any felony violation of sections 922 and 924 of title 18, United States Code (relating to firearms);

(o) any violation of section 5861 of the Internal Revenue Code of 1986 (relating to firearms);

(p) a felony violation of section 1028 (relating to production of false identification documents), section 1542 (relating to false statements in passport applications), section 1546 (relating to fraud and misuse of visas, permits, and other documents), section 1028A (relating to aggravated identity theft) of this title or a violation of section 274, 277, or 278 of the Immigration and Nationality Act (relating to the smuggling of aliens); or

(q) any criminal violation of section 229 (relating to chemical weapons) or sections 2332, 2332a, 2332b, 2332d, 2332f, 2332g, 2332h, 2339, 2339A, 2339B, 2339C, or 2339D of this title (relating to terrorism);

(r) any criminal violation of section 1 (relating to illegal restraints of trade or commerce), 2 (relating to illegal monopolizing of trade or commerce), or 3 (relating to illegal restraints of trade or commerce in territories or the District of Columbia) of the Sherman Act (15 U.S.C. 1, 2, 3); or

(s) any conspiracy to commit any offense described in any subparagraph of this paragraph.

(2) The principal prosecuting attorney of any State, or the principal prosecuting attorney of any political subdivision thereof, if such attorney is authorized by a statute of that State to make application to a State court judge of competent jurisdiction for an order authorizing or approving the interception of wire, oral, or electronic communications, may apply to such judge for, and such judge may grant in conformity with section 2518 of this chapter and with the applicable State statute an order authorizing, or approving the interception of wire, oral, or electronic communications by investigative or law enforcement officers having responsibility for the investigation of the offense as to which the application is made, when such interception may provide or has provided evidence of the commission of the offense of murder, kidnapping, gambling, robbery, bribery, extortion, or dealing in narcotic drugs, marihuana or other dangerous drugs, or other crime dangerous to life, limb, or property, and punishable by imprisonment for more than one year, designated in any applicable State statute authorizing such interception, or any conspiracy to commit any of the foregoing offenses.

(3) Any attorney for the Government (as such term is defined for the purposes of the Federal Rules of Criminal Procedure) may authorize an application to a Federal judge of competent jurisdiction for, and such judge may grant, in conformity with section 2518 of this title, an order authorizing or approving the interception of electronic communications by an investigative or law enforcement officer having responsibility for the investigation of the offense as to which the application is made, when such interception may provide or has provided evidence of any Federal felony.

18 U.S.C. § 2517. Authorization for Disclosure and Use of Intercepted Wire, Oral, or Electronic Communications

(1) Any investigative or law enforcement officer who, by any means authorized by this chapter, has obtained knowledge of the contents of any wire, oral, or electronic communication, or evidence derived therefrom, may disclose such contents to another investigative or law enforcement officer to the extent that such disclosure is appropriate to the proper performance of the official duties of the officer making or receiving the disclosure.

(2) Any investigative or law enforcement officer who, by any means authorized by this chapter, has obtained knowledge of the contents of any wire, oral, or electronic communication or evidence derived therefrom may use such contents to the extent such use is appropriate to the proper performance of his official duties.

(3) Any person who has received, by any means authorized by this chapter, any information concerning a wire, oral, or electronic communication, or evidence derived therefrom intercepted in accordance with the provisions of this chapter may disclose the contents of that communication or such derivative evidence while giving testimony under

oath or affirmation in any proceeding held under the authority of the United States or of any State or political subdivision thereof.

(4) No otherwise privileged wire, oral, or electronic communication intercepted in accordance with, or in violation of, the provisions of this chapter shall lose its privileged character.

(5) When an investigative or law enforcement officer, while engaged in intercepting wire, oral, or electronic communications in the manner authorized herein, intercepts wire, oral, or electronic communications relating to offenses other than those specified in the order of authorization or approval, the contents thereof, and evidence derived therefrom, may be disclosed or used as provided in subsections (1) and (2) of this section. Such contents and any evidence derived therefrom may be used under subsection (3) of this section when authorized or approved by a judge of competent jurisdiction where such judge finds on subsequent application that the contents were otherwise intercepted in accordance with the provisions of this chapter. Such application shall be made as soon as practicable.

(6) Any investigative or law enforcement officer, or attorney for the Government, who by any means authorized by this chapter, has obtained knowledge of the contents of any wire, oral, or electronic communication, or evidence derived therefrom, may disclose such contents to any other Federal law enforcement, intelligence, protective, immigration, national defense, or national security official to the extent that such contents include foreign intelligence or counterintelligence (as defined in section 3 of the National Security Act of 1947 (50 U.S.C. 401a)), or foreign intelligence information (as defined in subsection (19) of section 2510 of this title), to assist the official who is to receive that information in the performance of his official duties. Any Federal official who receives information pursuant to this provision may use that information only as necessary in the conduct of that person's official duties subject to any limitations on the unauthorized disclosure of such information.

(7) Any investigative or law enforcement officer, or other Federal official in carrying out official duties as such Federal official, who by any means authorized by this chapter, has obtained knowledge of the contents of any wire, oral, or electronic communication, or evidence derived therefrom, may disclose such contents or derivative evidence to a foreign investigative or law enforcement officer to the extent that such disclosure is appropriate to the proper performance of the official duties of the officer making or receiving the disclosure, and foreign investigative or law enforcement officers may use or disclose such contents or derivative evidence to the extent such use or disclosure is appropriate to the proper performance of their official duties.

(8) Any investigative or law enforcement officer, or other Federal official in carrying out official duties as such Federal official, who by any means authorized by this chapter, has obtained knowledge of the contents of any wire, oral, or electronic communication, or evidence derived therefrom, may disclose such contents or derivative evidence to any appropriate Federal, State, local, or foreign government official to the extent that such contents or derivative evidence reveals a threat of actual or potential attack or other grave hostile acts of a foreign power or an agent of a foreign power, domestic or international sabotage, domestic or international terrorism, or clandestine intelligence gathering activities by an intelligence service or network of a foreign power or by an agent of a foreign power, within the United States or elsewhere, for the purpose of preventing or responding to such a threat. Any official who receives information pursuant to this provision may use that information only as necessary in the conduct of that person's official duties subject to any limitations on the unauthorized disclosure of such information, and any State, local, or foreign official who receives information pursuant to this provision may use that information only consistent with such guidelines as the Attorney General and Director of Central Intelligence shall jointly issue.

18 U.S.C. § 2518. PROCEDURE FOR INTERCEPTION OF WIRE, ORAL, OR ELECTRONIC COMMUNICATIONS

(1) Each application for an order authorizing or approving the interception of a wire, oral, or electronic communication under this chapter shall be made in writing upon oath or affirmation to a judge of competent jurisdiction and shall state the applicant's authority to make such application. Each application shall include the following information:

(a) the identity of the investigative or law enforcement officer making the application, and the officer authorizing the application;

(b) a full and complete statement of the facts and circumstances relied upon by the applicant, to justify his belief that an order should be issued, including (i) details as to the particular offense that has been, is being, or is about to be committed, (ii) except as provided in subsection (11), a particular description of the nature and location of the facilities from which or the place where the communication is to be intercepted, (iii) a particular description of the type of communications sought to be intercepted, (iv) the identity of the person, if known, committing the offense and whose communications are to be intercepted;

(c) a full and complete statement as to whether or not other investigative procedures have been tried and failed or why they reasonably appear to be unlikely to succeed if tried or to be too dangerous;

(d) a statement of the period of time for which the interception is required to be maintained. If the nature of the investigation is such that the authorization for interception should not automatically terminate when the described type of communication has been first obtained, a particular description of facts establishing probable cause to believe that additional communications of the same type will occur thereafter;

(e) a full and complete statement of the facts concerning all previous applications known to the individual authorizing and making the application, made to any judge for authorization to intercept, or for approval of interceptions of, wire, oral, or electronic communications involving any of the same persons, facilities or places specified in the application, and the action taken by the judge on each such application; and

(f) where the application is for the extension of an order, a statement setting forth the results thus far obtained from the interception, or a reasonable explanation of the failure to obtain such results.

(2) The judge may require the applicant to furnish additional testimony or documentary evidence in support of the application.

(3) Upon such application the judge may enter an ex parte order, as requested or as modified, authorizing or approving interception of wire, oral, or electronic communications within the territorial jurisdiction of the court in which the judge is sitting (and outside that jurisdiction but within the United States in the case of a mobile interception device authorized by a Federal court within such jurisdiction), if the judge determines on the basis of the facts submitted by the applicant that—

(a) there is probable cause for belief that an individual is committing, has committed, or is about to commit a particular offense enumerated in section 2516 of this chapter;

(b) there is probable cause for belief that particular communications concerning that offense will be obtained through such interception;

(c) normal investigative procedures have been tried and have failed or reasonably appear to be unlikely to succeed if tried or to be too dangerous;

(d) except as provided in subsection (11), there is probable cause for belief that the facilities from which, or the place where, the wire, oral, or electronic communications are to be intercepted are being used, or are about to be used, in connection with the commission of such offense, or are leased to, listed in the name of, or commonly used by such person.

(4) Each order authorizing or approving the interception of any wire, oral, or electronic communication under this chapter shall specify—

    (a) the identity of the person, if known, whose communications are to be intercepted;

    (b) the nature and location of the communications facilities as to which, or the place where, authority to intercept is granted;

    (c) a particular description of the type of communication sought to be intercepted, and a statement of the particular offense to which it relates;

    (d) the identity of the agency authorized to intercept the communications, and of the person authorizing the application; and

    (e) the period of time during which such interception is authorized, including a statement as to whether or not the interception shall automatically terminate when the described communication has been first obtained.

An order authorizing the interception of a wire, oral, or electronic communication under this chapter shall, upon request of the applicant, direct that a provider of wire or electronic communication service, landlord, custodian or other person shall furnish the applicant forthwith all information, facilities, and technical assistance necessary to accomplish the interception unobtrusively and with a minimum of interference with the services that such service provider, landlord, custodian, or person is according the person whose communications are to be intercepted. Any provider of wire or electronic communication service, landlord, custodian or other person furnishing such facilities or technical assistance shall be compensated therefor by the applicant for reasonable expenses incurred in providing such facilities or assistance. Pursuant to section 2522 of this chapter, an order may also be issued to enforce the assistance capability and capacity requirements under the Communications Assistance for Law Enforcement Act.

(5) No order entered under this section may authorize or approve the interception of any wire, oral, or electronic communication for any period longer than is necessary to achieve the objective of the authorization, nor in any event longer than thirty days. Such thirty-day period begins on the earlier of the day on which the investigative or law enforcement officer first begins to conduct an interception under the order or ten days after the order is entered. Extensions of an order may be granted, but only upon application for an extension made in accordance with subsection (1) of this section and the court making the findings required by subsection (3) of this section. The period of extension shall be no longer than the authorizing judge deems necessary to achieve the purposes for which it was granted and in no event for longer than thirty days. Every order and extension thereof shall contain a provision that the authorization to intercept shall be executed as soon as practicable, shall be conducted in such a way as to minimize the interception of communications not otherwise subject to interception under this chapter, and must terminate upon attainment of the authorized objective, or in any event in thirty days. In the event the intercepted communication is in a code or foreign language, and an expert in that foreign language or code is not reasonably available during the interception period, minimization may be accomplished as soon as practicable after such interception. An interception under this chapter may be conducted in whole or in part by Government personnel, or by an individual operating under a contract with the Government, acting under the supervision of an investigative or law enforcement officer authorized to conduct the interception.

(6) Whenever an order authorizing interception is entered pursuant to this chapter, the order may require reports to be made to the judge who issued the order showing what progress has been made toward achievement of the authorized objective and the need for continued interception. Such reports shall be made at such intervals as the judge may require.

(7) Notwithstanding any other provision of this chapter, any investigative or law enforcement officer, specially designated by the Attorney General, the Deputy Attorney General, the Associate Attorney General, or by the principal prosecuting attorney of any State or subdivision thereof acting pursuant to a statute of that State, who reasonably determines that—

(a) an emergency situation exists that involves—

(i) immediate danger of death or serious physical injury to any person,

(ii) conspiratorial activities threatening the national security interest, or

(iii) conspiratorial activities characteristic of organized crime,

that requires a wire, oral, or electronic communication to be intercepted before an order authorizing such interception can, with due diligence, be obtained, and

(b) there are grounds upon which an order could be entered under this chapter to authorize such interception,

may intercept such wire, oral, or electronic communication if an application for an order approving the interception is made in accordance with this section within forty-eight hours after the interception has occurred, or begins to occur. In the absence of an order, such interception shall immediately terminate when the communication sought is obtained or when the application for the order is denied, whichever is earlier. In the event such application for approval is denied, or in any other case where the interception is terminated without an order having been issued, the contents of any wire, oral, or electronic communication intercepted shall be treated as having been obtained in violation of this chapter, and an inventory shall be served as provided for in subsection (d) of this section on the person named in the application.

(8)(a)   The contents of any wire, oral, or electronic communication intercepted by any means authorized by this chapter shall, if possible, be recorded on tape or wire or other comparable device. The recording of the contents of any wire, oral, or electronic communication under this subsection shall be done in such a way as will protect the recording from editing or other alterations. Immediately upon the expiration of the period of the order, or extensions thereof, such recordings shall be made available to the judge issuing such order and sealed under his directions. Custody of the recordings shall be wherever the judge orders. They shall not be destroyed except upon an order of the issuing or denying judge and in any event shall be kept for ten years. Duplicate recordings may be made for use or disclosure pursuant to the provisions of subsections (1) and (2) of section 2517 of this chapter for investigations. The presence of the seal provided for by this subsection, or a satisfactory explanation for the absence thereof, shall be a prerequisite for the use or disclosure of the contents of any wire, oral, or electronic communication or evidence derived therefrom under subsection (3) of section 2517.

(b) Applications made and orders granted under this chapter shall be sealed by the judge. Custody of the applications and orders shall be wherever the judge directs. Such applications and orders shall be disclosed only upon a showing of good cause before a judge of competent jurisdiction and shall not be destroyed except on order of the issuing or denying judge, and in any event shall be kept for ten years.

(c) Any violation of the provisions of this subsection may be punished as contempt of the issuing or denying judge.

(d) Within a reasonable time but not later than ninety days after the filing of an application for an order of approval under section 2518(7)(b) which is denied or the termination of the period of an order or extensions thereof, the issuing or denying judge shall cause to be served, on the persons named in the order or the application, and such other parties to intercepted communications as the judge may determine in his discretion that is in the interest of justice, an inventory which shall include notice of—

(1) the fact of the entry of the order or the application;

(2) the date of the entry and the period of authorized, approved or disapproved interception, or the denial of the application; and

(3) the fact that during the period wire, oral, or electronic communications were or were not intercepted.

The judge, upon the filing of a motion, may in his discretion make available to such person or his counsel for inspection such portions of the intercepted communications, applications and orders as the judge determines to be in the interest of justice. On an ex parte showing of good cause to a judge of competent jurisdiction the serving of the inventory required by this subsection may be postponed.

(9) The contents of any wire, oral, or electronic communication intercepted pursuant to this chapter or evidence derived therefrom shall not be received in evidence or otherwise disclosed in any trial, hearing, or other proceeding in a Federal or State court unless each party, not less than ten days before the trial, hearing, or proceeding, has been furnished with a copy of the court order, and accompanying application, under which the interception was authorized or approved. This ten-day period may be waived by the judge if he finds that it was not possible to furnish the party with the above information ten days before the trial, hearing, or proceeding and that the party will not be prejudiced by the delay in receiving such information.

(10)(a) Any aggrieved person in any trial, hearing, or proceeding in or before any court, department, officer, agency, regulatory body, or other authority of the United States, a State, or a political subdivision thereof, may move to suppress the contents of any wire or oral communication intercepted pursuant to this chapter, or evidence derived therefrom, on the grounds that—

(i) the communication was unlawfully intercepted;

(ii) the order of authorization or approval under which it was intercepted is insufficient on its face; or

(iii) the interception was not made in conformity with the order of authorization or approval.

Such motion shall be made before the trial, hearing, or proceeding unless there was no opportunity to make such motion or the person was not aware of the grounds of the motion. If the motion is granted, the contents of the intercepted wire or oral communication, or evidence derived therefrom, shall be treated as having been obtained in violation of this chapter. The judge, upon the filing of such motion by the aggrieved person, may in his discretion make available to the aggrieved person or his counsel for inspection such portions of the intercepted communication or evidence derived therefrom as the judge determines to be in the interests of justice.

(b) In addition to any other right to appeal, the United States shall have the right to appeal from an order granting a motion to suppress made under paragraph (a) of this subsection, or the denial of an application for an order of approval, if the United States attorney shall certify to the judge or other official granting such motion or denying such application that the appeal is not taken for purposes of delay. Such appeal shall be taken within thirty days after the date the order was entered and shall be diligently prosecuted.

(c) The remedies and sanctions described in this chapter with respect to the interception of electronic communications are the only judicial remedies and sanctions for nonconstitutional violations of this chapter involving such communications.

(11) The requirements of subsections (1)(b)(ii) and (3)(d) of this section relating to the specification of the facilities from which, or the place where, the communication is to be intercepted do not apply if—

(a) in the case of an application with respect to the interception of an oral communication—

(i) the application is by a Federal investigative or law enforcement officer and is approved by the Attorney General, the Deputy Attorney General, the Associate Attorney General, an Assistant Attorney General, or an acting Assistant Attorney General;

(ii) the application contains a full and complete statement as to why such specification is not practical and identifies the person committing the offense and whose communications are to be intercepted; and

(iii) the judge finds that such specification is not practical; and

(b) in the case of an application with respect to a wire or electronic communication—

(i) the application is by a Federal investigative or law enforcement officer and is approved by the Attorney General, the Deputy Attorney General, the Associate Attorney General, an Assistant Attorney General, or an acting Assistant Attorney General;

(ii) the application identifies the person believed to be committing the offense and whose communications are to be intercepted and the applicant makes a showing that there is probable cause to believe that the person's actions could have the effect of thwarting interception from a specified facility;

(iii) the judge finds that such showing has been adequately made; and

(iv) the order authorizing or approving the interception is limited to interception only for such time as it is reasonable to presume that the person identified in the application is or was reasonably proximate to the instrument through which such communication will be or was transmitted.

(12) An interception of a communication under an order with respect to which the requirements of subsections (1)(b)(ii) and (3)(d) of this section do not apply by reason of subsection (11)(a) shall not begin until the place where the communication is to be intercepted is ascertained by the person implementing the interception order. A provider of wire or electronic communications service that has received an order as provided for in subsection (11)(b) may move the court to modify or quash the order on the ground that its assistance with respect to the interception cannot be performed in a timely or reasonable fashion. The court, upon notice to the government, shall decide such a motion expeditiously.

18 U.S.C. § 2519. REPORTS CONCERNING INTERCEPTED WIRE, ORAL, OR ELECTRONIC COMMUNICATIONS

(1) Within thirty days after the expiration of an order (or each extension thereof) entered under section 2518, or the denial of an order approving an interception, the issuing or denying judge shall report to the Administrative Office of the United States Courts—

(a) the fact that an order or extension was applied for;

(b) the kind of order or extension applied for (including whether or not the order was an order with respect to which the requirements of sections 2518(1)(b)(ii) and 2518(3)(d) of this title did not apply by reason of section 2518(11) of this title);

(c) the fact that the order or extension was granted as applied for, was modified, or was denied;

(d) the period of interceptions authorized by the order, and the number and duration of any extensions of the order;

(e) the offense specified in the order or application, or extension of an order;

(f) the identity of the applying investigative or law enforcement officer and agency making the application and the person authorizing the application; and

(g) the nature of the facilities from which or the place where communications were to be intercepted.

(2) In January of each year the Attorney General, an Assistant Attorney General specially designated by the Attorney General, or the principal prosecuting attorney of a State, or the principal prosecuting attorney for any political subdivision of a State, shall report to the Administrative Office of the United States Courts—

(a) the information required by paragraphs (a) through (g) of subsection (1) of this section with respect to each application for an order or extension made during the preceding calendar year;

(b) a general description of the interceptions made under such order or extension, including (i) the approximate nature and frequency of incriminating communications intercepted, (ii) the approximate nature and frequency of other communications intercepted, (iii) the approximate number of persons whose communications were intercepted, (iv) the number of orders in which encryption was encountered and whether such encryption prevented law enforcement from obtaining the plain text of communications intercepted pursuant to such order, and (v) the approximate nature, amount, and cost of the manpower and other resources used in the interceptions;

(c) the number of arrests resulting from interceptions made under such order or extension, and the offenses for which arrests were made;

(d) the number of trials resulting from such interceptions;

(e) the number of motions to suppress made with respect to such interceptions, and the number granted or denied;

(f) the number of convictions resulting from such interceptions and the offenses for which the convictions were obtained and a general assessment of the importance of the interceptions; and

(g) the information required by paragraphs (b) through (f) of this subsection with respect to orders or extensions obtained in a preceding calendar year.

(3) In April of each year the Director of the Administrative Office of the United States Courts shall transmit to the Congress a full and complete report concerning the number of applications for orders authorizing or approving the interception of wire, oral, or electronic communications pursuant to this chapter and the number of orders and extensions granted or denied pursuant to this chapter during the preceding calendar year. Such report shall include a summary and analysis of the data required to be filed with the Administrative Office by subsections (1) and (2) of this section. The Director of the Administrative Office of the United States

Courts is authorized to issue binding regulations dealing with the content and form of the reports required to be filed by subsections (1) and (2) of this section.

18 U.S.C. § 2520. RECOVERY OF CIVIL DAMAGES AUTHORIZED

(a) In general. Except as provided in section 2511(2)(a)(ii), any person whose wire, oral, or electronic communication is intercepted, disclosed, or intentionally used in violation of this chapter may in a civil action recover from the person or entity, other than the United States, which engaged in that violation such relief as may be appropriate.

(b) Relief. In an action under this section, appropriate relief includes—

(1) such preliminary and other equitable or declaratory relief as may be appropriate;

(2) damages under subsection (c) and punitive damages in appropriate cases; and

(3) a reasonable attorney's fee and other litigation costs reasonably incurred.

(c) Computation of damages.

(1) In an action under this section, if the conduct in violation of this chapter is the private viewing of a private satellite video communication that is not scrambled or encrypted or if the communication is a radio communication that is transmitted on frequencies allocated under subpart D of part 74 of the rules of the Federal Communications Commission that is not scrambled or encrypted and the conduct is not for a tortious or illegal purpose or for purposes of direct or indirect commercial advantage or private commercial gain, then the court shall assess damages as follows:

(A) If the person who engaged in that conduct has not previously been enjoined under section 2511(5) and has not been found liable in a prior civil action under this section, the court shall assess the greater of the sum of actual damages suffered by the plaintiff, or statutory damages of not less than $50 and not more than $500.

(B) If, on one prior occasion, the person who engaged in that conduct has been enjoined under section 2511(5) or has been found liable in a civil action under this section, the court shall assess the greater of the sum of actual damages suffered by the plaintiff, or statutory damages of not less than $100 and not more than $1000.

(2) In any other action under this section, the court may assess as damages whichever is the greater of—

(A) the sum of the actual damages suffered by the plaintiff and any profits made by the violator as a result of the violation; or

(B) statutory damages of whichever is the greater of $100 a day for each day of violation or $10,000.

(d) Defense. A good faith reliance on—

(1) a court warrant or order, a grand jury subpoena, a legislative authorization, or a statutory authorization;

(2) a request of an investigative or law enforcement officer under section 2518(7) of this title; or

(3) a good faith determination that section 2511(3), 2511(2)(i), or 2511(2)(j) of this title permitted the conduct complained of;

is a complete defense against any civil or criminal action brought under this chapter or any other law.

(e) Limitation. A civil action under this section may not be commenced later than two years after the date upon which the claimant first has a reasonable opportunity to discover the violation.

(f) Administrative discipline. If a court or appropriate department or agency determines that the United States or any of its departments or agencies has violated any provision of this chapter, and the court or appropriate department or agency finds that the circumstances surrounding the violation raise serious questions about whether or not an officer or employee of the United States acted willfully or intentionally with respect to the violation, the department or agency shall, upon receipt of a true and correct copy of the decision and findings of the court or appropriate department or agency promptly initiate a proceeding to determine whether disciplinary action against the officer or employee is warranted. If the head of the department or agency involved determines that disciplinary action is not warranted, he or she shall notify the Inspector General with jurisdiction over the department or agency concerned and shall provide the Inspector General with the reasons for such determination.

(g) Improper disclosure is violation. Any willful disclosure or use by an investigative or law enforcement officer or governmental entity of information beyond the extent permitted by section 2517 is a violation of this chapter for purposes of section 2520(a).

18 U.S.C. § 2521. INJUNCTION AGAINST ILLEGAL INTERCEPTION

Whenever it shall appear that any person is engaged or is about to engage in any act which constitutes or will constitute a felony violation of this chapter, the Attorney General may initiate a civil action in a district court of the United States to enjoin such violation. The court shall proceed as soon as practicable to the hearing and determination of such an action, and may, at any time before final determination, enter such a restraining order or prohibition, or take such other action, as is warranted to prevent a continuing and substantial injury to the United States or to any person or class of persons for whose protection the action is brought. A proceeding under this section is governed by the Federal Rules of Civil Procedure, except that, if an indictment has been returned against the respondent, discovery is governed by the Federal Rules of Criminal Procedure.

18 U.S.C. § 2522. ENFORCEMENT OF THE COMMUNICATIONS ASSISTANCE FOR LAW ENFORCEMENT ACT

(a) **Enforcement by court issuing surveillance order.** If a court authorizing an interception under this chapter, a State statute, or the Foreign Intelligence Surveillance Act of 1978 (50 U.S.C. 1801 et seq.) or authorizing use of a pen register or a trap and trace device under chapter 206 or a State statute finds that a telecommunications carrier has failed to comply with the requirements of the Communications Assistance for Law Enforcement Act, the court may, in accordance with section 108 of such Act, direct that the carrier comply forthwith and may direct that a provider of support services to the carrier or the manufacturer of the carrier's transmission or switching equipment furnish forthwith modifications necessary for the carrier to comply.

(b) **Enforcement upon application by Attorney General.** The Attorney General may, in a civil action in the appropriate United States district court, obtain an order, in accordance with section 108 of the Communications Assistance for Law Enforcement Act, directing that a telecommunications carrier, a manufacturer of telecommunications transmission or switching equipment, or a provider of telecommunications support services comply with such Act.

(c) **Civil penalty.—**

(1) **In general.** A court issuing an order under this section against a telecommunications carrier, a manufacturer of telecommunications transmission or switching equipment, or a provider of telecommunications support services may impose a civil penalty of up to $10,000 per day for each day in violation after the issuance of the order or after such future date as the court may specify.

(2) **Considerations.** In determining whether to impose a civil penalty and in determining its amount, the court shall take into account—

(A) the nature, circumstances, and extent of the violation;

(B) the violator's ability to pay, the violator's good faith efforts to comply in a timely manner, any effect on the violator's ability to continue to do business, the degree of culpability, and the length of any delay in undertaking efforts to comply; and

(C) such other matters as justice may require.

(d) Definitions. As used in this section, the terms defined in section 102 of the Communications Assistance for Law Enforcement Act have the meanings provided, respectively, in such section.

18 U.S.C. § 2523. EXECUTIVE AGREEMENTS ON ACCESS TO DATA BY FOREIGN GOVERNMENTS

(a) Definitions. In this section—

(1) the term "lawfully admitted for permanent residence" has the meaning given the term in section 101(a) of the Immigration and Nationality Act (8 U.S.C. 1101(a)); and

(2) the term "United States person" means a citizen or national of the United States, an alien lawfully admitted for permanent residence, an unincorporated association a substantial number of members of which are citizens of the United States or aliens lawfully admitted for permanent residence, or a corporation that is incorporated in the United States.

(b) Executive agreement requirements.—For purposes of this chapter, chapter 121, and chapter 206, an executive agreement governing access by a foreign government to data subject to this chapter, chapter 121, or chapter 206 shall be considered to satisfy the requirements of this section if the Attorney General, with the concurrence of the Secretary of State, determines, and submits a written certification of such determination to Congress, including a written certification and explanation of each consideration in paragraphs (1), (2), (3), and (4), that—

(1) the domestic law of the foreign government, including the implementation of that law, affords robust substantive and procedural protections for privacy and civil liberties in light of the data collection and activities of the foreign government that will be subject to the agreement, if—

(A) such a determination under this section takes into account, as appropriate, credible information and expert input; and

(B) the factors to be met in making such a determination include whether the foreign government—

(i) has adequate substantive and procedural laws on cybercrime and electronic evidence, as demonstrated by being a party to the Convention on Cybercrime, done at Budapest November 23, 2001, and entered into force January 7, 2004, or through domestic laws that are consistent with definitions and the requirements set forth in chapters I and II of that Convention;

(ii) demonstrates respect for the rule of law and principles of nondiscrimination;

(iii) adheres to applicable international human rights obligations and commitments or demonstrates respect for international universal human rights, including—

(I) protection from arbitrary and unlawful interference with privacy;

(II) fair trial rights;

(III) freedom of expression, association, and peaceful assembly;

(IV) prohibitions on arbitrary arrest and detention; and

(V) prohibitions against torture and cruel, inhuman, or degrading treatment or punishment;

(iv) has clear legal mandates and procedures governing those entities of the foreign government that are authorized to seek data under the executive agreement, including procedures through which those authorities collect, retain, use, and share data, and effective oversight of these activities;

(v) has sufficient mechanisms to provide accountability and appropriate transparency regarding the collection and use of electronic data by the foreign government; and

(vi) demonstrates a commitment to promote and protect the global free flow of information and the open, distributed, and interconnected nature of the Internet;

(2) the foreign government has adopted appropriate procedures to minimize the acquisition, retention, and dissemination of information concerning United States persons subject to the agreement;

(3) the terms of the agreement shall not create any obligation that providers be capable of decrypting data or limitation that prevents providers from decrypting data; and

(4) the agreement requires that, with respect to any order that is subject to the agreement—

(A) the foreign government may not intentionally target a United States person or a person located in the United States, and shall adopt targeting procedures designed to meet this requirement;

(B) the foreign government may not target a non-United States person located outside the United States if the purpose is to obtain information concerning a United States person or a person located in the United States;

(C) the foreign government may not issue an order at the request of or to obtain information to provide to the United States Government or a third-party government, nor shall the foreign government be required to share any information produced with the United States Government or a third-party government;

(D) an order issued by the foreign government—

(i) shall be for the purpose of obtaining information relating to the prevention, detection, investigation, or prosecution of serious crime, including terrorism;

(ii) shall identify a specific person, account, address, or personal device, or any other specific identifier as the object of the order;

(iii) shall be in compliance with the domestic law of that country, and any obligation for a provider of an electronic communications service or a remote computing service to produce data shall derive solely from that law;

(iv) shall be based on requirements for a reasonable justification based on articulable and credible facts, particularity, legality, and severity regarding the conduct under investigation;

(v) shall be subject to review or oversight by a court, judge, magistrate, or other independent authority prior to, or in proceedings regarding, enforcement of the order; and

(vi) in the case of an order for the interception of wire or electronic communications, and any extensions thereof, shall require that the interception order—

(I) be for a fixed, limited duration; and

(II) may not last longer than is reasonably necessary to accomplish the approved purposes of the order; and

(III) be issued only if the same information could not reasonably be obtained by another less intrusive method;

(E) an order issued by the foreign government may not be used to infringe freedom of speech;

(F) the foreign government shall promptly review material collected pursuant to the agreement and store any unreviewed communications on a secure system accessible only to those persons trained in applicable procedures;

(G) the foreign government shall, using procedures that, to the maximum extent possible, meet the definition of minimization procedures in section 101 of the Foreign Intelligence Surveillance Act of 1978 (50 U.S.C. 1801), segregate, seal, or delete, and not disseminate material found not to be information that is, or is necessary to understand or assess the importance of information that is, relevant to the prevention, detection, investigation, or prosecution of serious crime, including terrorism, or necessary to protect against a threat of death or serious bodily harm to any person;

(H) the foreign government may not disseminate the content of a communication of a United States person to United States authorities unless the communication may be disseminated pursuant to subparagraph (G) and relates to significant harm, or the threat thereof, to the United States or United States persons, including crimes involving national security such as terrorism, significant violent crime, child exploitation, transnational organized crime, or significant financial fraud;

(I) the foreign government shall afford reciprocal rights of data access, to include, where applicable, removing restrictions on communications service providers, including providers subject to United States jurisdiction, and thereby allow them to respond to valid legal process sought by a governmental entity (as defined in section 2711) if foreign law would otherwise prohibit communications-service providers from disclosing the data;

(J) the foreign government shall agree to periodic review of compliance by the foreign government with the terms of the agreement to be conducted by the United States Government; and

(K) the United States Government shall reserve the right to render the agreement inapplicable as to any order for which the United States Government concludes the agreement may not properly be invoked.

(c) Limitation on judicial review.—A determination or certification made by the Attorney General under subsection (b) shall not be subject to judicial or administrative review.

(d) Effective date of certification.—

(1) Notice.—Not later than 7 days after the date on which the Attorney General certifies an executive agreement under subsection (b), the Attorney General shall provide notice of the determination under subsection (b) and a copy of the executive agreement to Congress, including—

> **(A)** the Committee on the Judiciary and the Committee on Foreign Relations of the Senate; and

> **(B)** the Committee on the Judiciary and the Committee on Foreign Affairs of the House of Representatives.

(2) Entry into force.—An executive agreement that is determined and certified by the Attorney General to satisfy the requirements of this section shall enter into force not earlier than the date that is 180 days after the date on which notice is provided under paragraph (1), unless Congress enacts a joint resolution of disapproval in accordance with paragraph (4).

(3) Requests for information.—Upon request by the Chairman or Ranking Member of a congressional committee described in paragraph (1), the head of an agency shall promptly furnish a summary of factors considered in determining that the foreign government satisfies the requirements of this section.

(4) Congressional review.—

> **(A) Joint resolution defined.**—In this paragraph, the term "joint resolution" means only a joint resolution—

>> **(i)** introduced during the 180-day period described in paragraph (2);

>> **(ii)** which does not have a preamble;

>> **(iii)** the title of which is as follows: "Joint resolution disapproving the executive agreement signed by the United States and ___.", the blank space being appropriately filled in; and

>> **(iv)** the matter after the resolving clause of which is as follows: "That Congress disapproves the executive agreement governing access by ___ to certain electronic data as submitted by the Attorney General on ___", the blank spaces being appropriately filled in.

> **(B) Joint resolution enacted.**—Notwithstanding any other provision of this section, if not later than 180 days after the date on which notice is provided to Congress under paragraph (1), there is enacted into law a joint resolution disapproving of an executive agreement under this section, the executive agreement shall not enter into force.

(C) Introduction.—During the 180-day period described in subparagraph (B), a joint resolution of disapproval may be introduced—

> **(i)** in the House of Representatives, by the majority leader or the minority leader; and

> **(ii)** in the Senate, by the majority leader (or the majority leader's designee) or the minority leader (or the minority leader's designee).

(5) Floor consideration in House of Representatives.—If a committee of the House of Representatives to which a joint resolution of disapproval has been referred has not reported the joint resolution within 120 days after the date of referral, that committee shall be discharged from further consideration of the joint resolution.

(6) Consideration in the Senate.—

> **(A) Committee referral.**—A joint resolution of disapproval introduced in the Senate shall be referred jointly—

> > **(i)** to the Committee on the Judiciary; and

> > **(ii)** to the Committee on Foreign Relations.

> **(B) Reporting and discharge.**—If a committee to which a joint resolution of disapproval was referred has not reported the joint resolution within 120 days after the date of referral of the joint resolution, that committee shall be discharged from further consideration of the joint resolution and the joint resolution shall be placed on the appropriate calendar.

> **(C) Proceeding to consideration.**—It is in order at any time after both the Committee on the Judiciary and the Committee on Foreign Relations report a joint resolution of disapproval to the Senate or have been discharged from consideration of such a joint resolution (even though a previous motion to the same effect has been disagreed to) to move to proceed to the consideration of the joint resolution, and all points of order against the joint resolution (and against consideration of the joint resolution) are waived. The motion is not debatable or subject to a motion to postpone. A motion to reconsider the vote by which the motion is agreed to or disagreed to shall not be in order.

> **(D) Consideration in the Senate.**—In the Senate, consideration of the joint resolution, and on all debatable motions and appeals in connection therewith, shall be limited to not more than 10 hours, which shall be divided equally between those favoring and those opposing the joint resolution. A motion further to limit debate is in order and not debatable. An amendment to,

or a motion to postpone, or a motion to proceed to the consideration of other business, or a motion to recommit the joint resolution is not in order.

(E) Consideration of veto messages.—Debate in the Senate of any veto message with respect to a joint resolution of disapproval, including all debatable motions and appeals in connection with the joint resolution, shall be limited to 10 hours, to be equally divided between, and controlled by, the majority leader and the minority leader or their designees.

(7) Rules relating to Senate and House of Representatives.—

(A) Treatment of Senate Joint Resolution in House.— In the House of Representatives, the following procedures shall apply to a joint resolution of disapproval received from the Senate (unless the House has already passed a joint resolution relating to the same proposed action):

(i) The joint resolution shall be referred to the appropriate committees.

(ii) If a committee to which a joint resolution has been referred has not reported the joint resolution within 7 days after the date of referral, that committee shall be discharged from further consideration of the joint resolution.

(iii) Beginning on the third legislative day after each committee to which a joint resolution has been referred reports the joint resolution to the House or has been discharged from further consideration thereof, it shall be in order to move to proceed to consider the joint resolution in the House. All points of order against the motion are waived. Such a motion shall not be in order after the House has disposed of a motion to proceed on the joint resolution. The previous question shall be considered as ordered on the motion to its adoption without intervening motion. The motion shall not be debatable. A motion to reconsider the vote by which the motion is disposed of shall not be in order.

(iv) The joint resolution shall be considered as read. All points of order against the joint resolution and against its consideration are waived. The previous question shall be considered as ordered on the joint resolution to final passage without intervening motion except 2 hours of debate equally divided and controlled by the sponsor of the joint resolution (or a designee) and an opponent. A motion to reconsider the vote on passage of the joint resolution shall not be in order.

(B) Treatment of House Joint Resolution in Senate.—

(i) If, before the passage by the Senate of a joint resolution of disapproval, the Senate receives an identical joint resolution from the House of Representatives, the following procedures shall apply:

(I) That joint resolution shall not be referred to a committee.

(II) With respect to that joint resolution—

(aa) the procedure in the Senate shall be the same as if no joint resolution had been received from the House of Representatives; but

(bb) the vote on passage shall be on the joint resolution from the House of Representatives.

(ii) If, following passage of a joint resolution of disapproval in the Senate, the Senate receives an identical joint resolution from the House of Representatives, that joint resolution shall be placed on the appropriate Senate calendar.

(iii) If a joint resolution of disapproval is received from the House, and no companion joint resolution has been introduced in the Senate, the Senate procedures under this subsection shall apply to the House joint resolution.

(C) Application to revenue measures.—The provisions of this paragraph shall not apply in the House of Representatives to a joint resolution of disapproval that is a revenue measure.

(8) Rules of House of Representatives and Senate.—This subsection is enacted by Congress—

(A) as an exercise of the rulemaking power of the Senate and the House of Representatives, respectively, and as such is deemed a part of the rules of each House, respectively, and supersedes other rules only to the extent that it is inconsistent with such rules; and

(B) with full recognition of the constitutional right of either House to change the rules (so far as relating to the procedure of that House) at any time, in the same manner, and to the same extent as in the case of any other rule of that House.

(e) Renewal of determination.—

(1) In general.—The Attorney General, with the concurrence of the Secretary of State, shall review and may renew a determination under subsection (b) every 5 years.

(2) Report.—Upon renewing a determination under subsection (b), the Attorney General shall file a report with the Committee on the Judiciary and the Committee on Foreign Relations of the Senate and the Committee on the Judiciary and the Committee on Foreign Affairs of the House of Representatives describing—

(A) the reasons for the renewal;

(B) any substantive changes to the agreement or to the relevant laws or procedures of the foreign government since the original determination or, in the case of a second or subsequent renewal, since the last renewal; and

(C) how the agreement has been implemented and what problems or controversies, if any, have arisen as a result of the agreement or its implementation.

(3) Nonrenewal.—If a determination is not renewed under paragraph (1), the agreement shall no longer be considered to satisfy the requirements of this section.

(f) Revisions to agreement.—A revision to an agreement under this section shall be treated as a new agreement for purposes of this section and shall be subject to the certification requirement under subsection (b), and to the procedures under subsection (d), except that for purposes of a revision to an agreement—

(1) the applicable time period under paragraphs (2), (4)(A)(i), (4)(B), and (4)(C) of subsection (d) shall be 90 days after the date notice is provided under subsection (d)(1); and

(2) the applicable time period under paragraphs (5) and (6)(B) of subsection (d) shall be 60 days after the date notice is provided under subsection (d)(1).

(g) Publication.—Any determination or certification under subsection (b) regarding an executive agreement under this section, including any termination or renewal of such an agreement, shall be published in the Federal Register as soon as is reasonably practicable.

(h) Minimization procedures.—A United States authority that receives the content of a communication described in subsection (b)(4)(H) from a foreign government in accordance with an executive agreement under this section shall use procedures that, to the maximum extent possible, meet the definition of minimization procedures in section 101 of the Foreign Intelligence Surveillance Act of 1978 (50 U.S.C. 1801) to appropriately protect nonpublicly available information concerning United States persons.

18 U.S.C. § 2701. UNLAWFUL ACCESS TO STORED COMMUNICATIONS

(a) Offense. Except as provided in subsection (c) of this section whoever—

(1) intentionally accesses without authorization a facility through which an electronic communication service is provided; or

(2) intentionally exceeds an authorization to access that facility;

and thereby obtains, alters, or prevents authorized access to a wire or electronic communication while it is in electronic storage in such system

shall be punished as provided in subsection (b) of this section.

(b) Punishment. The punishment for an offense under subsection (a) of this section is—

(1) if the offense is committed for purposes of commercial advantage, malicious destruction or damage, or private commercial gain, or in furtherance of any criminal or tortious act in violation of the Constitution or laws of the United States or any State—

(A) a fine under this title or imprisonment for not more than 5 years, or both, in the case of a first offense under this subparagraph; and

(B) a fine under this title or imprisonment for not more than 10 years, or both, for any subsequent offense under this subparagraph; and

(2) in any other case—

(A) a fine under this title or imprisonment for not more than 1 year or both, in the case of a first offense under this paragraph; and

(B) a fine under this title or imprisonment for not more than 5 years, or both, in the case of an offense under this subparagraph that occurs after a conviction of another offense under this section.

(c) Exceptions. Subsection (a) of this section does not apply with respect to conduct authorized—

(1) by the person or entity providing a wire or electronic communications service;

(2) by a user of that service with respect to a communication of or intended for that user; or

(3) in section 2703, 2704 or 2518 of this title.

18 U.S.C. § 2702. VOLUNTARY DISCLOSURE OF CUSTOMER COMMUNICATIONS OR RECORDS

(a) Prohibitions. Except as provided in subsection (b) or (c)—

(1) a person or entity providing an electronic communication service to the public shall not knowingly divulge to any person or entity the contents of a communication while in electronic storage by that service; and

(2) a person or entity providing remote computing service to the public shall not knowingly divulge to any person or entity the contents of any communication which is carried or maintained on that service—

> **(A)** on behalf of, and received by means of electronic transmission from (or created by means of computer processing of communications received by means of electronic transmission from), a subscriber or customer of such service;

> **(B)** solely for the purpose of providing storage or computer processing services to such subscriber or customer, if the provider is not authorized to access the contents of any such communications for purposes of providing any services other than storage or computer processing; and

(3) a provider of remote computing service or electronic communication service to the public shall not knowingly divulge a record or other information pertaining to a subscriber to or customer of such service (not including the contents of communications covered by paragraph (1) or (2)) to any governmental entity.

(b) Exceptions for disclosure of communications. A provider described in subsection (a) may divulge the contents of a communication—

(1) to an addressee or intended recipient of such communication or an agent of such addressee or intended recipient;

(2) as otherwise authorized in section 2517, 2511(2)(a), or 2703 of this title;

(3) with the lawful consent of the originator or an addressee or intended recipient of such communication, or the subscriber in the case of remote computing service;

(4) to a person employed or authorized or whose facilities are used to forward such communication to its destination;

(5) as may be necessarily incident to the rendition of the service or to the protection of the rights or property of the provider of that service;

(6) to the National Center for Missing and Exploited Children, in connection with a report submitted thereto under section 2258A;

(7) to a law enforcement agency—

(A) if the contents—

(i) were inadvertently obtained by the service provider; and

(ii) appear to pertain to the commission of a crime; or

(8) to a governmental entity, if the provider, in good faith, believes that an emergency involving danger of death or serious physical injury to any person requires disclosure without delay of communications relating to the emergency;

(9) to a foreign government pursuant to an order from a foreign government that is subject to an executive agreement that the Attorney General has determined and certified to Congress satisfies section 2523.

(c) **Exceptions for disclosure of customer records.** A provider described in subsection (a) may divulge a record or other information pertaining to a subscriber to or customer of such service (not including the contents of communications covered by subsection (a)(1) or (a)(2))—

(1) as otherwise authorized in section 2703;

(2) with the lawful consent of the customer or subscriber;

(3) as may be necessarily incident to the rendition of the service or to the protection of the rights or property of the provider of that service;

(4) to a governmental entity, if the provider, in good faith, believes that an emergency involving danger of death or serious physical injury to any person requires disclosure without delay of information relating to the emergency;

(5) to the National Center for Missing and Exploited Children, in connection with a report submitted thereto under section 2258A;

(6) to any person other than a governmental entity;

(7) to a foreign government pursuant to an order from a foreign government that is subject to an executive agreement that the Attorney General has determined and certified to Congress satisfies section 2523.

(d) **Reporting of emergency disclosures.** On an annual basis, the Attorney General shall submit to the Committee on the Judiciary of the House of Representatives and the Committee on the Judiciary of the Senate a report containing—

(1) the number of accounts from which the Department of Justice has received voluntary disclosures under subsection (b)(8); and

(2) a summary of the basis for disclosure in those instances where—

(A) voluntary disclosures under subsection (b)(8) were made to the Department of Justice; and

(B) the investigation pertaining to those disclosures was closed without the filing of criminal charges.

18 U.S.C. § 2703. REQUIRED DISCLOSURE OF CUSTOMER COMMUNICATIONS OR RECORDS

(a) Contents of wire or electronic communications in electronic storage. A governmental entity may require the disclosure by a provider of electronic communication service of the contents of a wire or electronic communication, that is in electronic storage in an electronic communications system for one hundred and eighty days or less, only pursuant to a warrant issued using the procedures described in the Federal Rules of Criminal Procedure (or, in the case of a State court, issued using State warrant procedures) by a court of competent jurisdiction. A governmental entity may require the disclosure by a provider of electronic communications services of the contents of a wire or electronic communication that has been in electronic storage in an electronic communications system for more than one hundred and eighty days by the means available under subsection (b) of this section.

(b) Contents of wire or electronic communications in a remote computing service.

(1) A governmental entity may require a provider of remote computing service to disclose the contents of any wire or electronic communication to which this paragraph is made applicable by paragraph (2) of this subsection—

(A) without required notice to the subscriber or customer, if the governmental entity obtains a warrant issued using the procedures described in the Federal Rules of Criminal Procedure (or, in the case of a State court, issued using State warrant procedures) by a court of competent jurisdiction; or

(B) with prior notice from the governmental entity to the subscriber or customer if the governmental entity—

(i) uses an administrative subpoena authorized by a Federal or State statute or a Federal or State grand jury or trial subpoena; or

(ii) obtains a court order for such disclosure under subsection (d) of this section;

except that delayed notice may be given pursuant to section 2705 of this title.

(2) Paragraph (1) is applicable with respect to any wire or electronic communication that is held or maintained on that service—

(A) on behalf of, and received by means of electronic transmission from (or created by means of computer processing of communications received by means of electronic transmission from), a subscriber or customer of such remote computing service; and

(B) solely for the purpose of providing storage or computer processing services to such subscriber or customer, if the provider is not authorized to access the contents of any such communications for purposes of providing any services other than storage or computer processing.

(c) Records concerning electronic communication service or remote computing service.

(1) A governmental entity may require a provider of electronic communication service or remote computing service to disclose a record or other information pertaining to a subscriber to or customer of such service (not including the contents of communications) only when the governmental entity—

(A) obtains a warrant issued using the procedures described in the Federal Rules of Criminal Procedure (or, in the case of a State court, issued using State warrant procedures) by a court of competent jurisdiction;

(B) obtains a court order for such disclosure under subsection (d) of this section;

(C) has the consent of the subscriber or customer to such disclosure;

(D) submits a formal written request relevant to a law enforcement investigation concerning telemarketing fraud for the name, address, and place of business of a subscriber or customer of such provider, which subscriber or customer is engaged in telemarketing (as such term is defined in section 2325 of this title); or

(E) seeks information under paragraph (2).

(2) A provider of electronic communication service or remote computing service shall disclose to a governmental entity the—

(A) name;

(B) address;

(C) local and long distance telephone connection records, or records of session times and durations;

    (D) length of service (including start date) and types of service utilized;

    (E) telephone or instrument number or other subscriber number or identity, including any temporarily assigned network address; and

    (F) means and source of payment for such service (including any credit card or bank account number),

of a subscriber to or customer of such service when the governmental entity uses an administrative subpoena authorized by a Federal or State statute or a Federal or State grand jury or trial subpoena or any means available under paragraph (1).

    (3) A governmental entity receiving records or information under this subsection is not required to provide notice to a subscriber or customer.

    (d) Requirements for court order. A court order for disclosure under subsection (b) or (c) may be issued by any court that is a court of competent jurisdiction and shall issue only if the governmental entity offers specific and articulable facts showing that there are reasonable grounds to believe that the contents of a wire or electronic communication, or the records or other information sought, are relevant and material to an ongoing criminal investigation. In the case of a State governmental authority, such a court order shall not issue if prohibited by the law of such State. A court issuing an order pursuant to this section, on a motion made promptly by the service provider, may quash or modify such order, if the information or records requested are unusually voluminous in nature or compliance with such order otherwise would cause an undue burden on such provider.

    (e) No cause of action against a provider disclosing information under this chapter. No cause of action shall lie in any court against any provider of wire or electronic communication service, its officers, employees, agents, or other specified persons for providing information, facilities, or assistance in accordance with the terms of a court order, warrant, subpoena, statutory authorization, or certification under this chapter.

    (f) Requirement to preserve evidence.

    (1) In general. A provider of wire or electronic communication services or a remote computing service, upon the request of a governmental entity, shall take all necessary steps to preserve records and other evidence in its possession pending the issuance of a court order or other process.

(2) Period of retention. Records referred to in paragraph (1) shall be retained for a period of 90 days, which shall be extended for an additional 90-day period upon a renewed request by the governmental entity.

(g) Presence of officer not required. Notwithstanding section 3105 of this title, the presence of an officer shall not be required for service or execution of a search warrant issued in accordance with this chapter requiring disclosure by a provider of electronic communications service or remote computing service of the contents of communications or records or other information pertaining to a subscriber to or customer of such service.

(h) Comity analysis and disclosure of information regarding legal process seeking contents of wire or electronic communication.

    (1) Definitions.—In this subsection—

        (A) the term "qualifying foreign government" means a foreign government—

            (i) with which the United States has an executive agreement that has entered into force under section 2523; and

            (ii) the laws of which provide to electronic communication service providers and remote computing service providers substantive and procedural opportunities similar to those provided under paragraphs (2) and (5); and

        (B) the term "United States person" has the meaning given the term in section 2523.

    (2) Motions to quash or modify.—

        (A) A provider of electronic communication service to the public or remote computing service, including a foreign electronic communication service or remote computing service, that is being required to disclose pursuant to legal process issued under this section the contents of a wire or electronic communication of a subscriber or customer, may file a motion to modify or quash the legal process where the provider reasonably believes—

            (i) that the customer or subscriber is not a United States person and does not reside in the United States; and

            (ii) that the required disclosure would create a material risk that the provider would violate the laws of a qualifying foreign government.

Such a motion shall be filed not later than 14 days after the date on which the provider was served with the legal process, absent agreement with the government or permission from the court to extend the deadline based on an application made within the 14 days. The right to move to quash is without prejudice to any other grounds to move to quash or defenses thereto, but it shall be the sole basis for moving to quash on the grounds of a conflict of law related to a qualifying foreign government.

(B) Upon receipt of a motion filed pursuant to subparagraph (A), the court shall afford the governmental entity that applied for or issued the legal process under this section the opportunity to respond. The court may modify or quash the legal process, as appropriate, only if the court finds that—

(i) the required disclosure would cause the provider to violate the laws of a qualifying foreign government;

(ii) based on the totality of the circumstances, the interests of justice dictate that the legal process should be modified or quashed; and

(iii) the customer or subscriber is not a United States person and does not reside in the United States.

(3) Comity analysis.—For purposes of making a determination under paragraph (2)(B)(ii), the court shall take into account, as appropriate—

(A) the interests of the United States, including the investigative interests of the governmental entity seeking to require the disclosure;

(B) the interests of the qualifying foreign government in preventing any prohibited disclosure;

(C) the likelihood, extent, and nature of penalties to the provider or any employees of the provider as a result of inconsistent legal requirements imposed on the provider;

(D) the location and nationality of the subscriber or customer whose communications are being sought, if known, and the nature and extent of the subscriber or customer's connection to the United States, or if the legal process has been sought on behalf of a foreign authority pursuant to section 3512, the nature and extent of the subscriber or customer's connection to the foreign authority's country;

(E) the nature and extent of the provider's ties to and presence in the United States;

(F) the importance to the investigation of the information required to be disclosed;

(G) the likelihood of timely and effective access to the information required to be disclosed through means that would cause less serious negative consequences; and

(H) if the legal process has been sought on behalf of a foreign authority pursuant to section 3512, the investigative interests of the foreign authority making the request for assistance.

(4) Disclosure obligations during pendency of challenge.—A service provider shall preserve, but not be obligated to produce, information sought during the pendency of a motion brought under this subsection, unless the court finds that immediate production is necessary to prevent an adverse result identified in section 2705(a)(2).

(5) Disclosure to qualifying foreign Government.

(A) It shall not constitute a violation of a protective order issued under section 2705 for a provider of electronic communication service to the public or remote computing service to disclose to the entity within a qualifying foreign government, designated in an executive agreement under section 2523, the fact of the existence of legal process issued under this section seeking the contents of a wire or electronic communication of a customer or subscriber who is a national or resident of the qualifying foreign government.

(B) Nothing in this paragraph shall be construed to modify or otherwise affect any other authority to make a motion to modify or quash a protective order issued under section 2705.

18 U.S.C. § 2704. BACKUP PRESERVATION

(a) Backup preservation.

(1) A governmental entity acting under section 2703(b)(2) may include in its subpoena or court order a requirement that the service provider to whom the request is directed create a backup copy of the contents of the electronic communications sought in order to preserve those communications. Without notifying the subscriber or customer of such subpoena or court order, such service provider shall create such backup copy as soon as practicable consistent with its regular business practices and shall confirm to the governmental entity that such backup copy has been made. Such backup copy shall be created within two business days after receipt by the service provider of the subpoena or court order.

(2) Notice to the subscriber or customer shall be made by the governmental entity within three days after receipt of such confirmation, unless such notice is delayed pursuant to section 2705(a).

(3) The service provider shall not destroy such backup copy until the later of—

(A) the delivery of the information; or

(B) the resolution of any proceedings (including appeals of any proceeding) concerning the government's subpoena or court order.

(4) The service provider shall release such backup copy to the requesting governmental entity no sooner than fourteen days after the governmental entity's notice to the subscriber or customer if such service provider—

(A) has not received notice from the subscriber or customer that the subscriber or customer has challenged the governmental entity's request; and

(B) has not initiated proceedings to challenge the request of the governmental entity.

(5) A governmental entity may seek to require the creation of a backup copy under subsection (a)(1) of this section if in its sole discretion such entity determines that there is reason to believe that notification under section 2703 of this title of the existence of the subpoena or court order may result in destruction of or tampering with evidence. This determination is not subject to challenge by the subscriber or customer or service provider.

(b) Customer challenges.

(1) Within fourteen days after notice by the governmental entity to the subscriber or customer under subsection (a)(2) of this section, such subscriber or customer may file a motion to quash such subpoena or vacate such court order, with copies served upon the governmental entity and with written notice of such challenge to the service provider. A motion to vacate a court order shall be filed in the court which issued such order. A motion to quash a subpoena shall be filed in the appropriate United States district court or State court. Such motion or application shall contain an affidavit or sworn statement—

(A) stating that the applicant is a customer or subscriber to the service from which the contents of electronic communications maintained for him have been sought; and

(B) stating the applicant's reasons for believing that the records sought are not relevant to a legitimate law enforcement inquiry or that there has not been substantial compliance with the provisions of this chapter in some other respect.

(2) Service shall be made under this section upon a governmental entity by delivering or mailing by registered or certified mail a copy of the papers to the person, office, or department specified in the notice which the customer has received pursuant to this chapter. For the purposes of this section, the term "delivery" has the meaning given that term in the Federal Rules of Civil Procedure.

(3) If the court finds that the customer has complied with paragraphs (1) and (2) of this subsection, the court shall order the governmental entity to file a sworn response, which may be filed in camera if the governmental entity includes in its response the reasons which make in camera review appropriate. If the court is unable to determine the motion or application on the basis of the parties' initial allegations and response, the court may conduct such additional proceedings as it deems appropriate. All such proceedings shall be completed and the motion or application decided as soon as practicable after the filing of the governmental entity's response.

(4) If the court finds that the applicant is not the subscriber or customer for whom the communications sought by the governmental entity are maintained, or that there is a reason to believe that the law enforcement inquiry is legitimate and that the communications sought are relevant to that inquiry, it shall deny the motion or application and order such process enforced. If the court finds that the applicant is the subscriber or customer for whom the communications sought by the governmental entity are maintained, and that there is not a reason to believe that the communications sought are relevant to a legitimate law enforcement inquiry, or that there has not been substantial compliance with the provisions of this chapter, it shall order the process quashed.

(5) A court order denying a motion or application under this section shall not be deemed a final order and no interlocutory appeal may be taken therefrom by the customer.

18 U.S.C. § 2705. DELAYED NOTICE

(a) Delay of notification.

(1) A governmental entity acting under section 2703(b) of this title may—

(A) where a court order is sought, include in the application a request, which the court shall grant, for an order delaying the notification required under section 2703(b) of this title for a period not to exceed ninety days, if the court determines that there is reason to believe that notification of the existence of the court order may have an adverse result described in paragraph (2) of this subsection; or

(B) where an administrative subpoena authorized by a Federal or State statute or a Federal or State grand jury subpoena is obtained, delay the notification required under section 2703(b) of this title for a period not to exceed ninety days upon the execution of a written certification of a supervisory official that there is reason to believe that notification of the existence of the subpoena may have an adverse result described in paragraph (2) of this subsection.

(2) An adverse result for the purposes of paragraph (1) of this subsection is—

(A) endangering the life or physical safety of an individual;

(B) flight from prosecution;

(C) destruction of or tampering with evidence;

(D) intimidation of potential witnesses; or

(E) otherwise seriously jeopardizing an investigation or unduly delaying a trial.

(3) The governmental entity shall maintain a true copy of certification under paragraph (1)(B).

(4) Extensions of the delay of notification provided in section 2703 of up to ninety days each may be granted by the court upon application, or by certification by a governmental entity, but only in accordance with subsection (b) of this section.

(5) Upon expiration of the period of delay of notification under paragraph (1) or (4) of this subsection, the governmental entity shall serve upon, or deliver by registered or first-class mail to, the customer or subscriber a copy of the process or request together with notice that—

(A) states with reasonable specificity the nature of the law enforcement inquiry; and

(B) informs such customer or subscriber—

(i) that information maintained for such customer or subscriber by the service provider named in such process or request was supplied to or requested by that governmental authority and the date on which the supplying or request took place;

(ii) that notification of such customer or subscriber was delayed;

(iii) what governmental entity or court made the certification or determination pursuant to which that delay was made; and

(iv) which provision of this chapter allowed such delay.

(6) As used in this subsection, the term "supervisory official" means the investigative agent in charge or assistant investigative agent in charge or an equivalent of an investigating agency's headquarters or regional office, or the chief prosecuting attorney or the first assistant prosecuting attorney or an equivalent of a prosecuting attorney's headquarters or regional office.

(b) **Preclusion of notice to subject of governmental access.** A governmental entity acting under section 2703, when it is not required to notify the subscriber or customer under section 2703(b)(1), or to the extent that it may delay such notice pursuant to subsection (a) of this section, may apply to a court for an order commanding a provider of electronic communications service or remote computing service to whom a warrant, subpoena, or court order is directed, for such period as the court deems appropriate, not to notify any other person of the existence of the warrant, subpoena, or court order. The court shall enter such an order if it determines that there is reason to believe that notification of the existence of the warrant, subpoena, or court order will result in—

(1) endangering the life or physical safety of an individual;

(2) flight from prosecution;

(3) destruction of or tampering with evidence;

(4) intimidation of potential witnesses; or

(5) otherwise seriously jeopardizing an investigation or unduly delaying a trial.

18 U.S.C. § 2706. COST REIMBURSEMENT

(a) **Payment.** Except as otherwise provided in subsection (c), a governmental entity obtaining the contents of communications, records, or other information under section 2702, 2703, or 2704 of this title shall pay to the person or entity assembling or providing such information a fee for reimbursement for such costs as are reasonably necessary and which have been directly incurred in searching for, assembling, reproducing, or otherwise providing such information. Such reimbursable costs shall include any costs due to necessary disruption of normal operations of any electronic communication service or remote computing service in which such information may be stored.

(b) **Amount.** The amount of the fee provided by subsection (a) shall be as mutually agreed by the governmental entity and the person or entity providing the information, or, in the absence of agreement, shall be as determined by the court which issued the order for production of such information (or the court before which a criminal prosecution relating to such information would be brought, if no court order was issued for production of the information).

(c) Exception. The requirement of subsection (a) of this section does not apply with respect to records or other information maintained by a communications common carrier that relate to telephone toll records and telephone listings obtained under section 2703 of this title. The court may, however, order a payment as described in subsection (a) if the court determines the information required is unusually voluminous in nature or otherwise caused an undue burden on the provider.

18 U.S.C. § 2707. CIVIL ACTION

(a) Cause of action. Except as provided in section 2703(e), any provider of electronic communication service, subscriber, or other person aggrieved by any violation of this chapter in which the conduct constituting the violation is engaged in with a knowing or intentional state of mind may, in a civil action, recover from the person or entity, other than the United States, which engaged in that violation such relief as may be appropriate.

(b) Relief. In a civil action under this section, appropriate relief includes—

(1) such preliminary and other equitable or declaratory relief as may be appropriate;

(2) damages under subsection (c); and

(3) a reasonable attorney's fee and other litigation costs reasonably incurred.

(c) Damages. The court may assess as damages in a civil action under this section the sum of the actual damages suffered by the plaintiff and any profits made by the violator as a result of the violation, but in no case shall a person entitled to recover receive less than the sum of $1,000. If the violation is willful or intentional, the court may assess punitive damages. In the case of a successful action to enforce liability under this section, the court may assess the costs of the action, together with reasonable attorney fees determined by the court.

(d) Administrative discipline. If a court or appropriate department or agency determines that the United States or any of its departments or agencies has violated any provision of this chapter, and the court or appropriate department or agency finds that the circumstances surrounding the violation raise serious questions about whether or not an officer or employee of the United States acted willfully or intentionally with respect to the violation, the department or agency shall, upon receipt of a true and correct copy of the decision and findings of the court or appropriate department or agency promptly initiate a proceeding to determine whether disciplinary action against the officer or employee is warranted. If the head of the department or agency involved determines that disciplinary action is not warranted, he or she shall notify the Inspector General with jurisdiction over the department or agency concerned and shall provide the Inspector General with the reasons for such determination.

(e) Defense. A good faith reliance on—

(1) a court warrant or order, a grand jury subpoena, a legislative authorization, or a statutory authorization (including a request of a governmental entity under section 2703(f) of this title);

(2) a request of an investigative or law enforcement officer under section 2518(7) of this title; or

(3) a good faith determination that section 2511(3), section 2702(b)(9), or section 2702(c)(7) of this title permitted the conduct complained of;

is a complete defense to any civil or criminal action brought under this chapter or any other law.

(f) Limitation. A civil action under this section may not be commenced later than two years after the date upon which the claimant first discovered or had a reasonable opportunity to discover the violation.

(g) Improper disclosure. Any willful disclosure of a 'record', as that term is defined in section 552a(a) of title 5, United States Code, obtained by an investigative or law enforcement officer, or a governmental entity, pursuant to section 2703 of this title, or from a device installed pursuant to section 3123 or 3125 of this title, that is not a disclosure made in the proper performance of the official functions of the officer or governmental entity making the disclosure, is a violation of this chapter. This provision shall not apply to information previously lawfully disclosed (prior to the commencement of any civil or administrative proceeding under this chapter) to the public by a Federal, State, or local governmental entity or by the plaintiff in a civil action under this chapter.

18 U.S.C. § 2708. EXCLUSIVITY OF REMEDIES

The remedies and sanctions described in this chapter are the only judicial remedies and sanctions for nonconstitutional violations of this chapter.

18 U.S.C. § 2711. DEFINITIONS FOR CHAPTER

As used in this chapter—

(1) the terms defined in section 2510 of this title have, respectively, the definitions given such terms in that section;

(2) the term "remote computing service" means the provision to the public of computer storage or processing services by means of an electronic communications system;

(3) the term "court of competent jurisdiction" includes—

(A) any district court of the United States (including a magistrate judge of such a court) or any United States court of appeals that—(i) has jurisdiction over the offense being investigated; (ii) is in or for a district in which the provider of a wire or electronic communication service is located or in which the wire or electronic communications, records, or other information are stored; or (iii) is acting on a request for foreign assistance pursuant to section 3512 of this title; or

(B) a court of general criminal jurisdiction of a State authorized by the law of that State to issue search warrants; and

(4) the term "governmental entity" means a department or agency of the United States or any State or political subdivision thereof.

18 U.S.C. § 2713. REQUIRED PRESERVATION AND DISCLOSURE OF COMMUNICATIONS AND RECORDS

A provider of electronic communication service or remote computing service shall comply with the obligations of this chapter to preserve, backup, or disclose the contents of a wire or electronic communication and any record or other information pertaining to a customer or subscriber within such provider's possession, custody, or control, regardless of whether such communication, record, or other information is located within or outside of the United States.

18 U.S.C. § 3121. GENERAL PROHIBITION ON PEN REGISTER AND TRAP AND TRACE DEVICE USE; EXCEPTION

(a) In general. Except as provided in this section, no person may install or use a pen register or a trap and trace device without first obtaining a court order under section 3123 of this title or under the Foreign Intelligence Surveillance Act of 1978 (50 U.S.C. 1801 et seq.) or an order from a foreign government that is subject to an executive agreement that the Attorney General has determined and certified to Congress satisfies section 2523.

(b) Exception. The prohibition of subsection (a) does not apply with respect to the use of a pen register or a trap and trace device by a provider of electronic or wire communication service—

(1) relating to the operation, maintenance, and testing of a wire or electronic communication service or to the protection of the rights or property of such provider, or to the protection of users of that service from abuse of service or unlawful use of service; or

(2) to record the fact that a wire or electronic communication was initiated or completed in order to protect such provider, another provider furnishing service toward the completion of the wire communication, or a user of that service, from fraudulent, unlawful or abusive use of service; or

(3) where the consent of the user of that service has been obtained.

(c) Limitation. A government agency authorized to install and use a pen register or trap and trace device under this chapter or under State law shall use technology reasonably available to it that restricts the recording or decoding of electronic or other impulses to the dialing, routing, addressing, and signaling information utilized in the processing and transmitting of wire or electronic communications so as not to include the contents of any wire or electronic communications.

(d) Penalty. Whoever knowingly violates subsection (a) shall be fined under this title or imprisoned not more than one year, or both.

18 U.S.C. § 3122. APPLICATION FOR AN ORDER FOR A PEN REGISTER OR A TRAP AND TRACE DEVICE

(a) Application.

(1) An attorney for the Government may make application for an order or an extension of an order under section 3123 of this title authorizing or approving the installation and use of a pen register or a trap and trace device under this chapter, in writing under oath or equivalent affirmation, to a court of competent jurisdiction.

(2) Unless prohibited by State law, a State investigative or law enforcement officer may make application for an order or an extension of an order under section 3123 of this title authorizing or approving the installation and use of a pen register or a trap and trace device under this chapter, in writing under oath or equivalent affirmation, to a court of competent jurisdiction of such State.

(b) Contents of application. An application under subsection (a) of this section shall include—

(1) the identity of the attorney for the Government or the State law enforcement or investigative officer making the application and the identity of the law enforcement agency conducting the investigation; and

(2) a certification by the applicant that the information likely to be obtained is relevant to an ongoing criminal investigation being conducted by that agency.

18 U.S.C. § 3123. ISSUANCE OF AN ORDER FOR A PEN REGISTER OR A TRAP AND TRACE DEVICE

(a) In general.

(1) **Attorney for the Government.** Upon an application made under section 3122(a)(1), the court shall enter an ex parte order authorizing the installation and use of a pen register or trap and trace device anywhere within the United States, if the court finds that the attorney for the Government has certified to the court that the information likely to be obtained by such installation and use is relevant to an ongoing criminal investigation. The order, upon service of that order, shall apply to any person or entity providing wire or electronic communication service in the United States whose assistance may facilitate the execution of the order. Whenever such an order is served on any person or entity not specifically named in the order, upon request of such person or entity, the attorney for the Government or law enforcement or investigative officer that is serving the order shall provide written or electronic certification that the order applies to the person or entity being served.

(2) **State investigative or law enforcement officer.** Upon an application made under section 3122(a)(2), the court shall enter an ex parte order authorizing the installation and use of a pen register or trap and trace device within the jurisdiction of the court, if the court finds that the State law enforcement or investigative officer has certified to the court that the information likely to be obtained by such installation and use is relevant to an ongoing criminal investigation.

(3)(A)   Where the law enforcement agency implementing an ex parte order under this subsection seeks to do so by installing and using its own pen register or trap and trace device on a packet-switched data network of a provider of electronic communication service to the public, the agency shall ensure that a record will be maintained which will identify—

> (i)   any officer or officers who installed the device and any officer or officers who accessed the device to obtain information from the network;

> (ii)   the date and time the device was installed, the date and time the device was uninstalled, and the date, time, and duration of each time the device is accessed to obtain information;

> (iii) the configuration of the device at the time of its installation and any subsequent modification thereof; and

> (iv) any information which has been collected by the device.

To the extent that the pen register or trap and trace device can be set automatically to record this information electronically, the record shall be maintained electronically throughout the installation and use of such device.

(B) The record maintained under subparagraph (A) shall be provided ex parte and under seal to the court which entered the ex parte order authorizing the installation and use of the device within 30 days after termination of the order (including any extensions thereof).

(b) **Contents of order.** An order issued under this section—

(1) shall specify—

(A) the identity, if known, of the person to whom is leased or in whose name is listed the telephone line or other facility to which the pen register or trap and trace device is to be attached or applied;

(B) the identity, if known, of the person who is the subject of the criminal investigation;

(C) the attributes of the communications to which the order applies, including the number or other identifier and, if known, the location of the telephone line or other facility to which the pen register or trap and trace device is to be attached or applied, and, in the case of an order authorizing installation and use of a trap and trace device under subsection (a)(2), the geographic limits of the order; and

(D) a statement of the offense to which the information likely to be obtained by the pen register or trap and trace device relates; and

(2) shall direct, upon the request of the applicant, the furnishing of information, facilities, and technical assistance necessary to accomplish the installation of the pen register or trap and trace device under section 3124 of this title.

(c) **Time period and extensions.**

(1) An order issued under this section shall authorize the installation and use of a pen register or a trap and trace device for a period not to exceed sixty days.

(2) Extensions of such an order may be granted, but only upon an application for an order under section 3122 of this title and upon the judicial finding required by subsection (a) of this section. The period of extension shall be for a period not to exceed sixty days.

(d) Nondisclosure of existence of pen register or a trap and trace device. An order authorizing or approving the installation and use of a pen register or a trap and trace device shall direct that

(1) the order be sealed until otherwise ordered by the court; and

(2) the person owning or leasing the line or other facility to which the pen register or a trap and trace device is attached, or applied, or who is obligated by the order to provide assistance to the applicant, not disclose the existence of the pen register or trap and trace device or the existence of the investigation to the listed subscriber, or to any other person, unless or until otherwise ordered by the court.

18 U.S.C. § 3124. ASSISTANCE IN INSTALLATION AND USE OF A PEN REGISTER OR A TRAP AND TRACE DEVICE

(a) Pen registers. Upon the request of an attorney for the Government or an officer of a law enforcement agency authorized to install and use a pen register under this chapter, a provider of wire or electronic communication service, landlord, custodian, or other person shall furnish such investigative or law enforcement officer forthwith all information, facilities, and technical assistance necessary to accomplish the installation of the pen register unobtrusively and with a minimum of interference with the services that the person so ordered by the court accords the party with respect to whom the installation and use is to take place, if such assistance is directed by a court order as provided in section 3123(b)(2) of this title.

(b) Trap and trace device. Upon the request of an attorney for the Government or an officer of a law enforcement agency authorized to receive the results of a trap and trace device under this chapter, a provider of a wire or electronic communication service, landlord, custodian, or other person shall install such device forthwith on the appropriate line or other facility and shall furnish such investigative or law enforcement officer all additional information, facilities and technical assistance including installation and operation of the device unobtrusively and with a minimum of interference with the services that the person so ordered by the court accords the party with respect to whom the installation and use is to take place, if such installation and assistance is directed by a court order as provided in section 3123(b)(2) of this title. Unless otherwise ordered by the court, the results of the trap and trace device shall be furnished, pursuant to section 3123(b) or section 3125 of this title, to the officer of a law enforcement agency, designated in the court order, at reasonable intervals during regular business hours for the duration of the order.

(c) Compensation. A provider of a wire or electronic communication service, landlord, custodian, or other person who furnishes facilities or technical assistance pursuant to this section shall be reasonably compensated for such reasonable expenses incurred in providing such facilities and assistance.

(d) No cause of action against a provider disclosing information under this chapter. No cause of action shall lie in any court against any provider of a wire or electronic communication service, its officers, employees, agents, or other specified persons for providing information, facilities, or assistance in accordance with a court order under this chapter, request pursuant to section 3125 of this title, or an order from a foreign government that is subject to an executive agreement that the Attorney General has determined and certified to Congress satisfies section 2523.

(e) Defense. A good faith reliance on a court order under this chapter, a request pursuant to section 3125 of this title, a legislative authorization, a statutory authorization, or a good faith determination that the conduct complained of was permitted by an order from a foreign government that is subject to executive agreement that the Attorney General has determined and certified to Congress satisfies section 2523, is a complete defense against any civil or criminal action brought under this chapter or any other law.

(f) Communications assistance enforcement orders. Pursuant to section 2522, an order may be issued to enforce the assistance capability and capacity requirements under the Communications Assistance for Law Enforcement Act.

18 U.S.C. § 3125. EMERGENCY PEN REGISTER AND TRAP AND TRACE DEVICE INSTALLATION

(a) Notwithstanding any other provision of this chapter, any investigative or law enforcement officer, specially designated by the Attorney General, the Deputy Attorney General, the Associate Attorney General, any Assistant Attorney General, any acting Assistant Attorney General, or any Deputy Assistant Attorney General, or by the principal prosecuting attorney of any State or subdivision thereof acting pursuant to a statute of that State, who reasonably determines that—

    (1) an emergency situation exists that involves—

        (A) immediate danger of death or serious bodily injury to any person;

        (B) conspiratorial activities characteristic of organized crime;

        (C) an immediate threat to a national security interest; or

        (D) an ongoing attack on a protected computer (as defined in section 1030) that constitutes a crime punishable by a term of imprisonment greater than one year;

that requires the installation and use of a pen register or a trap and trace device before an order authorizing such installation and use can, with due diligence, be obtained, and

(2) there are grounds upon which an order could be entered under this chapter to authorize such installation and use;

may have installed and use a pen register or trap and trace device if, within forty-eight hours after the installation has occurred, or begins to occur, an order approving the installation or use is issued in accordance with section 3123 of this title.

(b) In the absence of an authorizing order, such use shall immediately terminate when the information sought is obtained, when the application for the order is denied or when forty-eight hours have lapsed since the installation of the pen register or trap and trace device, whichever is earlier.

(c) The knowing installation or use by any investigative or law enforcement officer of a pen register or trap and trace device pursuant to subsection (a) without application for the authorizing order within forty-eight hours of the installation shall constitute a violation of this chapter.

(d) A provider of a wire or electronic service, landlord, custodian, or other person who furnished facilities or technical assistance pursuant to this section shall be reasonably compensated for such reasonable expenses incurred in providing such facilities and assistance.

18 U.S.C. § 3126. REPORTS CONCERNING PEN REGISTERS AND TRAP AND TRACE DEVICES

The Attorney General shall annually report to Congress on the number of pen register orders and orders for trap and trace devices applied for by law enforcement agencies of the Department of Justice, which report shall include information concerning—

(1) the period of interceptions authorized by the order, and the number and duration of any extensions of the order;

(2) the offense specified in the order or application, or extension of an order;

(3) the number of investigations involved;

(4) the number and nature of the facilities affected; and

(5) the identity, including district, of the applying investigative or law enforcement agency making the application and the person authorizing the order.

18 U.S.C. § 3127. DEFINITIONS FOR CHAPTER

As used in this chapter—

(1) the terms "wire communication", "electronic communication", "electronic communication service", and "contents" have the meanings set forth for such terms in section 2510 of this title;

(2) the term "court of competent jurisdiction" means—

    (A) any district court of the United States (including a magistrate judge of such a court) or any United States court of appeals that—(i) has jurisdiction over the offense being investigated; (ii) is in or for a district in which the provider of a wire or electronic communication service is located; (iii) is in or for a district in which a landlord, custodian, or other person subject to subsections (a) or (b) of section 3124 of this title is located; or (iv) is acting on a request for foreign assistance pursuant to section 3512 of this title; or

    (B) a court of general criminal jurisdiction of a State authorized by the law of that State to enter orders authorizing the use of a pen register or a trap and trace device;

(3) the term "pen register" means a device or process which records or decodes dialing, routing, addressing, or signaling information transmitted by an instrument or facility from which a wire or electronic communication is transmitted, provided, however, that such information shall not include the contents of any communication, but such term does not include any device or process used by a provider or customer of a wire or electronic communication service for billing, or recording as an incident to billing, for communications services provided by such provider or any device or process used by a provider or customer of a wire communication service for cost accounting or other like purposes in the ordinary course of its business;

(4) the term "trap and trace device" means a device or process which captures the incoming electronic or other impulses which identify the originating number or other dialing, routing, addressing, and signaling information reasonably likely to identify the source of a wire or electronic communication, provided, however, that such information shall not include the contents of any communication;

(5) the term "attorney for the Government" has the meaning given such term for the purposes of the Federal Rules of Criminal Procedure; and

(6) the term "State" means a State, the District of Columbia, Puerto Rico, and any other possession or territory of the United States.

47 U.S.C. § 223. Obscene or Harassing Telephone Calls in the District of Columbia or in Interstate or Foreign Communications

(a) **Prohibited acts generally.** Whoever—

(1) in interstate or foreign communications—

(A) by means of a telecommunications device knowingly—

(i) makes, creates, or solicits, and

(ii) initiates the transmission of,

any comment, request, suggestion, proposal, image, or other communication which is obscene or child pornography, with intent to annoy, abuse, threaten, or harass another person;

(B) by means of a telecommunications device knowingly—

(i) makes, creates, or solicits, and

(ii) initiates the transmission of,

any comment, request, suggestion, proposal, image, or other communication which is obscene or child pornography, knowing that the recipient of the communication is under 18 years of age, regardless of whether the maker of such communication placed the call or initiated the communication;

(C) makes a telephone call or utilizes a telecommunications device, whether or not conversation or communication ensues, without disclosing his identity and with intent to annoy, abuse, threaten, or harass any person at the called number or who receives the communications;

(D) makes or causes the telephone of another repeatedly or continuously to ring, with intent to harass any person at the called number; or

(E) makes repeated telephone calls or repeatedly initiates communication with a telecommunications device, during which conversation or communication ensues, solely to harass any person at the called number or who receives the communication; or

(2) knowingly permits any telecommunications facility under his control to be used for any activity prohibited by paragraph (1) with the intent that it be used for such activity,

shall be fined under Title 18 or imprisoned not more than two years, or both.

(b) **Prohibited acts for commercial purposes; defense to prosecution.**

(1) Whoever knowingly—

(A) within the United States, by means of telephone, makes (directly or by recording device) any obscene communication for commercial purposes to any person, regardless of whether the maker of such communication placed the call; or

(B) permits any telephone facility under such person's control to be used for an activity prohibited by subparagraph (A),

shall be fined in accordance with Title 18 or imprisoned not more than two years, or both.

(2) Whoever knowingly—

(A) within the United States, by means of telephone, makes (directly or by recording device) any indecent communication for commercial purposes which is available to any person under 18 years of age or to any other person without that person's consent, regardless of whether the maker of such communication placed the call; or

(B) permits any telephone facility under such person's control to be used for an activity prohibited by subparagraph (A), shall be fined not more than $50,000 or imprisoned not more than six months, or both.

(3) It is a defense to prosecution under paragraph (2) of this subsection that the defendant restricted access to the prohibited communication to persons 18 years of age or older in accordance with subsection (c) of this section and with such procedures as the Commission may prescribe by regulation.

(4) In addition to the penalties under paragraph (1), whoever, within the United States, intentionally violates paragraph (1) or (2) shall be subject to a fine of not more than $50,000 for each violation. For purposes of this paragraph, each day of violation shall constitute a separate violation.

(5)(A) In addition to the penalties under paragraphs (1), (2), and (5), whoever, within the United States, violates paragraph (1) or (2) shall be subject to a civil fine of not more than $50,000 for each violation. For purposes of this paragraph, each day of violation shall constitute a separate violation.

(B) A fine under this paragraph may be assessed either—

(i) by a court, pursuant to civil action by the Commission or any attorney employed by the Commission who is designated by the Commission for such purposes, or

(ii) by the Commission after appropriate administrative proceedings.

(6) The Attorney General may bring a suit in the appropriate district court of the United States to enjoin any act or practice which violates paragraph (1) or (2). An injunction may be granted in accordance with the Federal Rules of Civil Procedure.

(c) Restriction on access to subscribers by common carriers; judicial remedies respecting restrictions.

(1) A common carrier within the District of Columbia or within any State, or in interstate or foreign commerce, shall not, to the extent technically feasible, provide access to a communication specified in subsection (b) of this section from the telephone of any subscriber who has not previously requested in writing the carrier to provide access to such communication if the carrier collects from subscribers an identifiable charge for such communication that the carrier remits, in whole or in part, to the provider of such communication.

(2) Except as provided in paragraph (3), no cause of action may be brought in any court or administrative agency against any common carrier, or any of its affiliates, including their officers, directors, employees, agents, or authorized representatives on account of—

(A) any action which the carrier demonstrates was taken in good faith to restrict access pursuant to paragraph (1) of this subsection; or

(B) any access permitted—

(i) in good faith reliance upon the lack of any representation by a provider of communications that communications provided by that provider are communications specified in subsection (b) of this section, or

(ii) because a specific representation by the provider did not allow the carrier, acting in good faith, a sufficient period to restrict access to communications described in subsection (b) of this section.

(3) Notwithstanding paragraph (2) of this subsection, a provider of communications services to which subscribers are denied access pursuant to paragraph (1) of this subsection may bring an action for a declaratory judgment or similar action in a court. Any such action shall be limited to the question of whether the communications which the provider seeks to provide fall within the category of communications to which the carrier will provide access only to subscribers who have previously requested such access.

(d) Sending or displaying offensive material to persons under 18. Whoever—

> **(1)** in interstate or foreign communications knowingly—
>
> > **(A)** uses an interactive computer service to send to a specific person or persons under 18 years of age, or
> >
> > **(B)** uses any interactive computer service to display in a manner available to a person under 18 years of age,
>
> any comment, request, suggestion, proposal, image, or other communication that, is obscene or child pornography, regardless of whether the user of such service placed the call or initiated the communication; or
>
> **(2)** knowingly permits any telecommunications facility under such person's control to be used for an activity prohibited by paragraph (1) with the intent that it be used for such activity,

shall be fined under Title 18 or imprisoned not more than two years, or both.

(e) Defenses. In addition to any other defenses available by law:

> **(1)** No person shall be held to have violated subsection (a) or (d) of this section solely for providing access or connection to or from a facility, system, or network not under that person's control, including transmission, downloading, intermediate storage, access software, or other related capabilities that are incidental to providing such access or connection that does not include the creation of the content of the communication.
>
> **(2)** The defenses provided by paragraph (1) of this subsection shall not be applicable to a person who is a conspirator with an entity actively involved in the creation or knowing distribution of communications that violate this section, or who knowingly advertises the availability of such communications.
>
> **(3)** The defenses provided in paragraph (1) of this subsection shall not be applicable to a person who provides access or connection to a facility, system, or network engaged in the violation of this section that is owned or controlled by such person.
>
> **(4)** No employer shall be held liable under this section for the actions of an employee or agent unless the employee's or agent's conduct is within the scope of his or her employment or agency and the employer (A) having knowledge of such conduct, authorizes or ratifies such conduct, or (B) recklessly disregards such conduct.
>
> **(5)** It is a defense to a prosecution under subsection (a)(1)(B) or (d) of this section, or under subsection (a)(2) of this section with respect

to the use of a facility for an activity under subsection (a)(1)(B) of this section that a person—

(A) has taken, in good faith, reasonable, effective, and appropriate actions under the circumstances to restrict or prevent access by minors to a communication specified in such subsections, which may involve any appropriate measures to restrict minors from such communications, including any method which is feasible under available technology; or

(B) has restricted access to such communication by requiring use of a verified credit card, debit account, adult access code, or adult personal identification number.

(6) The Commission may describe measures which are reasonable, effective, and appropriate to restrict access to prohibited communications under subsection (d) of this section. Nothing in this section authorizes the Commission to enforce, or is intended to provide the Commission with the authority to approve, sanction, or permit, the use of such measures. The Commission shall have no enforcement authority over the failure to utilize such measures. The Commission shall not endorse specific products relating to such measures. The use of such measures shall be admitted as evidence of good faith efforts for purposes of paragraph (5) in any action arising under subsection (d) of this section. Nothing in this section shall be construed to treat interactive computer services as common carriers or telecommunications carriers.

(f) Violations of law required; commercial entities, nonprofit libraries, or institutions of higher education.

(1) No cause of action may be brought in any court or administrative agency against any person on account of any activity that is not in violation of any law punishable by criminal or civil penalty, and that the person has taken in good faith to implement a defense authorized under this section or otherwise to restrict or prevent the transmission of, or access to, a communication specified in this section.

(2) No State or local government may impose any liability for commercial activities or actions by commercial entities, nonprofit libraries, or institutions of higher education in connection with an activity or action described in subsection (a)(2) or (d) of this section that is inconsistent with the treatment of those activities or actions under this section: *Provided, however,* That nothing herein shall preclude any State or local government from enacting and enforcing complementary oversight, liability, and regulatory systems, procedures, and requirements, so long as such systems, procedures, and requirements govern only intrastate services and do not result in the imposition of inconsistent rights, duties or obligations on the provision of interstate services. Nothing in this subsection shall preclude any State or local government from governing conduct not covered by this section.

(g) Application and enforcement of other Federal law. Nothing in subsection (a), (d), (e), or (f) of this section or in the defenses to prosecution under subsection (a) or (d) of this section shall be construed to affect or limit the application or enforcement of any other Federal law.

(h) Definitions. For purposes of this section—

(1) The use of the term "telecommunications device" in this section—

(A) shall not impose new obligations on broadcasting station licensees and cable operators covered by obscenity and indecency provisions elsewhere in this chapter;

(B) does not include an interactive computer service; and

(C) in the case of subparagraph (C) of subsection (a)(1), includes any device or software that can be used to originate telecommunications or other types of communications that are transmitted, in whole or in part, by the Internet (as such term is defined in section 1104 of the Internet Tax Freedom Act (47 U.S.C. 151 note)).

(2) The term "interactive computer service" has the meaning provided in section 230(f)(2) of this title.

(3) The term "access software" means software (including client or server software) or enabling tools that do not create or provide the content of the communication but that allow a user to do any one or more of the following:

(A) filter, screen, allow, or disallow content;

(B) pick, choose, analyze, or digest content; or

(C) transmit, receive, display, forward, cache, search, subset, organize, reorganize, or translate content.

(4) The term "institution of higher education" has the meaning provided in section 1001 of Title 20.

(5) The term "library" means a library eligible for participation in State-based plans for funds under title III of the Library Services and Construction Act (20 U.S.C. 355e et seq.).

CYBERSECURITY ACT OF 2015

6 U.S.C. § 1501. DEFINITIONS

In this subchapter:

* * *

(4) Cybersecurity purpose

The term "cybersecurity purpose" means the purpose of protecting an information system or information that is stored on, processed by, or transiting an information system from a cybersecurity threat or security vulnerability.

(5) Cybersecurity threat

(A) In general

Except as provided in subparagraph (B), the term "cybersecurity threat" means an action, not protected by the First Amendment to the Constitution of the United States, on or through an information system that may result in an unauthorized effort to adversely impact the security, availability, confidentiality, or integrity of an information system or information that is stored on, processed by, or transiting an information system.

(B) Exclusion

The term "cybersecurity threat" does not include any action that solely involves a violation of a consumer term of service or a consumer licensing agreement.

(6) Cyber threat indicator

The term "cyber threat indicator" means information that is necessary to describe or identify—

(A) malicious reconnaissance, including anomalous patterns of communications that appear to be transmitted for the purpose of gathering technical information related to a cybersecurity threat or security vulnerability;

(B) a method of defeating a security control or exploitation of a security vulnerability;

(C) a security vulnerability, including anomalous activity that appears to indicate the existence of a security vulnerability;

(D) a method of causing a user with legitimate access to an information system or information that is stored on, processed by, or transiting an information system to unwittingly enable the defeat of a security control or exploitation of a security vulnerability;

(E) malicious cyber command and control;

(F) the actual or potential harm caused by an incident, including a description of the information exfiltrated as a result of a particular cybersecurity threat;

(G) any other attribute of a cybersecurity threat, if disclosure of such attribute is not otherwise prohibited by law; or

(H) any combination thereof.

(7) Defensive measure

(A) In general

Except as provided in subparagraph (B), the term "defensive measure" means an action, device, procedure, signature, technique, or other measure applied to an information system or information that is stored on, processed by, or transiting an information system that detects, prevents, or mitigates a known or suspected cybersecurity threat or security vulnerability.

(B) Exclusion

The term "defensive measure" does not include a measure that destroys, renders unusable, provides unauthorized access to, or substantially harms an information system or information stored on, processed by, or transiting such information system not owned by—

(i) the private entity operating the measure; or

(ii) another entity or Federal entity that is authorized to provide consent and has provided consent to that private entity for operation of such measure.

(8) Federal entity

The term "Federal entity" means a department or agency of the United States or any component of such department or agency.

(9) Information system

The term "information system"—

(A) has the meaning given the term in section 3502 of Title 44; and

(B) includes industrial control systems, such as supervisory control and data acquisition systems, distributed control systems, and programmable logic controllers.

(10) Local government

The term "local government" means any borough, city, county, parish, town, township, village, or other political subdivision of a State.

(11) Malicious cyber command and control

The term "malicious cyber command and control" means a method for unauthorized remote identification of, access to, or use of, an information system or information that is stored on, processed by, or transiting an information system.

(12) Malicious reconnaissance

The term "malicious reconnaissance" means a method for actively probing or passively monitoring an information system for the purpose of discerning security vulnerabilities of the information system, if such method is associated with a known or suspected cybersecurity threat.

(13) Monitor

The term "monitor" means to acquire, identify, or scan, or to possess, information that is stored on, processed by, or transiting an information system.

(14) Non-Federal entity

(A) In general

Except as otherwise provided in this paragraph, the term "non-Federal entity" means any private entity, non-Federal government agency or department, or State, tribal, or local government (including a political subdivision, department, or component thereof).

(B) Inclusions

The term "non-Federal entity" includes a government agency or department of the District of Columbia, the Commonwealth of Puerto Rico, the United States Virgin Islands, Guam, American Samoa, the Northern Mariana Islands, and any other territory or possession of the United States.

(C) Exclusion

The term "non-Federal entity" does not include a foreign power as defined in section 1801 of Title 50.

(15) Private entity

(A) In general

Except as otherwise provided in this paragraph, the term "private entity" means any person or private group, organization, proprietorship, partnership, trust, cooperative, corporation, or other commercial or nonprofit entity, including an officer, employee, or agent thereof.

(B) Inclusion

The term "private entity" includes a State, tribal, or local government performing utility services, such as electric, natural gas, or water services.

(C) Exclusion

The term "private entity" does not include a foreign power as defined in section 1801 of Title 50.

(16) Security control

The term "security control" means the management, operational, and technical controls used to protect against an unauthorized effort to adversely affect the confidentiality, integrity, and availability of an information system or its information.

(17) Security vulnerability

The term "security vulnerability" means any attribute of hardware, software, process, or procedure that could enable or facilitate the defeat of a security control.

6 U.S.C. § 1503. AUTHORIZATIONS FOR PREVENTING, DETECTING, ANALYZING, AND MITIGATING CYBERSECURITY THREATS

(a) Authorization for monitoring

(1) In general

Notwithstanding any other provision of law, a private entity may, for cybersecurity purposes, monitor—

(A) an information system of such private entity;

(B) an information system of another non-Federal entity, upon the authorization and written consent of such other entity;

(C) an information system of a Federal entity, upon the authorization and written consent of an authorized representative of the Federal entity; and

(D) information that is stored on, processed by, or transiting an information system monitored by the private entity under this paragraph.

(2) Construction

Nothing in this subsection shall be construed—

(A) to authorize the monitoring of an information system, or the use of any information obtained through such monitoring, other than as provided in this subchapter; or

(B) to limit otherwise lawful activity.

(b) Authorization for operation of defensive measures

(1) In general

Notwithstanding any other provision of law, a private entity may, for cybersecurity purposes, operate a defensive measure that is applied to—

(A) an information system of such private entity in order to protect the rights or property of the private entity;

(B) an information system of another non-Federal entity upon written consent of such entity for operation of such defensive measure to protect the rights or property of such entity; and

(C) an information system of a Federal entity upon written consent of an authorized representative of such Federal entity for operation of such defensive measure to protect the rights or property of the Federal Government.

(2) Construction

Nothing in this subsection shall be construed—

(A) to authorize the use of a defensive measure other than as provided in this subsection; or

(B) to limit otherwise lawful activity.

(c) Authorization for sharing or receiving cyber threat indicators or defensive measures

(1) In general

Except as provided in paragraph (2) and notwithstanding any other provision of law, a non-Federal entity may, for a cybersecurity purpose and consistent with the protection of classified information, share with, or receive from, any other non-Federal entity or the Federal Government a cyber threat indicator or defensive measure.

(2) Lawful restriction

A non-Federal entity receiving a cyber threat indicator or defensive measure from another non-Federal entity or a Federal entity shall comply with otherwise lawful restrictions placed on the sharing or use of such cyber threat indicator or defensive measure by the sharing non-Federal entity or Federal entity.

(3) Construction

Nothing in this subsection shall be construed—

(A) to authorize the sharing or receiving of a cyber threat indicator or defensive measure other than as provided in this subsection; or

(B) to limit otherwise lawful activity.

(d) Protection and use of information

(1) Security of information

A non-Federal entity monitoring an information system, operating a defensive measure, or providing or receiving a cyber threat indicator or defensive measure under this section shall implement and utilize a security control to protect against unauthorized access to or acquisition of such cyber threat indicator or defensive measure.

(2) Removal of certain personal information

A non-Federal entity sharing a cyber threat indicator pursuant to this subchapter shall, prior to such sharing—

(A) review such cyber threat indicator to assess whether such cyber threat indicator contains any information not directly related to a cybersecurity threat that the non-Federal entity knows at the time of sharing to be personal information of a specific individual or information that identifies a specific individual and remove such information; or

(B) implement and utilize a technical capability configured to remove any information not directly related to a cybersecurity threat that the non-Federal entity knows at the time of sharing to be personal information of a specific individual or information that identifies a specific individual.

(3) Use of cyber threat indicators and defensive measures by non-Federal entities

(A) In general

Consistent with this subchapter, a cyber threat indicator or defensive measure shared or received under this section may, for cybersecurity purposes—

(i) be used by a non-Federal entity to monitor or operate a defensive measure that is applied to—

(I) an information system of the non-Federal entity; or

(II) an information system of another non-Federal entity or a Federal entity upon the written consent of that other non-Federal entity or that Federal entity; and

(ii) be otherwise used, retained, and further shared by a non-Federal entity subject to—

(I) an otherwise lawful restriction placed by the sharing non-Federal entity or Federal entity on such cyber threat indicator or defensive measure; or

(II) an otherwise applicable provision of law.

(B) Construction

Nothing in this paragraph shall be construed to authorize the use of a cyber threat indicator or defensive measure other than as provided in this section.

(4) Use of cyber threat indicators by State, tribal, or local government

(A) Law enforcement use

A State, tribal, or local government that receives a cyber threat indicator or defensive measure under this subchapter may use such cyber threat indicator or defensive measure for the purposes described in section 1504(d)(5)(A) of this title.

(B) Exemption from disclosure

A cyber threat indicator or defensive measure shared by or with a State, tribal, or local government, including a component of a State, tribal, or local government that is a private entity, under this section shall be—

(i)   deemed voluntarily shared information; and

(ii) exempt from disclosure under any provision of State, tribal, or local freedom of information law, open government law, open meetings law, open records law, sunshine law, or similar law requiring disclosure of information or records.

(C) State, tribal, and local regulatory authority

(i) In general

Except as provided in clause (ii), a cyber threat indicator or defensive measure shared with a State, tribal, or local government under this subchapter shall not be used by any State, tribal, or local government to regulate, including an enforcement action, the lawful activity of any non-Federal entity or any activity taken by a non-Federal entity pursuant to mandatory standards, including an activity relating to monitoring, operating a defensive measure, or sharing of a cyber threat indicator.

(ii) Regulatory authority specifically relating to prevention or mitigation of cybersecurity threats

A cyber threat indicator or defensive measure shared as described in clause (i) may, consistent with a State, tribal, or local government regulatory authority specifically relating to the prevention or mitigation of cybersecurity threats to information systems, inform the development or implementation of a regulation relating to such information systems.

(e) Antitrust exemption

(1) In general

Except as provided in section 1507(e) of this title, it shall not be considered a violation of any provision of antitrust laws for 2 or more private entities to exchange or provide a cyber threat indicator or defensive measure, or assistance relating to the prevention, investigation, or mitigation of a cybersecurity threat, for cybersecurity purposes under this subchapter.

(2) Applicability

Paragraph (1) shall apply only to information that is exchanged or assistance provided in order to assist with—

(A) facilitating the prevention, investigation, or mitigation of a cybersecurity threat to an information system or information that is stored on, processed by, or transiting an information system; or

(B) communicating or disclosing a cyber threat indicator to help prevent, investigate, or mitigate the effect of a cybersecurity threat to an information system or information that is stored on, processed by, or transiting an information system.

(f) No right or benefit

The sharing of a cyber threat indicator or defensive measure with a non-Federal entity under this subchapter shall not create a right or benefit to similar information by such non-Federal entity or any other non-Federal entity.

6 U.S.C. § 1505. PROTECTION FROM LIABILITY

(a) Monitoring of information systems

No cause of action shall lie or be maintained in any court against any private entity, and such action shall be promptly dismissed, for the monitoring of an information system and information under section 1503(a) of this title that is conducted in accordance with this subchapter.

(b) Sharing or receipt of cyber threat indicators

No cause of action shall lie or be maintained in any court against any private entity, and such action shall be promptly dismissed, for the sharing or receipt of a cyber threat indicator or defensive measure under section 1503(c) of this title if—

(1) such sharing or receipt is conducted in accordance with this subchapter; and

(2) in a case in which a cyber threat indicator or defensive measure is shared with the Federal Government, the cyber threat indicator or defensive measure is shared in a manner that is consistent with section 1504(c)(1)(B) of this title and the sharing or receipt, as the case may be, occurs after the earlier of—

(A) the date on which the interim policies and procedures are submitted to Congress under section 1504(a)(1) of this title and guidelines are submitted to Congress under section 1504(b)(1) of this title; or

(B) the date that is 60 days after December 18, 2015.

(c) Construction

Nothing in this subchapter shall be construed—

(1) to create—

(A) a duty to share a cyber threat indicator or defensive measure; or

(B) a duty to warn or act based on the receipt of a cyber threat indicator or defensive measure; or

(2) to undermine or limit the availability of otherwise applicable common law or statutory defenses.

6 U.S.C. § 1507. CONSTRUCTION AND PREEMPTION

(a) Otherwise lawful disclosures

Nothing in this subchapter shall be construed—

(1) to limit or prohibit otherwise lawful disclosures of communications, records, or other information, including reporting of known or suspected criminal activity, by a non-Federal entity to any other non-Federal entity or the Federal Government under this subchapter; or

(2) to limit or prohibit otherwise lawful use of such disclosures by any Federal entity, even when such otherwise lawful disclosures duplicate or replicate disclosures made under this subchapter.

(b) Whistle blower protections

Nothing in this subchapter shall be construed to prohibit or limit the disclosure of information protected under section 2302(b)(8) of Title 5 (governing disclosures of illegality, waste, fraud, abuse, or public health or safety threats), section 7211 of Title 5 (governing disclosures to Congress), section 1034 of Title 10 (governing disclosure to Congress by members of the military), section 3234 of Title 50 (governing disclosure by employees of elements of the intelligence community), or any similar provision of Federal or State law.

(c) Protection of sources and methods

Nothing in this subchapter shall be construed—

(1) as creating any immunity against, or otherwise affecting, any action brought by the Federal Government, or any agency or department thereof, to enforce any law, executive order, or procedure governing the appropriate handling, disclosure, or use of classified information;

(2) to affect the conduct of authorized law enforcement or intelligence activities; or

(3) to modify the authority of a department or agency of the Federal Government to protect classified information and sources and methods and the national security of the United States.

(d) Relationship to other laws

Nothing in this subchapter shall be construed to affect any requirement under any other provision of law for a non-Federal entity to provide information to the Federal Government.

(e) Prohibited conduct

Nothing in this subchapter shall be construed to permit price-fixing, allocating a market between competitors, monopolizing or attempting to monopolize a market, boycotting, or exchanges of price or cost information, customer lists, or information regarding future competitive planning.

(f) Information sharing relationships

Nothing in this subchapter shall be construed—

(1) to limit or modify an existing information sharing relationship;

(2) to prohibit a new information sharing relationship;

(3) to require a new information sharing relationship between any non-Federal entity and a Federal entity or another non-Federal entity; or

(4) to require the use of the capability and process within the Department of Homeland Security developed under section 1504(c) of this title.

(g) Preservation of contractual obligations and rights

Nothing in this subchapter shall be construed—

(1) to amend, repeal, or supersede any current or future contractual agreement, terms of service agreement, or other contractual relationship between any non-Federal entities, or between any non-Federal entity and a Federal entity; or

(2) to abrogate trade secret or intellectual property rights of any non-Federal entity or Federal entity.

(h) Anti-tasking restriction

Nothing in this subchapter shall be construed to permit a Federal entity—

> **(1)** to require a non-Federal entity to provide information to a Federal entity or another non-Federal entity;

> **(2)** to condition the sharing of cyber threat indicators with a non-Federal entity on such entity's provision of cyber threat indicators to a Federal entity or another non-Federal entity; or

> **(3)** to condition the award of any Federal grant, contract, or purchase on the provision of a cyber threat indicator to a Federal entity or another non-Federal entity.

(i) No liability for non-participation

Nothing in this subchapter shall be construed to subject any entity to liability for choosing not to engage in the voluntary activities authorized in this subchapter.

(j) Use and retention of information

Nothing in this subchapter shall be construed to authorize, or to modify any existing authority of, a department or agency of the Federal Government to retain or use any information shared under this subchapter for any use other than permitted in this subchapter.

(k) Federal preemption

(1) In general

This subchapter supersedes any statute or other provision of law of a State or political subdivision of a State that restricts or otherwise expressly regulates an activity authorized under this subchapter.

(2) State law enforcement

Nothing in this subchapter shall be construed to supersede any statute or other provision of law of a State or political subdivision of a State concerning the use of authorized law enforcement practices and procedures.

(*l*) Regulatory authority

Nothing in this subchapter shall be construed—

> **(1)** to authorize the promulgation of any regulations not specifically authorized to be issued under this subchapter;

> **(2)** to establish or limit any regulatory authority not specifically established or limited under this subchapter; or

(3) to authorize regulatory actions that would duplicate or conflict with regulatory requirements, mandatory standards, or related processes under another provision of Federal law.

(m) Authority of Secretary of Defense to respond to malicious cyber activity carried out by foreign powers

Nothing in this subchapter shall be construed to limit the authority of the Secretary of Defense under section 130g of Title 10.

(n) Criminal prosecution

Nothing in this subchapter shall be construed to prevent the disclosure of a cyber threat indicator or defensive measure shared under this subchapter in a case of criminal prosecution, when an applicable provision of Federal, State, tribal, or local law requires disclosure in such case.

6 U.S.C. § 1510. EFFECTIVE PERIOD

(a) In general

Except as provided in subsection (b), this title and the amendments made by this title shall be effective during the period beginning on December 18, 2015, and ending on September 30, 2025.

(b) Exception

With respect to any action authorized by this subchapter or information obtained pursuant to an action authorized by this subchapter, which occurred before the date on which the provisions referred to in subsection (a) cease to have effect, the provisions of this subchapter shall continue in effect.

FEDERAL RULE OF CRIMINAL PROCEDURE 41
[Rule 41]

SEARCH AND SEIZURE

(Effective December 1, 2016)

(a) Scope and Definitions.

(1) Scope. This rule does not modify any statute regulating search or seizure, or the issuance and execution of a search warrant in special circumstances.

(2) Definitions. The following definitions apply under this rule:

(A) "Property" includes documents, books, papers, any other tangible objects, and information.

(B) "Daytime" means the hours between 6:00 a.m. and 10:00 p.m. according to local time.

(C) "Federal law enforcement officer" means a government agent (other than an attorney for the government) who is engaged in enforcing the criminal laws and is within any category of officers authorized by the Attorney General to request a search warrant.

(D) "Domestic terrorism" and "international terrorism" have the meanings set out in 18 U.S.C. § 2331.

(E) "Tracking device" has the meaning set out in 18 U.S.C. § 3117(b).

(b) Venue for a Warrant Application. At the request of a federal law enforcement officer or an attorney for the government:

(1) a magistrate judge with authority in the district—or if none is reasonably available, a judge of a state court of record in the district—has authority to issue a warrant to search for and seize a person or property located within the district;

(2) a magistrate judge with authority in the district has authority to issue a warrant for a person or property outside the district if the person or property is located within the district when the warrant is issued but might move or be moved outside the district before the warrant is executed;

(3) a magistrate judge—in an investigation of domestic terrorism or international terrorism—with authority in any district in which activities related to the terrorism may have occurred has authority to issue a warrant for a person or property within or outside that district;

(4) a magistrate judge with authority in the district has authority to issue a warrant to install within the district a tracking device; the warrant may authorize use of the device to track the movement of a person or property located within the district, outside the district, or both; and

(5) a magistrate judge having authority in any district where activities related to the crime may have occurred, or in the District of Columbia, may issue a warrant for property that is located outside the jurisdiction of any state or district, but within any of the following:

(A) a United States territory, possession, or commonwealth;

(B) the premises—no matter who owns them—of a United States diplomatic or consular mission in a foreign state, including any appurtenant building, part of a building, or land used for the mission's purposes; or

(C) a residence and any appurtenant land owned or leased by the United States and used by United States personnel assigned to a United States diplomatic or consular mission in a foreign state.

(6) a magistrate judge with authority in any district where activities related to a crime may have occurred has authority to issue a warrant to use remote access to search electronic storage media and to seize or copy electronically stored information located within or outside that district if:

>   **(A)** the district where the media or information is located has been concealed through technological means; or

>   **(B)** in an investigation of a violation of 18 U.S.C. § 1030(a)(5), the media are protected computers that have been damaged without authorization and are located in five or more districts.

(c) Persons or Property Subject to Search or Seizure. A warrant may be issued for any of the following:

>   **(1)** evidence of a crime;

>   **(2)** contraband, fruits of crime, or other items illegally possessed;

>   **(3)** property designed for use, intended for use, or used in committing a crime; or

>   **(4)** a person to be arrested or a person who is unlawfully restrained.

(d) Obtaining a Warrant.

>   **(1)   In General.** After receiving an affidavit or other information, a magistrate judge—or if authorized by Rule 41(b), a judge of a state court of record—must issue the warrant if there is probable cause to search for and seize a person or property or to install and use a tracking device.

>   **(2)   Requesting a Warrant in the Presence of a Judge.**

>   >   **(A)** *Warrant on an Affidavit.* When a federal law enforcement officer or an attorney for the government presents an affidavit in support of a warrant, the judge may require the affiant to appear personally and may examine under oath the affiant and any witness the affiant produces.

>   >   **(B)** *Warrant on Sworn Testimony.* The judge may wholly or partially dispense with a written affidavit and base a warrant on sworn testimony if doing so is reasonable under the circumstances.

>   >   **(C)** *Recording Testimony.* Testimony taken in support of a warrant must be recorded by a court reporter or by a suitable

recording device, and the judge must file the transcript or recording with the clerk, along with any affidavit.

(3) Requesting a Warrant by Telephonic or Other Means.

(A) *In General.* A magistrate judge may issue a warrant based on information communicated by telephone or other reliable electronic means.

(B) *Recording Testimony.* Upon learning that an applicant is requesting a warrant under Rule 41(d)(3)(A), a magistrate judge must:

    (i) place under oath the applicant and any person on whose testimony the application is based; and

    (ii) make a verbatim record of the conversation with a suitable recording device, if available, or by a court reporter, or in writing.

(C) *Certifying Testimony.* The magistrate judge must have any recording or court reporter's notes transcribed, certify the transcription's accuracy, and file a copy of the record and the transcription with the clerk. Any written verbatim record must be signed by the magistrate judge and filed with the clerk.

(D) *Suppression Limited.* Absent a finding of bad faith, evidence obtained from a warrant issued under Rule 41(d)(3)(A) is not subject to suppression on the ground that issuing the warrant in that manner was unreasonable under the circumstances.

(e) Issuing the Warrant.

(1) In General. The magistrate judge or a judge of a state court of record must issue the warrant to an officer authorized to execute it.

(2) Contents of the Warrant.

(A) *Warrant to Search for and Seize a Person or Property.* Except for a tracking-device warrant, the warrant must identify the person or property to be searched, identify any person or property to be seized, and designate the magistrate judge to whom it must be returned. The warrant must command the officer to:

    (i) execute the warrant within a specified time no longer than 14 days;

    (ii) execute the warrant during the daytime, unless the judge for good cause expressly authorizes execution at another time; and

    (iii) return the warrant to the magistrate judge designated in the warrant.

(B) *Warrant Seeking Electronically Stored Information.* A warrant under Rule 41(e)(2)(A) may authorize the seizure of electronic storage media or the seizure or copying of electronically stored information. Unless otherwise specified, the warrant authorizes a later review of the media or information consistent with the warrant. The time for executing the warrant in Rule 41(e)(2)(A) and (f)(1)(A) refers to the seizure or on-site copying of the media or information, and not to any later off-site copying or review.

(C) *Warrant for a Tracking Device.* A tracking-device warrant must identify the person or property to be tracked, designate the magistrate judge to whom it must be returned, and specify a reasonable length of time that the device may be used. The time must not exceed 45 days from the date the warrant was issued. The court may, for good cause, grant one or more extensions for a reasonable period not to exceed 45 days each. The warrant must command the officer to:

(i) complete any installation authorized by the warrant within a specified time no longer than 10 calendar days;

(ii) perform any installation authorized by the warrant during the daytime, unless the judge for good cause expressly authorizes installation at another time; and

(iii) return the warrant to the judge designated in the warrant.

(3) Warrant by Telephonic or Other Means. If a magistrate judge decides to proceed under Rule 41(d)(3)(A), the following additional procedures apply:

(A) *Preparing a Proposed Duplicate Original Warrant.* The applicant must prepare a "proposed duplicate original warrant" and must read or otherwise transmit the contents of that document verbatim to the magistrate judge.

(B) *Preparing an Original Warrant.* If the applicant reads the contents of the proposed duplicate original warrant, the magistrate judge must enter those contents into an original warrant. If the applicant transmits the contents by reliable electronic means, that transmission may serve as the original warrant.

(C) *Modification.* The magistrate judge may modify the original warrant. The judge must transmit any modified warrant to the applicant by reliable electronic means under Rule 41(e)(3)(D) or direct the applicant to modify the proposed duplicate original warrant accordingly.

(D) *Signing the Warrant.* Upon determining to issue the warrant, the magistrate judge must immediately sign the original warrant, enter on its face the exact date and time it is issued, and transmit it by reliable electronic means to the applicant or direct the applicant to sign the judge's name on the duplicate original warrant.

(f) Executing and Returning the Warrant.

(1) Warrant to Search for and Seize a Person or Property.

(A) *Noting the Time.* The officer executing the warrant must enter on it the exact date and time it was executed.

(B) *Inventory.* An officer present during the execution of the warrant must prepare and verify an inventory of any property seized. The officer must do so in the presence of another officer and the person from whom, or from whose premises, the property was taken. If either one is not present, the officer must prepare and verify the inventory in the presence of at least one other credible person. In a case involving the seizure of electronic storage media or the seizure or copying of electronically stored information, the inventory may be limited to describing the physical storage media that were seized or copied. The officer may retain a copy of the electronically stored information that was seized or copied.

(C) *Receipt.* The officer executing the warrant must give a copy of the warrant and a receipt for the property taken to the person from whom, or from whose premises, the property was taken or leave a copy of the warrant and receipt at the place where the officer took the property. For a warrant to use remote access to search electronic storage media and seize or copy electronically stored information, the officer must make reasonable efforts to serve a copy of the warrant and receipt on the person whose property was searched or who possessed the information that was seized or copied. Service may be accomplished by any means, including electronic means, reasonably calculated to reach that person.

(D) *Return.* The officer executing the warrant must promptly return it—together with a copy of the inventory—to the magistrate judge designated on the warrant. The judge must, on request, give a copy of the inventory to the person from whom, or from whose premises, the property was taken and to the applicant for the warrant.

(2) Warrant for a Tracking Device.

(A) *Noting the Time.* The officer executing a tracking-device warrant must enter on it the exact date and time the device was installed and the period during which it was used.

(B) *Return.* Within 10 calendar days after the use of the tracking device has ended, the officer executing the warrant must return it to the judge designated in the warrant.

(C) *Service.* Within 10 calendar days after the use of the tracking device has ended, the officer executing a tracking-device warrant must serve a copy of the warrant on the person who was tracked or whose property was tracked. Service may be accomplished by delivering a copy to the person who, or whose property, was tracked; or by leaving a copy at the person's residence or usual place of abode with an individual of suitable age and discretion who resides at that location and by mailing a copy to the person's last known address. Upon request of the government, the judge may delay notice as provided in Rule 41(f)(3).

(3) Delayed Notice. Upon the government's request, a magistrate judge—or if authorized by Rule 41(b), a judge of a state court of record—may delay any notice required by this rule if the delay is authorized by statute.

(g) Motion to Return Property. A person aggrieved by an unlawful search and seizure of property or by the deprivation of property may move for the property's return. The motion must be filed in the district where the property was seized. The court must receive evidence on any factual issue necessary to decide the motion. If it grants the motion, the court must return the property to the movant, but may impose reasonable conditions to protect access to the property and its use in later proceedings.

(h) Motion to Suppress. A defendant may move to suppress evidence in the court where the trial will occur, as Rule 12 provides.

(i) Forwarding Papers to the Clerk. The magistrate judge to whom the warrant is returned must attach to the warrant a copy of the return, of the inventory, and of all other related papers and must deliver them to the clerk in the district where the property was seized.